WE OWN THIS CITY

WE OWN THIS CITY

A True Story of Crime, Cops, and Corruption

JUSTIN FENTON

RANDOM HOUSE
NEW YORK

Copyright © 2021 by Justin Fenton

Published in the United States by Random House,
an imprint and division of Penguin Random House LLC, New York.

RANDOM HOUSE and the HOUSE colophon are registered trademarks of
Penguin Random House LLC.

Library of Congress Cataloging-in-Publication Data
Names: Fenton, Justin, author.
Title: We own this city : a true story of crime,
cops, and corruption / Justin Fenton.
Description: First edition. | New York : Random House, [2021] |
Includes bibliographical references and index.
Identifiers: LCCN 2020020879 (print) | LCCN 2020020880 (ebook) |
ISBN 9780593133668 (hardcover ; alk. paper) | ISBN 9780593133675 (ebook)
Subjects: LCSH: Jenkins, Wayne, 1980– | Baltimore (Md.). Police Department—
Corrupt practices—Case studies. | Police corruption—Maryland—Baltimore—
Case studies. | Drug traffic—Maryland—Baltimore—Case studies. |
Racketeering—Maryland—Baltimore—Case studies. |
Crime—Maryland—Baltimore—Case studies.
Classification: LCC HV8148.B2 F46 2021 (print) |
LCC HV8148.B2 (ebook) | DDC 364.1/323097526—dc23
LC record available at https://lccn.loc.gov/2020020879
LC ebook record available at https://lccn.loc.gov/2020020880

Printed in the United States of America on acid-free paper

randomhousebooks.com

3 4 5 6 7 8 9

Book design by Edwin Vazquez

CONTENTS

LIST OF CHARACTERS

THE INVESTIGATED

Sergeant Wayne Jenkins

Detective Momodu Gondo

Detective Evodio Hendrix

Detective Daniel Hersl

Detective Marcus Taylor

Detective Maurice Ward

Sergeant Thomas Allers

Sergeant Keith Gladstone

THE INVESTIGATORS

Assistant U.S. Attorney Leo Wise

Assistant U.S. Attorney Derek Hines

Special Agent Erika Jensen

Sergeant John Sieracki

Corporal David McDougall

Detective Scott Kilpatrick

THE DECEASED

Detective Sean Suiter

WIND-UP

CHAPTER ONE

KNOCKERS

THE LETTER ARRIVED IN the chambers of a federal judge in Baltimore in the summer of 2017. It had been sent from the McDowell Federal Correctional Institution, which was nestled in the middle of nowhere, West Virginia, more than six hours from Baltimore. On the front of the envelope, the inmate had written: "Special mail."

Umar Burley had written his letter on lined notebook paper, in neat, bouncy print, using tildes to top his T's. Burley, inmate number 43787-037, was reaching out to the judge for a second time, begging for a court-appointed lawyer. His attorney had retired, and attempts to reach another had gone unanswered.

"Could you imagine how hard it is to be here for a crime I didn't commit and struggling to find clarity and justice on my own?" Burley wrote.

Months earlier, Burley had been in the recreation hall of a federal prison in Oklahoma, awaiting transportation to McDowell, when someone called to him: "Little Baltimore! Little Baltimore! Did you see that?" News from home flashed across the television screen: A group of eight Baltimore police officers had been charged with stealing from citizens and lying about their cases. The officers had carried out their alleged crimes undeterred by the fact that the police department was at the time under a broad civil rights investigation following the death of a young Black man from injuries sustained while in police custody. The revelations were breathtaking, though not entirely unbelievable: For years, accusations of misconduct—from illegal strip searches to broken bones—had been leveled against city police. But many claims lacked hard proof and came from people with long rap sheets and every incentive to level a false accusation. Such toss-ups tended to go in favor of the cops. With the deck so stacked against them, most victims didn't even bother to speak up. Often, they did have drugs or guns, and the fact that the cops lied about the details of the encounter or took some of the seized money for themselves, well, in Baltimore, it was a dirty game in which the ends justified the means.

But now a wiretap case back home was shining a light on the culture of the force, and the federal prosecutors who brought the charges were looking for more victims. And Umar Burley had a story to tell.

BURLEY'S STORY BEGINS ON the morning of April 28, 2010. Members of a plainclothes police squad had been summoned for an ad hoc roll call on the street. Their sergeant, running a little late, told them to stay put. But Detective Wayne Jenkins felt the itch. He told the others that the area around Belle Avenue, in Northwest Baltimore, was "hot" with reports of criminal activity.

"Let's go," Jenkins said.

You can tell some police officers to stand under a pole for ten hours. Check nine hours later, they'll still be there. Send them to Greenmount Avenue and order them to walk up and down the boulevard, and they'll pace until the soles of their shoes begin to wear thin. But others need to get into something. They want to sit in vacant houses peering through binoculars or chase suspects through alleys; they work ungodly amounts of overtime. These are the "10 percent" whom commanders in the Baltimore Police Department (BPD) rely on to get the job done.

These are also the officers most likely to make up the plainclothes units known around town as "knockers" or "jumpout boys," a reference to their aggressive tactics. Officers in plainclothes units often operate in the shadows of a police department. Their work is not to be confused with undercover operations, in which police officers assume a different identity and worm their way into a criminal organization. Plainclothes officers, as the description suggests, work in street clothes rather than uniforms. They drive unmarked vehicles. They are not typically tethered to specific posts or obligated to respond to 911 calls. Instead, they go out looking for illegal activity—people selling drugs or displaying bulges under clothing that could be guns—and they operate with a great deal of independence. They can let a suspect go if they think the suspect can lead them to bigger fish. Across the country, these plainclothes squads have often been where scandals are born, but police department leaders over the years have deemed them critical to the crime fight—they are the "Vikings" who go out into the field and return with a "bounty," as one Baltimore chief would later put it.

Jenkins seemed perpetually in motion, and his gung-ho attitude quickly won the white former marine early entry into the BPD's most elite units. By 2010, less than seven years into his time on the force, Jenkins had worked his way into a new "violent repeat offender" squad, a handpicked group of officers whose charge was to go after Baltimore's worst offenders. They would often be given names of elusive suspected criminals and allowed only thirty days to build their best case.

They headed to Grove Park, a leafy neighborhood on the city/county border featuring single-family homes and a constellation of apartment buildings connected by paths and lined with cherry trees. As Baltimore neighborhoods go, it was decidedly different from the dense, abandoned row home neighborhoods closer to the city core, but it was not without crime. From their unmarked cars, the officers would later write in court paperwork, they spotted Umar Burley sitting in his Acura in the 3800 block of Parkview Avenue when another man walked up carrying what appeared to be cash and climbed in. "At this time, due to my training and expertise, I believed a narcotic transaction was possibly taking place," Jenkins would write.

Jenkins was riding with Detective Ryan Guinn, a half-Irish, half-Vietnamese cop whose appearance nevertheless prompted people in the neighborhoods where he worked to call him "Puerto Rican Yo." Guinn reached for his radio.

"Hey Sean," he said in a low calm voice, addressing Sean Suiter, another member of the squad riding in a separate car. "We'll try to stop this Accord."

"I got you. I'm with you," said Suiter.

The officers moved in for an arrest, with Jenkins and Guinn pulling in front of Burley's car, and Suiter taking up the rear. Their emergency lights were activated, Jenkins wrote in the charging papers, and their badges were "clearly displayed." He said the officers saw movement in the vehicle and ordered the men to show their hands. Guinn jumped out of the car and drew his gun, ordering Burley not to move. Burley maneuvered his car around the police vehicles and raced out of view.

"Hey, we got one running," Guinn radioed to the other officers, Jenkins's voice audible in the background. "By Seton Park Apartments. Black Acura."

He called out the license plate: "One-Frank-Young-King-Zero-Eight."

The chase lasted less than a minute. Burley made it less than a mile down the road when the officers heard a loud crash. It sounded like a bomb going off, and when they arrived at the intersection of Belle and Gwynn Oak avenues, they saw water gushing out of a fire hydrant that had been struck. The front bumper had come away from the car; the hood was mangled. The officers wondered how badly the men inside were hurt, when suddenly they bolted out. Guinn gave chase after the passenger, Brent Matthews, while Jenkins and Suiter took on Burley.

An onlooker called 911, relaying a scene that did not appear to involve police officers.

"A car crash. Belle and Gwynn Oak. A guy—they're running, trying to shoot each other!"

"You said they're trying to shoot each other?" the 911 operator asked.

"Yes—the car's into a fire hydrant, they jumped out, they started running, one with a gun."

Burley was caught by Suiter about fifty feet from the crash site. "Why did you pull off?" Suiter asked, according to Burley. "Why didn't you just see what we wanted?"

"All you had to do was put on your lights," Burley responded.

Guinn caught the passenger, and a struggle ensued. He was able to overpower the man and walked him back to the scene in cuffs.

"The shit's in the car," Jenkins told Guinn.

Along with a patrol officer, Suiter searched Burley's vehicle and picked up a baggie on the floor containing thirty-two grams of heroin.

It would take a moment for those at the scene to take stock of the damage. But they soon realized that the boom the officers and neighbors had heard wasn't from the collision with the fire hydrant. It was the sound of Burley's car first smashing into a Chevrolet Monte Carlo being driven by an elderly couple passing through the intersection. That car had been thrown into the air and over a row of bushes.

A neighbor, who had been making breakfast when the crash shook his house, ran outside to the injured couple. The man was bleeding from the head; the woman was crying for help. "Hold on, help is coming," the neighbor told them.

Elbert Davis Sr., eighty-six, and his wife Phosa Cain, eighty-one, had left that morning to visit one of their ten children. The couple was taken downtown by ambulance to the University of Maryland Shock Trauma Center for treatment; Guinn followed to check on their condition and later said he was at the nurses' station when he heard Davis flatline. He went into Cain's hospital room and held her hand. She asked Guinn if her husband was okay. "They're doing everything they can," Guinn told her, seeking to calm her until the doctors could deliver the news.

Back at the scene of the crash, Joyce Fuller, a sixty-two-year-old woman whose home had been struck by the vehicle, denounced the fleeing men who'd been involved in the crash.

"I'd like to take all of these drug dealers and put them in a cargo plane and take them to Iraq," she told reporters. "That couple hadn't done anything. It's just so unfair."

BURLEY, FORTY, WAS HEADED back to prison. He had spent years in the game, with a record of prior drug arrests dating back to age thirteen, when he had taken a charge for a beloved uncle. He also had the rare distinction of having beaten a prior federal gun charge: In 2007, he'd been pulled over on the pretext of "exceeding the lawful amount of window tint." The arresting officer said he had smelled alcohol, reached down for a cup in the vehicle, and seen the butt of a handgun sticking out from under the armrest of the bench-style seat. Police would later say Burley and the other man in the car "had to have known" the weapon was there and would charge them both with possessing the one gun. Burley spent just shy of a year and a half locked up on those charges, first on a bail he couldn't afford to post, then on federal pretrial detention, only to be released when the other guy took responsibility for the gun and the case against Burley was abandoned.

This time, in addition to drugs, Burley would be charged with manslaughter. The crash might have been an accident, but fleeing police with drugs made it criminal. The drug charge was taken federal, a second bite at the apple for an office that had dropped the earlier case against Burley. He was ordered held without bond while awaiting trial.

But Burley swore to his court-appointed attorney that there had been no drugs in the car that day. He had been picking up Matthews on the way to attend the sentencing hearing of a man convicted of killing Burley's cousin. Burley, who had been shot twice before, said the officers had startled him when they boxed in his vehicle and pulled their guns. He had panicked, he said, and fled.

Burley's lawyer told a judge that his client disputed "much of Detective Jenkins' statement of probable cause." He said the detectives had seized and arrested Burley without legal basis and were justifying their actions by the after-the-fact discovery of drugs.

"Alleged law enforcement observations of an African American entering a parked car with money in a high crime area do not add up to probable cause," Burley's attorney wrote. Burley pleaded not guilty and was held pending trial.

Guinn later said he thought nothing of the men's assertion that the drugs were planted. Arrestees denied the charges against them all the time.

But Jenkins seemed obsessed with the case. Officers are able to listen in on calls inmates make from jail, and Jenkins was glued to the calls of Burley and his passenger, Matthews. They were telling others that the heroin had been planted.

"If this case goes to trial," Jenkins told Guinn, "I can't testify."

The bar that Burley needed to clear for acquittal was ultimately too high—he was a repeat offender, driving on a revoked license, and he had killed an old man while fleeing police officers who said they found heroin in the vehicle. A plea deal was worked out in which he received ten years' federal time on the drug charges; in state court, where the manslaughter charges were still in play, he received another ten years, the maximum. With no trial, the officers involved wouldn't have to discuss the case in court, and Burley was shipped off to prison.

Seven years later came a plot twist in what looked like a closed case. Burley appeared once again in a courtroom in Baltimore. This time he was being freed early, with a federal judge stepping off the bench to personally apologize and shake his hand. Meanwhile, Wayne Jenkins would soon be sent to a penitentiary in the desert outside of Tucson, Arizona, to serve a twenty-five-year prison sentence. And Sean Suiter lay crumpled in a West Baltimore alley with a bullet in his head.

CHAPTER TWO

WHATEVER IT TAKES

THE CITY OF BALTIMORE had been shrinking and struggling for most of Wayne Jenkins's life.

After a postwar boom in the 1940s, Baltimore's population peaked at nearly one million, but with the desegregation of public schools in the mid-1950s—and the expansion of streetcars and highways to the city's perimeter—white families began to flee the urban center for bigger yards and more homogenous communities. This white flight intensified with the rise of crime and unrest in the 1960s, culminating in riots that followed Martin Luther King's death in 1968, which left one thousand Baltimore businesses looted or damaged, and six dead and seven hundred injured. In 1950, the city had been 76 percent white; by the time Jenkins was born in 1980, that share had fallen to 44 percent. Meanwhile, the total population continued to decrease—falling below eight hundred thousand by 1980.

A month before Jenkins's birth in June 1980, the city had opened Harborplace, a shopping complex built on the formerly decrepit waterfront, to great fanfare celebrating it as the centerpiece of the city's downtown revival. Longtime mayor William Donald Schaefer was determined to reverse Baltimore's downward trend and focused relentlessly on boosting the city's tourism and sense of pride. "There was no question we had to build pride in a city that had none," Schaefer said in 1979. "To make it so people wouldn't be so ashamed to say they are Baltimoreans." And yet the flight would continue—fifty thousand more residents would leave the city over the course of the 1980s.

Jenkins grew up in Middle River, a bedroom community east of the city that hugged the northern neck of the Chesapeake Bay. It had grown as a receptacle of white flight and as a result of its proximity to several of the major industrial sites in the area: the Martin Aircraft plant, right in Middle River, which had employed fifty-three thousand during the war; just to the south, the massive Bethlehem Steel in Sparrows Point, which by the mid-1960s was one of the largest steel plants in the world with thirty thousand employees; and General Motors, just inside the city's eastern border, employing seven thousand people.

The community was quiet and close-knit, sustained by the steady jobs at these factories and others. Some cops lived in the neighborhood, with their take-home cars visible in their driveways. But in the years following Jenkins's birth, the inner-suburban stability began to fray as deindustrialization took hold across the city. General Motors and Bethlehem Steel alone cut twelve thousand jobs between 1978 and 1982. Beneath Middle River's clean-cut, All-American veneer, a hidden drug culture took root, spreading from the city that most of its families had escaped. It burst into public view in 1987 when two pregnant sisters and their husbands were shot execution-style in a house on Jenkins's street during a robbery of seventeen pounds of marijuana. Still, this kind of violence was rare, and so in turn were police crackdowns.

Jenkins was the youngest of five—three siblings as well as two cousins taken in by his family. His father, Lloyd "Lee" Jenkins, a former marine, often wouldn't get home until late at night after working at the Beth Steel plant and at his second job moonlighting as a handyman. Not only was Wayne the youngest child, he struggled with a speech impediment that required therapy. Perhaps this helped foster a certain toughness. "Wayne didn't take shit from no one," recalled Andy Janowich, who lived four doors down and remembered him sticking up for other kids. "I was always smaller; Wayne would take up for me. He wasn't going to go looking for a fight," but he was always quick to defend others. Janowich recalled Jenkins was given boxing gloves at a young age.

Jenkins attended Eastern Technical High School, where he was in a vocational program for heating, ventilation, and air conditioning. Eastern Tech was a well-regarded school, one of only eleven across the state designated as a "Blue Ribbon School of Excellence." Though it drew from some of Baltimore County's poorest areas, the school achieved excellent ratings in every category on the state's report card.

Jenkins developed an unlikely bond with an art teacher, Bob Brent—unlikely, because Brent was not one of Jenkins's teachers but rather had an open classroom during a period when Jenkins was often booted from a welding class held next door. Brent offered a refuge and said Jenkins would appear upset with himself after getting in trouble for mouthing off in class. "Not being his teacher, he and I could sit down and have a one-on-one human being conversation," Brent recalled. "My impression was that he wished he could take back what he did, but he seemed to have a pattern of recidivism with those kinds of behaviors." Brent recalled hearing that Jenkins's "home life was a little tough."

Jenkins played two sports: lacrosse and football. He didn't start on either team but had a strong enough work ethic that the other players called him "Rudy," after the walk-on player at Notre Dame whose extra effort earned him an opportunity to play in his last game as a senior. The football coach, Nick Arminio, recalled Jenkins as a hard worker who played on special teams. "I think he wanted to belong to part of the team and be a part of something," Arminio said.

At Eastern Tech, Jenkins began dating Kristy Myers. In his senior yearbook quote, he thanked his mother and father, along with Brent and another teacher, and told Kristy he loved her. He concluded with a sense of accomplishment at graduating: "I did it."

A few months later, on August 24, 1998, Jenkins followed in his father's footsteps and entered the Marines. After basic training, he was stationed in Camp Lejeune, a sprawling waterfront training facility in Jacksonville, North Carolina. He connected with a fellow Baltimore-area native named Patrick Armetta, and they became roommates. They had different styles: Armetta in those days liked to party, but Jenkins was a poster boy for the military with his razor-sharp creases and polished boots—a "squared-away marine." "He would always be the guy saying, 'Dawg, you gotta shine those boots,' 'You gonna put a hot rock [an iron] on that uniform?' Wayne was always that person who stuck out," Armetta recalled. He said Jenkins in those years had bad knees, sometimes tumbling to the ground when they were running in formation, but always kept going. In 2000, Jenkins reached the rank of corporal and specialized in driving tactical vehicles and transporting cargo. His sergeant remembered him, almost two decades later, as having "the utmost flawless character that I've ever ran into over my twenty years of serving this great country." The sergeant said Jenkins was a "shining example of the type of quality leader the Marine Corps creates."

Jenkins was perhaps most focused, though, about making the four-hundred-mile return trip home to see his family and Kristy as often as possible, offering to pay for gas and drive Armetta's car.

Jenkins left the Marines with an honorable discharge on August 15, 2001, one month before 9/11. The timing was life-altering: Had he stayed, he might have been launched into the war on terror, perhaps deployed to a combat zone. Instead, for the next year, Jenkins toiled away in menial jobs, laying tile and working as a line operator at a factory in Dundalk. When a tropical storm flooded the neighborhood, Jenkins showed up at the local volunteer fire company with a boat. "This is my community," he said. "How can I help?"

He was finished with the military but still wanted to serve, so he began applying for police jobs. Jenkins was rejected by the Maryland State Police in 2002 because he "failed to meet testing standards," though the precise reason is unclear. He turned his attention to the Baltimore police force. In the interview process, he admitted to some minor indiscretions, like smoking marijuana a handful of times as a teen and getting arrested for jaywalking once in Myrtle Beach. He got a "C" on his psychological evaluation. But the recruiter marveled at Jenkins's poise in his interview: "Applicant was by far the most polite applicant that I have ever had the opportunity to talk to. With every answer that he gave, it followed with either 'yes sir' or 'no sir.' He was very respectful. You could tell that he was very interested in the career."

He was ultimately accepted and joined the department as a cadet in February 2003. His military pedigree and toughness were on full display in the training academy, according to members of his class. Jason Rathell, another recruit, recalled the class going to watch him box competitively one night. Dan Horgan, an Air Force veteran selected as the class commander, said Jenkins, who stood five-foot-eleven with a slim build and chiseled jawline, was "a fighter, literally and figuratively. He loved to box; his mentality was your typical marine.... Let's get this done, but we're going to do it 100 percent. Nothing was 10 percent."

Jenkins was entering a police force that had seen constant leadership changes at the top and was trying to adopt new enforcement strategies. The nationwide crack epidemic saw violent crime in Baltimore rise by 53 percent from 1985 to 1993, and the city experienced more than three hundred homicides every year of the 1990s even as its population was declining. In the first half of the decade, the agency's struggle to reduce crime came against a backdrop of a hiring freeze and new morale challenges. Officers reported that the proliferation of drugs and a breakdown in internal discipline saw a rise in thefts by officers: "With drugs the way they are, there's so much cash around. It's hard for guys to see all this money out on the street and stay conscientious," one officer told *The Baltimore Sun*.

Meanwhile, New York City and its leaders had become national stars in the nineties for slashing crime using tough police tactics based on the "broken windows theory" that "disorder and crime are inextricably linked." Baltimore's commissioner in the late 1990s, a West Coast transplant named Thomas Frazier, warned that the policies were "one iota away from harassment and discrimination" and that in Baltimore using them would be like "trying to push a tennis ball through a garden hose." But a charismatic young councilman with national aspirations named Martin O'Malley wanted those New York crime stats for his city. In his successful campaign for mayor in 1999, he pledged to clean up ten notorious drug corners in the first six months of his administration and make low-income neighborhoods as safe as wealthier communities. Not content to merely duplicate New York's policies, he imported some of its personnel, such as NYPD's rising star deputy commissioner Ed Norris, whom O'Malley named commissioner in 2000. Norris was a cop's cop and had no interest in being "a social worker with a gun," as Frazier had called himself once. "We're the police," Norris said. "We're supposed to be protecting the public. If we don't actually make the city safer and a thousand people a month continue to leave, there will be no tax base to support any city services. So I think that crime reduction is our primary mission."

Black political leaders had concerns about the implications of the new approach, sparked in part after a member of the Maryland House of Delegates said he had been pulled over for "driving while Black." There was fear such incidents would become more prevalent under the new policing style. O'Malley met with twenty Black state legislators and members of the city council to assure them that crime fighting and accountability would go hand in hand. "We cannot hope to have effective policing unless we have a police department with integrity and one that is willing to police itself," O'Malley told them.

To help him, the mayor recruited the architects of New York's statistics-based crime fighting program, called CompStat, and asked them to do a top-to-bottom analysis of Baltimore's police department. Their eventual 152-page report, issued in April 2000, quoted residents saying police seemed unwilling to take on drug dealers, and officers saying they felt unsupported in their mission. The report also made this startling finding: In a survey of the 3,200 officers on the force, nearly a quarter said they believed the number of officers stealing money or drugs was greater than a quarter of the department. During the first three years of O'Malley's tenure, the police department's internal affairs unit ran more than two hundred stings in hopes of catching unethical officers in the act. Only four officers failed such an "integrity sting," a department spokesman said. "We have not come across that sort of beehive's nest of every officer on a shift in a particular precinct [involved in corruption], like they had in New York, where they had a couple of celebrated cases," O'Malley said in 2003.

That same year, during Jenkins's first months as a trainee, Keith Gladstone and Thomas Wilson, two officers he would later work with, were reprimanded by a federal judge, U.S. District Court Judge Andre Davis, who tossed out two cases in which he determined that the officers had carried out unlawful searches. Davis angrily described the police affidavit in one case as "packed with knowing lies." He said he "almost fell out of my chair" when he read that the officers had hand-cuffed the suspect and driven him back to his apartment, where they used his key and entered without a warrant. In the other case, the officers arrested a man and then went to his mother's West Baltimore home at 4 A.M. asking permission to search her residence. Such a move would never be tolerated in the city's wealthier white communities, he said.

"Where are they learning this stuff?" said Judge Davis. "It's sad. We deserve better."

The federal prosecutor on the case backed the officers, saying they were good cops who were getting unfairly questioned in their pursuit of bad guys. "I guess we are just looking through different prisms at the same evidence," the prosecutor told Davis. "Where you see mis-statements in the warrant as being evidence of perhaps a lack of ve-racity by the police, I look at it more as this was a function of police acting in a hasty fashion, being inexact—that being the function of an overworked group of police in a city with 60,000 addicts."

The judge disagreed. "They are not making cases," Davis said. "They're not building investigations. . . . They are just making arrests. They are just making seizures."

Though mistakes by officers were often forgiven internally, a dress-ing down from a federal judge was rare. It was supposed to carry weight. In some places, it could derail an officer's career. But in Balti-more, it was more often a speed bump.

Court records suggest that Gladstone and Wilson were briefly sidelined in the months after the hearing. Wilson was involved in just three arrests in the four months after Davis's remarks. Over the next eight months, however, he was back on the streets and made a stag-gering 230 lockups. Gladstone continued to work with an elite federal task force.

Jenkins's academy class graduated in November 2003, and his first assignment was walking a beat on Monument Street—the main street of East Baltimore, with a commercial strip that ran east from Johns Hopkins Hospital and bisected dense row home communities. Hor-gan, the recruit class commander, said the new officers' early experi-ences were eye-opening: "The open-air drug markets were ridiculous," he said. "You'd roll through an alley and see forty people hanging in the backyard of a vacant [building], waiting for 'testers.' Then they'd see you and scatter. Where else does that happen? It was almost like shooting fish in a barrel."

The police department was now on its second commissioner recruited from New York City, Kevin P. Clark. Mayor O'Malley was touting the third-largest decline in crime in the country, but there were questions about whether statistics were being juked, and the city had barely moved the needle on the homicide number. Commissioner Clark arrived vowing to drive open-air drug dealing indoors. The first prong of his attack was to train more undercover detectives to make drug purchases, so they could testify in court about personally buying the drugs as opposed to simply describing what they believed to be a transaction. The second prong was to constantly harass suspected drug dealers by citing them for petty offenses, like loitering. One night, with a reporter in tow, Clark urged a group of plainclothes officers to give citations to several young men sitting against the wall of a vacant building. Clark assumed the men were drug dealers. The officers resisted, saying they couldn't write a citation because they hadn't given the men a prior warning. "Write the violation!" Clark yelled.

This wasn't just going after drugs for the sake of going after drugs, officials said; drugs underpinned much of the continuing street violence. In the fall of 2002, the city had been stunned by a firebombing that wiped out an entire family of seven—Carnell, forty-three, and Angela Dawson, thirty-six, and five of their children. A twenty-one-year-old neighbor, upset that Angela Dawson had called the police about drug dealing on the block, had kicked in the front door and doused the first floor with gasoline. The five children and Angela had one funeral—six caskets, each topped by flowers and a photograph of the deceased. Carnell died a week later. "You think you have purchased half of us and intimidated the rest of us, but you are as foolish as you are cruel," O'Malley said during the service, speaking of the drug dealers. "As long as Baltimore remembers the Dawsons, we will never surrender to your hate. . . . The fight is not over. Love and justice will have the final word."

The turmoil in Baltimore would only get worse.

In December 2003, shortly after Jenkins joined the force, Commissioner Clark's predecessor, Norris, was federally indicted for abusing an off-the-books spending account while he was commissioner. He would plead guilty and be sentenced to six months in prison. Then, a year later, Clark himself was ousted by O'Malley, with his office raided by SWAT team members following a row over a domestic violence investigation.

About that time, in 2005, an underground DVD entitled *Stop Fucking Snitching,* in which people who spoke to police were called "rats" and "bitches," started circulating on the streets. Featuring a cameo by NBA star and Baltimore native Carmelo Anthony in the background of one scene, it gained widespread attention. The makers' stated message praised a code of honor among thieves, in which hustlers would do their time instead of taking down others along the way, but officials fretted about the implications as the title was put on T-shirts and as thousands of pirated copies spread beyond Baltimore.

In one scene of the video, a man complained that drug dealers who worked a particular corner in West Baltimore weren't "catching cases," or being arrested, because they had two Baltimore police officers looking out for them.

"Word is they work for King and Murray," the man said. "Don't nobody go to jail."

William King and Antonio Murray were partners working in the department's public housing unit, feared by drug dealers for their willingness to bend the rules. One of their targets was a seventeen-year-old whom they provided with drugs on the condition that he split the profits with them. Eventually they told him he would have to help bring down other dealers or he would face consequences. Feeling the squeeze, he decided he wanted out of the arrangement and went to the FBI. In a sting operation, agents placed a bag of fake crack cocaine in an alley in the West Baltimore neighborhood of Harlem Park and watched the officers pick it up.

At their trial, King testified that after he received training from police officials in New York, he changed the way he submitted evidence. It was tacitly approved within the department to let people go who provided information, or even to give them drugs and money to keep them working and providing information.

"Sometimes you submit the [seized drugs and money]," King said. "Sometimes you don't."

The practices were widespread in Baltimore and used by officers under pressure from their bosses to get results, he asserted. Federal prosecutors trying the case, and police officials who testified, insisted no such techniques were allowed.

King and Murray were convicted by a federal jury on nearly three dozen charges, including extortion, drug conspiracy, and handgun violations. King's sentence, mandated by federal sentencing guidelines, was 315 years and one month behind bars. Murray received 139 years.

City officials treated the case as an aberration, however, and continued to swat away claims of misconduct within the force. The aggressive policing philosophy had translated to more arrests; by 2005 it would result in over 100,000 lockups in a city of about 630,000 people. Prosecutors were declining to prosecute one in three cases at the point of arrest. One man that year told *The Baltimore Sun* that police had arrested him five times in a three-month span, within a two-block radius of his home. He said he had been taking the trash out when police arrested him during a drug sweep; another arrest was for "loitering" in front of his house. "How do you get arrested in front of [your] own house for loitering?" he asked.

City officials rejected the criticisms. "Let me be clear," O'Malley, who was reelected in 2003 with 87 percent of the vote, told residents at a boisterous community forum in January 2006. "We do not now, nor do we ever, encourage arrests for the sake of arrests. Nor have we, nor will we ever, encourage or turn a blind eye to the abuse of police powers, or arrests made outside the bounds of the Constitution." But former officers recall a culture that was aggressive about racking up stats. Former officer Eric Kowalczyk remembered attending roll calls in various districts early in his career where commanders gave directives such as "Lock up every swinging dick," "No free passes, everybody goes," and "Clear those corners. I don't care how you do it. Get it done."

"The message from up on high was clear. Do whatever it took to stem the tide of violence. Whatever. It. Took," Kowalczyk wrote in his

2019 book, *The Politics of Crisis*. An officer with a strong grasp of the law could justify all types of lockups. Another ugly truth, he said: Arresting everybody could actually be effective—at least for the short-term gains the department was looking for. "The violence drops, the homicide number goes down. Replicate this belief across an entire department and you can easily see how in one year we made more than 100,000 arrests."

In 2005 alone, Jenkins is listed in court records as having been personally involved in more than four hundred arrests, sometimes a half dozen in a single day.

One Saturday night in early October 2005, Tim O'Connor was out watching football with a friend, slinging back drinks at the Brewer's Hill Pub in Southeast Baltimore. Eventually, O'Connor was asked by the bartender to leave because he'd had too many. Outside on the sidewalk, his friends tried to coax him up the street, causing a minor commotion. A group of police officers, including Jenkins, who were at a Royal Farms convenience store across the street made their way over to see if they needed to intervene. Jenkins's supervisor, Sergeant Michael Fries, knew O'Connor from an adult soccer league where they both played. For no reason in particular—other than that he was sloshed—O'Connor yelled at Fries.

"Fuck you, Mike Fries," he said. "You ain't shit."

O'Connor was pulled to the ground from behind. One officer held a nightstick across his chest, while Jenkins jumped on top of him, punching him in the face. "It was like taking a hammer to the face," O'Connor later testified, slamming his fist into his palm three times. "I couldn't protect myself." Blood spilled from his eye. "It was a pain I've never felt before in my life," he said. His orbital bones were fractured, requiring surgery and causing him to miss extended time from work.

His friend called for an ambulance, and O'Connor was taken to the hospital, where his wife called the police to report what had happened. Jenkins and Fries hadn't made a report of their own or called for medical assistance. When a lieutenant from the Southeastern District showed up to take a report, he asked O'Connor what had happened. "Mikey Fries and the Baltimore City Police Department did this to me," O'Connor told him.

In 2006, O'Connor sued Jenkins and Fries for damages. When the case went to trial two years later, the officers said they had no idea how O'Connor had gotten hurt; they had had their backs turned when someone else must have hit him. And they hadn't called for help, they claimed, because O'Connor's friends had waved them off and wanted to just get him home.

Jenkins appeared engaged but nervous at the defense table throughout the proceedings. He wore a slightly oversized dress shirt and a tie. He joked to the jury that he got dressed up only for court and funerals. On the witness stand, however, he transformed. Confident and indignant, he pushed back at questions from O'Connor's attorney, Domenic Iamele, who accused Jenkins of being a "professional witness" experienced with manipulating jurors. Iamele said he had noticed Jenkins trying to work one female juror in particular. Jenkins turned and smiled at the jury, drawing laughs from them as he raised his hands in a "Who, me?" pose.

"You tried catching me all day, and you can't, because I'm telling the truth," Jenkins told Iamele. "You didn't catch me in nothing."

Despite his performance, the jury found in favor of O'Connor and awarded him $75,000. Taxpayers footed the bill. But nothing was added to Jenkins's personnel file, and he appeared to suffer no consequences.

A few months after the O'Connor incident, in January 2006, Jenkins and Fries were patrolling McElderry Park, a small neighborhood a few blocks east of Johns Hopkins Hospital. They passed a couple of men, brothers Charles and Robert Lee, sitting on the stoop of their grandmother's home and drinking beer. Police hadn't received any complaints, but the officers told them to go inside. When Jenkins and Fries circled back around later, the men were still there. Police authority was being challenged. Charles Lee started to walk into the home, but Jenkins charged after him and pulled him back out. They tumbled down the front steps and onto the sidewalk. Lee's brother, who was watching the scuffle, was also taken down.

"All this happened over nothing," Charles Lee later recalled. The two police officers "came over because they had nothing else to do."

A passerby, George Sneed, stopped to watch the altercation. Suddenly, another officer, Robert Cirello, who had arrived on the scene, ran toward him. Sneed took off. Cirello caught up to him, slammed him to the ground, and broke his jaw.

Sneed sued. At trial four years after the incident, the officers' story was that Sneed had been throwing bottles and yelling profanities at them from across the street while they were trying to bring a tense situation under control. "I saw defendant Sneed throw a bottle," Jenkins said in a deposition, "[then] another bottle, and that was winged at us. Winged at us. I mean, it had velocity. It was flying at us. As a patrol officer pulled up and officers exited, I instructed them he was under arrest."

"He's yelling fuck you, I'll kill all you police, fuck you bitches," Fries added.

Sneed's attorney had pulled video from the street corner, however, and it showed no such thing. Sneed had walked up and stood calmly, arms at his sides and watched what was unfolding, until Cirello charged him.

"In light of this evidence plainly demonstrating the officers' testimony is untrue," Sneed's attorney, Michael Pulver, wrote in a court filing, "the trier of fact could easily determine that the officers fabricated this story to hide the fact that they intentionally assaulted and falsely arrested and imprisoned Mr. Sneed."

Although the jury found against Cirello—since he was the one who assaulted Sneed—Jenkins was cleared. But for the second time he appeared to have been caught in lies. Once again, his personnel file remained clean.

Sneed's attorney Pulver was a former Baltimore County prosecutor—he had tried the sextuple murder case that occurred on Jenkins's block in the 1980s. He said he inherently trusted police but what he saw on surveillance footage of the Sneed assault disgusted him.

"They're just treating these people like animals," Pulver said. "And it was over drinking beer on the step. They run into this guy's house— hot pursuit of a beer drinker? They were in this mode of: There's no minor offense. Everything, we enforce. We're the law, and in their minds, they're doing patrols in Afghanistan."

Cirello, who has since left the police force, now admits that the assault on Sneed was unjustified. The officers at the scene "ordered me to fuck him up."

"So I fucked him up," Cirello said.

When Fries was promoted into the department's elite Organized Crime Division around 2007, he sized up his officers and decided that only Jenkins merited being promoted—the others were "worthless" and "didn't meet the standards" of the unit, he said. Jenkins, on the other hand, was "the best officer I had working under my command."

Jenkins's personal life was prospering as well. In late 2005, he and Kristy, who had been living together and then had gotten married the previous December, purchased a small split-level home for $289,000. It was not far from Jenkins's parents' place, in a residential neighborhood near the Gunpowder River and a state park—a good place to raise a family as he ventured into the city to do battle.

CHAPTER THREE

BAD GUYS WITH GUNS

A SHIFT IN POLICING strategy in 2007 would lead to the creation of a new unit: the Gun Trace Task Force.

The uptick in arrests was wearing on the long-frayed relationship between police and the community, without making the impact on killings that officials had envisioned. Martin O'Malley's goal of lowering the yearly number of homicides to 175 hadn't even been approached, and when he moved to the governor's mansion in Annapolis, gun violence was surging toward levels not seen since the 1990s, with the city on track to top 300 homicides yet again. The *Sun* ran a daily homicide count in a box on the front page. The acting mayor, Sheila Dixon, fired the police commissioner and replaced him with Frederick H. Bealefeld III, a veteran of Baltimore's narcotics and homicide units.

Bealefeld had been running the department for months, and Dixon said she was impressed with his tough questioning of police commanders during intelligence meetings. "We will make this city safe," Bealefeld said at a news conference. "The people of this city have high expectations of their leaders in the Police Department, and they should. I don't take it lightly. The citizens demand action, and the mayor expects results." He said he wanted to see officers "engaging gangbangers, not sitting in their cruisers."

Bealefeld wanted the department to focus more on guns and those who carried them. For too long, he said, police had been pursuing drugs, which was a crapshoot. Yes, drugs were tangled up with violence, but judges, inundated with such cases, were devaluing them because they couldn't tell which ones mattered. He wanted his officers to make fewer arrests but to go after the right people. He moved the department away from the zero tolerance policies of his predecessors, and arrests began to decline significantly. The department eventually settled a lawsuit brought by the ACLU and NAACP over zero tolerance policing, in which the city formally denounced the tactic.

Instead, police said they would focus on "repeat, violent offenders" who had been flagged for multiple serious crimes. Bealefeld insisted that police weren't going after everyone in Baltimore anymore, just those "bad guys with guns" who toted illegal firearms. They were the ones most likely to shoot someone, and to be shot.

To prove he was interested not just in fighting crime but in improving the quality of the police department, Bealefeld made a major push to emphasize training. The centerpiece of that effort was a program called Diamond Standard training, intended in part to drill into officers that they would need the help and respect of the people they served. Officers were sent to the training together as a shift, taken off the street for a month.

On the street, though, the department was aggressively pursuing its campaign against "bad guys with guns." The man put in charge of day-to-day operations was a West Baltimore native named Anthony Barksdale, who got into policing to clean up his grandfather's neighborhood. He became a disciple of the imported New York policing leaders preaching CompStat's philosophies of putting "cops on dots"—places where crime was known to historically occur—and ensuring accountability. Barksdale believed that tough policing was necessary and that, with rigorous oversight through the city's own Comstat program, the department could also police itself. At the same time, Internal Affairs was siloed away, and if it couldn't make cases against officers with complaints, the operations side would keep trotting them out. "Your harder working cops will get complaints. Some guy is going to say you did this, or you did that to him. That's part of the job. The guys who aren't afraid of that will rack up complaints. You have to sort out: are these good cops or bad cops," Barksdale recalled later. "Hearing things isn't enough; we have to make an actual case." "There was so much pressure—political pressure, social pressure, internal pressure—to do something about the murder rate that it became all-encompassing, and everything else slipped," added John Skinner, who became a commander in 2001 and retired as a deputy commissioner in 2014.

The agency put nearly three hundred of what it viewed as its best detectives into a new plainclothes unit called the Violent Crimes Impact Division. These were, in the eyes of leadership, their top flight officers, the upper 10 percent who worked hard and got results. The department, with help from academics, analyzed historical crime patterns and determined the areas of the city that, year after year, were plagued by the highest rates of gun violence. Instead of being shuttled around as crime flared up in different areas, they were ordered to stay in those zones and clamp down.

Shootings and killings began an immediate downward trend. Not only was the seemingly inevitable mark of three hundred homicides not reached in 2007, but within three years the number of people killed would dip below two hundred for the first time since the early 1980s. Major cities across the country had been seeing such declines for years, but Baltimore had been an outlier. Suddenly, a safer city seemed possible—even if the underlying sociological factors, the true bellwethers of progress, weren't keeping pace. Baltimore hadn't added thousands of jobs or made significant inroads on addiction. Was the crime drop a mirage, or had the department found a better way to police that could curb violence in the face of the city's deeply entrenched challenges?

While various categories of crime were declining, one concerning trend appeared: Police shootings spiked, from fifteen in 2006 to thirty-three in 2007—more than departments in Philadelphia and Washington, and only one fewer than in Los Angeles, a city of 3.8 million people. And while every shooting was investigated to determine if it was a legally justified use of force, there was no review for whether the officers complied with department rules and whether they followed training that could have prevented the shooting from occurring in the first place. Officers were often sent right back into the field after a shooting. "I don't want 2,900 scarecrows dressed up in police uniforms," Bealefeld said after one shooting by an officer. "I want people who are going to go out and do their jobs."

The city's top prosecutor at the time, Patricia C. Jessamy, was concerned enough about the department's general ability to police its own that she created an internal "do not call" list of cops who were known by her office to have integrity problems but who remained on the job. Her office refused to call them as witnesses, effectively forcing the police department to sideline them: Police could continue to let the flagged officers roam the streets, but their cases would be immediately pitched. Police brass and the union fumed.

Though such lists exist now in other cities, Jessamy may have been the first. Police "went years without any trial boards and refused to take any complaint of wrongdoing seriously," Jessamy, who was the chief prosecutor from 1995 until 2010, recalled later. "It was the only card I had to play. . . . This was my own solution to a very serious officer credibility problem."

The department pushed its gun-first priority through a number of initiatives, such as "GunStat" meetings where officials reviewed gun seizure cases and discussed the creation of a gun offender registry, which would require people convicted of gun offenses to register their address with the city, subjecting them to check-ins to ensure compliance with gun-possession and other restrictions.

Another signature program was the creation in 2007 of a unit called the Gun Tracing Task Force (GTTF). One of the inaugural members was Detective Ryan Guinn. At the time, he was investigating shootings, robberies, and other serious crimes out of the city's Southern District, where he had started his career as a drug cop and built up a strong network of informants. Guinn enjoyed the pace of the district detective job and the freedom to more methodically assemble cases. One day he was pulled aside in the headquarters parking garage by his sergeant, who said Commissioner Bealefeld had a new assignment for them.

"It's the mayor's baby—it's going to be a new task force with us [and] neighboring jurisdictions," the sergeant told him.

"We're not doing street rips and shit, are we?" Guinn asked.

"Nope, no street rips," the sergeant said. "That's an order."

Soon Guinn was in Bealefeld's office with others who had been tapped for the squad. Bealefeld reiterated to them that the work was to be focused and deliberate, then directed them to a sixth-floor office where a group of state troopers was ready to get to work with them. The Maryland State Police had sent some of their best to take part in the GTTF as well, including a trooper who had worked executive protection for the governor, and another who had been recognized for his bravery after being wounded in the line of duty. The Baltimore County Police and the Bureau of Alcohol, Tobacco, and Firearms were also providing officers.

The task force's mission was to trace guns back to distributors and straw purchasers. Instead of prowling neighborhoods and taking one gun out of circulation at a time, they were going to seize weapons in bunches by tracing them to the people who were putting them onto the street. The work would take them around the state, whether executing raids on the Eastern Shore or on a pawnshop just outside the city in Glen Burnie.

"We were like one big unit," Guinn recalled, "and we went everywhere."

In its first full year, the task force was getting big results through fewer but more deliberate investigations, seizing 268 guns through just forty-one arrests. After they took down a gun dealer who had executed an illegal sale at a gun show, the weapons they seized were spread out at a table at a news conference with mayors from around the Mid-Atlantic region, including New York City mayor Michael Bloomberg.

JENKINS HAD BEEN THRIVING in the aggressive atmosphere of the plainclothes enforcement units. He had been working regularly alongside other detectives who went on to federal task forces, the pinnacle for plainclothes officers. Asked on the stand in one trial about what type of training he had to go through, Jenkins responded that he had learned by doing and by studying under other officers whom he considered "legends," such as Mike Fries and Keith Gladstone: "They've got more narcotics seizures in their careers than any narcotics officers," he said. "On a consistent basis, they're getting 'weight.' When I say 'weight,' I'm talking large-scale seizures of marijuana, large-scale seizures of cocaine, seizures of hundreds of grams of heroin." Jenkins claimed that he was now carrying the torch: "I constantly, on a regular basis, get the largest seizures in our unit. On a regular basis." In early 2009, he and another detective who would later go on to work with the Drug Enforcement Administration found forty-one kilograms of cocaine—worth $3 million—in the back of a flatbed truck. "To get a 41-kilo seizure, that's extraordinary by anyone's measure," Commissioner Bealefeld said at a news conference with the packaged bricks lined up on a table. It was considered the largest cocaine seizure without federal assistance in the city's history, and it earned Jenkins a Bronze Star. It was his second award in two years.

One officer recalled standing in a long line to submit evidence at police headquarters and watching Jenkins stomp up and down "like King Kong," berating the other officers about not getting enough guns.

"I got two guns," Jenkins crowed, according to this officer. "I can get another. What the fuck are you guys doing? You're not doing shit."

The officer remembered being in awe of Jenkins from afar, likening the feeling to that of watching Mark McGwire and Sammy Sosa the year they were chasing the single-season home run record: "How is he doing it? Why can't I be like this guy?"

Another recalled him this way: "That dude was like the messiah of drugs. You'd hear stories; people would say, 'Bro, I've seen Wayne stop a junkie, flip that guy to who sold it, flip that guy to who he's getting packs from, [up to the person who was dealing] the raw form.' All in the course of a day. It was like goddamn, dude, that's fucking crazy." The same officer described a personal interaction in which Jenkins displayed his prowess: "We're driving a pretty quick pace, and like literally, we just left the district parking lot two minutes before. He slams on the brakes. He says, 'You see that, that guy had a stack of cash.' He did it so quick. He throws the car in reverse. . . . It was like, 'How the fuck? How the fuck did you see this?'"

Others, however, were skeptical: "It just didn't seem possible he could run the pace he ran and do it by the book," one said. "If you could get away from him, you got away from him, and if it wasn't affecting you, you just let it be."

The onetime stutterer who'd been called "Rudy" on the high school football team was no longer the underdog. In Jenkins's spare time he participated in mixed martial arts, where his nickname was "Silverback" and he went 7-0 as an amateur. He won the "Battle of Baltimore" grappling title in 2009 and took thirty-eight seconds at another event to knock out his opponent in a cage-fighting match during an event called "Barbarian Fight Club."

"Fuck his ass up, Wayne!" a man in the crowd yelled on a video clip of the fight posted to YouTube, as Jenkins, his head completely shaved, pummeled his opponent with punches and kicks. After Jenkins was declared the victor, a young relative entered the ring wearing an American flag like a cape.

"I saw you over here jumping up and down and screaming at the top of your lungs. What do you think about this guy's win right now?" the ring announcer asked the boy.

"He's awesome!" the boy said, before being lifted in the air by Jenkins and pumping his fists.

ONE ATTORNEY WAS DETERMINED to slow Jenkins down. Richard C. B. Woods had taken on two cases in which clients vigorously disputed the account put forward by Jenkins and his fellow plainclothes officers. One was a criminal case in federal court, another a civil case in the city. The first to go forward was the criminal case.

One drizzly afternoon in February 2008, Rodney Baylor stepped onto a woman's front porch in Northeast Baltimore. It was about 2 P.M. on a Friday, and he was looking for some side work beyond his job cutting grass for the State Highway Administration. Baylor was providing the woman an estimate for her lawn when he heard tires screeching and a crash. He turned to see men carrying guns jump out of a blue Nissan that had just smashed into an Acura SUV as it was pulling into a parking space. One of the men started beating on the passenger side window of the SUV with his gun, shattering it, and the driver was pulled out of the car through the window.

"I got on the ground once I'd seen all of that," Baylor said. "I thought they were going to stick the guy up or shoot him. I didn't see any badges or anything."

The men with the guns were Jenkins and a crew of officers that included Daniel Hersl. They were after Mickey Oakley, a forty-two-year-old man who, they said they'd been told, stored and sold drugs. Oakley was caught that day with four hundred gelcaps of heroin in a paper bag. The officers then took his keys and raided his apartment, where they found guns, more drugs, and packaging material. Oakley said they had made entry before obtaining a warrant; officially, Jenkins said he had entered the apartment with a warrant at 5:50 P.M.— almost four hours after the detectives swooped in on Oakley in the street. Other officers would later say Jenkins had merely tried Oakley's keys in the door to see if they worked, and had not entered.

Four months later Oakley was indicted on federal drug charges. Though he didn't dispute having drugs when he was arrested, he wanted to fight the case. The officers had lied in their account of what led them to him, he claimed, and how the arrest had unfolded: Jenkins had written in a sworn affidavit that Oakley was carrying a brown paper bag, which Jenkins said he had been told by an informant would contain heroin. Oakley did have such a bag, but he asserted it was underneath his hoodie and never visible. A suspect admitting to having drugs in hopes of beating his case was all but unheard of, but that's exactly what Oakley was doing—his own guilt, he was arguing, didn't mean police could bypass the rules or make things up.

Woods sought to ding Jenkins's credibility. His clients in another case involving Jenkins claimed Jenkins had left out key facts about the circumstances of a search inside a West Baltimore bar. In this case, they had video evidence. Jenkins and his squad had detained everyone inside the bar. Although Jenkins had written that one of the men turned over his car keys, the video showed Jenkins searching him and taking the keys out of his pocket after slapping a phone out of his hands. It was perhaps a small lie, but a lie nonetheless.

"The suspect didn't voluntarily produce a key. It was taken out of his pockets within seconds of the police officers entering. I gave the tape to the government because I wanted them to realize there was a good faith basis for these questions," Woods told the judge in Oakley's case. "I think they go to the very heart of the truth of his statement of probable cause, and I think that in that particular instance, he fabricated information and included it on a sworn statement."

When Jenkins took the stand, he shrugged off the questions about the bar case. He said it was a simple mistake and he'd been cleared of wrongdoing by police and prosecutors in the bar case.

"As far as you know, did they investigate you personally?" the federal prosecutor asked Jenkins.

"Yes, ma'am."

"What were the results of their investigation of you?"

"The Internal Affairs case was open and closed," Jenkins said. The city prosecutor overseeing the narcotics units had also "cleared me of any intent-related issues," he added.

Woods pressed forward with trying to quiz the officers about their actions arresting Oakley, trying to get someone to slip up. The officers presented a united front, saying they hadn't rammed Oakley's car; rather, Oakley had reversed into them before throwing the bag of drugs out of his car window.

Judge Catherine Blake said the claims of Oakley and Baylor didn't "make any sense" when compared to the officers' account.

"It appears that not just Detective Jenkins, but virtually all the other officers . . . would have to be inaccurate in their testimony if it is to be believed that Detective Jenkins was manufacturing information for the affidavit," Blake said.

Frustrated, Oakley took a guilty plea but stood his ground at his sentencing.

"I would like to say I'm feeling a lot of remorse for my actions I have led through my life," Oakley said, "and I also feel kind of torn between feelings because I came forth with the truth about the incident that happened, as far as what the officers had done. I think that if I am held responsible for my actions, then the same should be with the officers for their wrongdoing."

Woods still had another chance at Jenkins, when the bar case went before a civil jury a year later. Two months earlier the officers' target in the raid, Antonio Lee, had been murdered. The other bar patrons still wanted justice for the unjustified encounter. The attorney representing Jenkins and his unit told the jurors that the officers were the "best of the best," who had "not and will not ever give up on the war on drugs."

Woods delivered an impassioned rebuttal, saying that officers couldn't do whatever they wanted in their quest to stop crime. The officers had been caught in "lie after lie after lie," he said. "You decide if you want the elite of the elite to get a rubber stamp on constitutional deprivation. You, the citizens of Baltimore, say no. No! These constitutional rights people bled for and died for, upon which our government was founded, these liberties we hold so dear, you cannot ignore them. You cannot assume that because a man is in an impoverished neighborhood, surrounded by drugs and violence, that he is a criminal. You cannot! You cannot invade his personal space, and touch him and go in his pockets with a reasonable belief.

"You break a man's jaw, the bone heals. You break a man's spirit, you take away his faith in his own liberty, his own right to express his constitutional freedom from unreasonable search and seizures, you make him feel powerless and humiliated and afraid that every police officer he sees is going to do whatever he wants."

The jury considered thirty-nine counts in the lawsuit and acquitted the officers of every count except one: battery, against Jenkins. Woods had asked for $250,000 to each of four plaintiffs.

Instead, the jury awarded one dollar.

Woods picked up his bag, tucked the verdict sheet inside, closed it, and stretched out his arms to push the bag away. He clasped his hands together, looking down. The jury had determined the encounter was simply collateral damage of the drug war.

"They have free rein to do whatever they want now," one of the plaintiffs said after the verdict.

GUINN HAD BEEN WORKING on the commissioner's Gun Trace Task Force when he was tabbed for another priority initiative—a "violent repeat offender" squad tasked with building cases against high-priority targets. Jenkins was also among those selected for the detail. The two had never worked together before. Guinn said Jenkins refused to follow rules and was always going out on his own and floating between assignments.

"I was told I wouldn't like Wayne—that he was arrogant, a loudmouth," Guinn recalled. "Right off the bat, I hated the guy."

Also joining the new squad were Sean Suiter and Keith Gladstone. The latter, Guinn observed, "was like Wayne's sensei."

The crash involving Umar Burley happened a few weeks into their new assignment, and Guinn recalls that afterward Jenkins started acting paranoid: In addition to listening to Burley's jail calls and saying he didn't want to testify if the case went to trial, he said he believed a car was parked outside his home, watching him. Guinn brushed it off as more high-strung behavior from Jenkins. No one in command seemed to spend too much time dwelling on Burley either, as the special unit kept making cases. In August, the new mayor, Stephanie Rawlings-Blake, held a news conference to highlight their work. Jenkins, Suiter, and Gladstone had just raided a car wash in Northwest Baltimore, where they reported seizing two pounds of cocaine, six weapons including an assault pistol, $4,000 cash, and a twenty-four-foot powerboat. At the mayor's press conference, the drugs and weapons were spread out on a table for the media. "We're targeting violent offenders," the mayor told reports. "We're getting drugs off the street."

Guinn had left the squad just before that big hit—he had been told from the start that his stint would be short, and he returned to the Gun Trace Task Force. But it wasn't the same GTTF he had left. There was a new commander who was urging more street rips, which went against the unit's original goal of selectively targeting key players in the gun-trafficking trade. The Maryland State Police and county police, not interested in having their officers roaming city neighborhoods, had also pulled their officers out of the GTTF, dropping the number of officers from fourteen to just five. The once-elite unit had lost its luster.

ONE DETECTIVE WHO WORKED with Jenkins during this time period said that when Jenkins debriefed suspects he had a particular way of asking them about who police should target next. He didn't ask them who their supplier was or who the biggest players in town were. Instead, he asked, "If you was going to rob somebody, who would it be?" The officer figured Jenkins was just trying to speak in the vernacular, but in hindsight, the framing of the question was telling.

In addition to being brash, Jenkins was obsessed with speculating about other cops being dirty, and insisting—without provocation—that he wasn't.

A peculiar incident in January 2011 raised the possibility that he was being watched. The agency's plainclothes officers were often assigned late-model rental cars that would better blend in on the streets. Jenkins was assigned a 2010 Dodge Avenger as his departmental vehicle. Five weeks later, it suddenly shut down in the middle of the road, and Jenkins had it towed to a dealership to be fixed.

When Jenkins called to find out why the repairs were taking so long, he was told there was damage to the electrical system caused by an after-market GPS tracking system the mechanic had found installed under the car. According to an internal report written by one of Jenkins's supervisors at the time, the device was wallet-sized, with an antenna sticking out. The mechanic told Jenkins it had been hastily installed and the wiring job had caused electrical failures and malfunctions. Jenkins asked if it could be a LoJack-type device, installed by the rental company to track their property.

"I've been doing this type of work half my life, and I've never seen a device like this," the mechanic said, according to the report.

The next morning, the mechanic would tell the officers later, a mysterious man arrived at the dealership claiming he was from the "installation department" and was there to recover the device. The man walked straight to the car, got on his knees, and removed the device. "He did not provide his name, who he worked for, or what he was going to do about the damage caused to the vehicle," Jenkins's supervisor wrote in an internal report at the time. "Additionally the mechanic stated that the male seemed angry that the device had been discovered. As he removed the device he attempted to conceal it in a box, then stormed out of the dealership in a hurry. The mechanic stated that it all seemed very odd as the male got back into his truck which also had a white K-9 in it."

An officer friendly with Jenkins at the time said Jenkins was disturbed by the episode but never found out who had installed the device or why. There was reason for Jenkins to suspect it might have been the FBI or Internal Affairs. That might have spooked most officers, but not Jenkins.

CHAPTER FOUR
EYES AND EARS

IN THE BALTIMORE POLICE Department's paramilitary structure, the most crucial supervision occurs at the sergeant level. Sergeants are the bosses who directly observe and interact with the officers on the ground; they report their observations to a lieutenant who oversees multiple sergeants and their respective squads; the lieutenants report to captains who oversee multiple lieutenants; the captains to majors; the majors to lieutenant colonels; the lieutenant colonels to colonels; the colonels to deputy commissioners; the deputy commissioners to the commissioner. And just as good sergeants can ensure that information makes its way to the top, they can also screen problems and keep complaints from going any further.

Wayne Jenkins was promoted to sergeant on November 30, 2012. Now he joined those who were the department's eyes and ears.

There's a tradition in the BPD that officers in specialized units who are promoted return to patrol work, and for the first time since being a rookie a decade earlier, Jenkins donned a uniform and climbed into a patrol car. The return is meant to keep supervisors connected to patrol, the backbone of the department, and to spread their experience to new places. For young officers in the Northeastern District where he was assigned, this was seen as a chance to work with one of the department's best.

James Kostoplis had joined the BPD earlier that year. A native of northern New Jersey, he was twenty years old but looked even younger. His father and brothers were police officers, like other family members before them. Too young to join a police force right after high school, he worked retail security, chasing shoplifters. Kostoplis's first assignment as an officer was the midnight shift in the busiest and roughest sector of the sprawling and chronically understaffed Northeastern District: its southernmost portion, with neighborhoods like the "Four by Four," a tiny four-block-by-four-block area, and Coldstream-Homestead-Montbello, nicknamed "the CHUM." The overnight shift tended to be quiet, however, with cops mostly patrolling and responding to building alarm calls. After a few months, Kostoplis wrote his first warrant for a gun arrest. Writing warrants was an essential part of what was considered to be more sophisticated police work. He liked it.

Jenkins showed him the ropes, going over the department's general orders for search and seizures and how to check "deconfliction" databases to make sure no one else was investigating the target already. After their overnight shift ended, they'd often grab breakfast with other officers and continue talking shop.

"He was pretty squared away," Kostoplis said of his sergeant. "I had not heard about him until I met him, but once I met him, people were like, 'He's good,' and he *was* good. He had a very keen eye for drug activity. No matter where you put him. He knew what he saw when he saw it, and he could articulate it real well, and I think that's what made him successful."

As they drove around, Jenkins loved to put on old school rap music from another officer's playlist. Kostoplis remembers that when the Geto Boys' "Mind Playing Tricks on Me" came on, Jenkins shushed everyone and recited the lyrics about being successful but paranoid. (Another officer who worked with Jenkins years later also said Jenkins loved rap music and "would try to freestyle battle other officers and even citizens.")

Kostoplis remembered cruising the sector with Jenkins one night, looking for a shooting suspect's vehicle. When they spotted it, the driver hopped out and started running. Jenkins went one way and Kostoplis went another. The man, who was carrying a big gun—Kostoplis thought it might be a .357 Desert Eagle—ran into an alley, ditching the weapon. Now in the alley being pursued by Kostoplis, the man suddenly stopped running and turned. It was just him and Kostoplis. Kostoplis wasn't sure if the man was squaring up to fight or if he might have another weapon. He was nervous and gearing up for a confrontation. Suddenly, Jenkins came out of nowhere and grabbed the man from behind, placing him under arrest. Knowing you could trust your partners to have your back was one of the top-valued qualities among officers on the streets.

On another occasion he had a front-row seat as Jenkins responded to a fiery crash involving other officers who had embarked on a high-speed chase of a fleeing car that collided with another vehicle. Kostoplis recalled the intense heat of the flames and having to physically block Jenkins from climbing into the car in an attempt to save a woman inside.

In less intense scenarios, Kostoplis recalled Jenkins had the "gift of gab" with drug dealers they stopped. He knew the streets, and the dealers recognized it and respected him. The young officer wanted to be like that.

"It was pretty cool to watch, me being brand-new," he said.

Kostoplis remembered Jenkins giving him other advice as well.

"The first time I ever rode with him, he said, 'If we're going to work together, I have two rules: We don't put stuff on people, and we don't take money.'"

No problem there, Kostoplis thought to himself.

Two weeks after his promotion, Jenkins was driving home on Interstate 95 after playing blackjack at Delaware Park Casino with Donald Carroll Stepp Jr., an old family friend. Stepp had known the Jenkins family for close to forty years and had gotten to know Wayne through Texas Hold'em games hosted by Jenkins's brother that were attended by other police officers. During the casino trip, Jenkins had spoken of his skill at taking drugs off the street and the big busts he was making.

Now as they returned home, Jenkins had a proposition.

He asked if Stepp would know what to do "if something were to come his way"—whether Stepp would sell the drugs Jenkins was recovering during his police shifts. It would be pure profit, and they would split the proceeds. Stepp was interested.

"I felt comfortable with it because all the police officers that I met—which were many during the card games—in my opinion, they owned the city," Stepp said later. "I look at risk. I thought it was a winner."

Stepp had been in and out of trouble since the early 1980s. Former Baltimore County police commissioner James Johnson, whose career spanned four decades, said Stepp had stood out, even as a kid. He recalled arresting Stepp when he was fourteen years old for breaking into a supermarket on Thanksgiving. Johnson said he later used Stepp as an informant but cut him loose after learning that Stepp was tipping off the person he was supposedly snitching on. He also once encountered Stepp doing a ride-along with another officer and considered Stepp then to be a "police groupie" who sought to immerse himself in police tactics.

Addicted to cocaine and alcohol, Stepp would amass a lengthy rap sheet across the state for stealing things to support his addiction. He emerged from prison in 2002 clean and sober and worked hard to rebuild his life. At a sentence modification hearing a few years after his release, he spoke about his desire to make a change.

"Seven years ago, the state wanted to bury me and they asked you to put me underneath the jail," Stepp told the judge. "A lot of people come in front of you. It's easy to put people in jail. A lot of judges throughout the state, that's all they want to do. Prosecutors want to get convictions. Judges want to bury them in jail, but they never want to look at the real problem. Solving the problem is hard. It's hard for people that's addicted. . . . You told me, 'Mr. Stepp, it doesn't matter. With a record like yours, if you go out and do something wrong, break the law anywhere in this country, you're done for the rest of your life.' And you know what, I knew that from the first day I got locked up with my record. If I got out this time, I knew something would have to be really different, and I did that.

"There's a lot of people drowning in that same addiction. It got me for twenty years but today, your honor, it don't have me. Today is a whole different life. And you know, I've just started to live it. I'm going to turn 38 years old and just start life and it feels good."

The judge remarked: "Out of all the cases that I've had in recent years . . . you've probably made the greatest gains I've ever seen."

Stepp worked construction jobs at first, before landing with a mortgage lender as a loan officer. The real estate market was booming, and Stepp was good at his job. He became the top loan officer in the office, brimming with confidence and putting his powers of persuasion to use. By 2006 he was able to buy a home on the water with a private pier for $850,000. He got engaged and had a child.

Then the housing market crashed, and the Maryland legislature passed a law requiring loan officers to be licensed. Because of his criminal record, Stepp was disqualified. He remained employed with Metropolis, helping in any way he could around the office, but his salary was cut by half.

With a mortgage to pay and his job prospects dimming, Stepp returned to drug dealing, eventually connecting with Colombian and Dominican suppliers.

"It takes a lot of years to get up to people like that," Stepp would later testify.

Since at least the fall of 2011, Stepp had also been toying around with the idea of opening up a bail bonds company. He went to a crowdsourced online design site and asked for help drawing up a design for a company called "Double D Bail Bonds":

"What I am Looking for is a unique, original, sexy, catchy logo that will be able to be copyrighted & trademarked," he wrote. "You should be concentrating on the 'D' in Double D. . . . Target audience: Drug addicts, Criminals, pimps, prostitutes, gangsters, drug dealers, and also just simple good people that just make a mistake.

"COMPANY SLOGAN: 'Everyone loves Double D's'

"(Our company slogan is sexual)"

Dennis Danielczyk, Stepp's boss at the mortgage company, incorporated the business in the summer of that year, and by the fall they had a storefront in downtown Towson, the county seat of Baltimore County and just north of the city. The company logo caused a stir among locals: It depicted an extremely large-chested woman with a

"D" on each breast. When a reporter for a community news website stopped by to ask about the controversy, Stepp talked up his plans to "revolutionize" the bail bonds industry by pairing with local groups to provide rehabilitation and mental health treatment. He brushed off concerns about the logo.

"I guess there are some feminists here," he told the reporter. "I guess that's why it's called America. We all have to get along with different aspects of life, and it's not meant to be taken in an offensive way."

In order for Stepp to officially take over the bail bonds company, he needed to get a waiver to have his criminal past overlooked. In his application to the state insurance agency, he said he'd turned his life around and, through his new company, hoped to do right and give back to the community—he said he planned to use his experiences with addiction to help clients obtain treatment.

He included three character-recommendation letters in his application. One came from his attorney. Another was from Danielczyk. The third was sent on Baltimore Police Department letterhead from Sergeant Wayne Jenkins.

In a two-page typed letter, Jenkins asserted that Stepp had become a model citizen:

Fifteen years ago, I didn't think I'd ever be able to say this, but Donny Stepp is now one of the good guys.

Growing up, our families lived in Essex and were close, and Donny went to school with my siblings. In those days he was smart and funny, and he couldn't sit still! Everything was always a mile a minute, but anything he really set his mind to do, he did well.

Then he started using drugs and developed a really severe habit. Like so many young people, he got caught up in the hustle of stealing to support his habit. I wasn't in touch with him much in those days, but talk in the neighborhood was that he was a mess, in and out of jail for years. It got to the point where I just figured he would wind up dead or doing life in installments.

I went on with my life, became a cop, and have been with the

Baltimore City Police Department for 10 years. I have spent much of my career locking up people like Donny—like the person he was, that is.

After Donny got out of prison the last time, well over a decade ago, I had just gotten honorably discharged from the Marine Corps. Rumor had it that he had walked away from drugs and the drug lifestyle. I was skeptical, knowing how few people ever really do, but as time went on people kept saying he really was changed. Eventually, we ran into each other and I got to see for myself.

I was wary at first, because I have a street mentality perspective, but it didn't take long to see that he had truly changed, and that he was on the right side of the law. Our families began to socialize together. It's hard to explain, because so few people truly make it back from the abyss, but there was something about Donny that left no doubt that he wasn't that person any more. . . .

I hope you will consider granting Donny his license. He truly is a changed man, clean and sober going on 16 years. I trust him with my children. I would trust him with my money. I trust him in my house. I don't even think in terms of whether he is trustworthy any more. He is just Donny, my friend, and a good guy.

By April 2013, Stepp took over the business as a licensed bail bondsman and could be seen driving around a black Ford Raptor pickup truck covered with "Double D Bail Bonds" decals that read "1% Down," "24 Hr Service," and his phone number and website address.

Since their Delaware Park Casino trip in late 2012, a few months before Stepp's waiver application was approved, the dope dropoffs from Jenkins had been occurring regularly in small amounts, with Stepp giving Jenkins hundreds of dollars as his share. Sometimes he and Jenkins would meet up for lunch or breakfast. Other times, if it was late at night, Jenkins would deposit the drugs in a shed outside Stepp's home or ask him to open the garage. Stepp had a client base for cocaine, but Jenkins was eventually dropping off a wide array of narcotics, more than he could handle. "It was just over the top," Stepp said. "Everything and anything that could be imagined. I didn't even know what some of the stuff was. It was coming in such an abundance that I didn't even know what it was."

Business appeared to be going well: A few months after pairing up, Jenkins and Stepp flew to New Orleans to watch the Ravens defeat the 49ers in Super Bowl XLVII. Stepp snapped a selfie of them smiling in their Ravens jerseys and beaded necklaces.

But Jenkins was again playing with fire. Since the spring of 2012, county cops had been quietly pursuing Stepp. Two detectives had separately learned from informants that Stepp was a big cocaine dealer on the east side of Baltimore County. Investigators had surveilled his business. They also watched his home and twice crept up in the middle of the night to search his garbage for evidence of drugs. They even went so far as to secure a "trap and trace" warrant from a judge to review call logs for his business cellphone. In the warrant, Stepp was referred to as an "upper level drug dealer."

He was being watched.

CHAPTER FIVE
DON'T FREEZE UP

IN JANUARY 2014, UMAR BURLEY was escorted into a downtown Baltimore courtroom. With his hands shackled in front of him, he held a manila folder full of papers against his chest. It had been four years since Burley had fled from Jenkins, Suiter, and Guinn and gotten into the crash that killed Elbert Davis. Burley had always insisted privately that he didn't have drugs in his car, but, facing a squeeze from both state and federal prosecutors, he'd pleaded guilty and was serving his time in a western Maryland prison.

He was emotionally destroyed. He'd been a shell of himself since his mother passed away from cancer—he had cared for her and watched her take her last breaths. He now had a granddaughter, but he refused to let her visit because he didn't want her to see him locked up. "Grandad, I've never seen you before—why are you not home? Why have I never seen you before?" she'd ask over the phone. He tried to make the most of the time away. He was able to clear his head and refocus on what was important to him, and he also helped tutor other inmates. Eventually he would be transferred to federal custody to serve out the final years of his sentence, and he hoped that from there he could mount a case to have his conviction overturned or his sentence reduced.

In the courtroom were six of Elbert Davis's adult children and their two attorneys, who were seeking damages for their father's death. No one sat on Burley's side. A gang fight had prompted an extended lockdown at the facility—there'd been no phone, no visitors, and no access to the library, and he'd been unable to secure legal representation. He wasn't quite sure what the hearing was about.

Judge John Carroll Byrnes, who was retired but continuing to hear cases, began the proceedings by announcing their purpose was to assess the amount of damages against Burley, following the entry of a default judgment against him months earlier.

"What's a 'default judgment'?" Burley asked, interrupting the judge.

"First of all, sir, do you have an attorney, or any representation at all in this civil suit?" Byrnes asked.

"I was coming to ask for a postponement or continuance in this matter, because I didn't—I don't understand the language and nature of the laws and stuff that's being brung before me," Burley said. "Uh, furthermore, um, I have litigating"—he meant mitigating—"circumstances as far as where I'm housed at and stuff like that caused me not to have an attorney at this time." Burley thought that, as in criminal court, he would get an attorney appointed to represent him.

Burley didn't realize he'd already lost the case. Byrnes said Burley hadn't responded to the civil suit, and by default the court had ruled in favor of the Davis children.

"You're aware a default judgment was entered against you?"

"I don't even know what a default judgment is," Burley reiterated. "A lot of things have been done in this case, and this, what I understand, this can affect me not just for now but for my whole lifetime. So this is a very serious matter, so I'm throwing my mercy on the court, so I can get an attorney in this matter."

"It's not unreasonable that you thought maybe you'd get a free attorney in a case like this," Byrnes said, "but the answer is you don't."

Byrnes continued explaining the process of how the judgment came to be.

"Do you understand what I'm saying so far?" Byrnes asked Burley. "I'm not asking you to agree with me, but do you understand it?"

"No, I don't understand."

"What part don't you understand, sir?"

"I don't understand none of it."

"I think you understand it, to be honest with you, because what I said is really not that complicated," the judge said.

Burley looked uncomfortable. He wobbled his legs occasionally. Still handcuffed, he continued to hold his papers against his body.

"Is there anything about 'foreseen circumstances,' or something like that?" Burley said, meaning to say "unforeseen circumstances."

Byrnes brushed off the question and moved to have Burley sworn in.

"Everything you say from now on will be under oath, so if you falsify anything—this is true of any person presenting information—it would be considered perjury, which is a crime. So listen carefully to the clerk," Byrnes said.

The courtroom clerk rose and asked Burley to raise his right hand.

"No, hold up," Burley said.

"That's good enough," Byrnes said to the clerk.

"I don't even understand what we're doing right now," Burley protested.

"Sir, you're going to be given the oath right now. Let's go step by step. The first step, I've taken. The second step, you're going to be administered an oath. . . . It's not complicated," Byrnes said.

"I'm trying to figure how we got from me asking you about that, to now—"

"You don't have to understand how we got there," Byrnes said. "You are there. So, your right hand, as far as I'm concerned, is in the air. . . ." Burley's hand was under the table.

The clerk read the oath, and told Burley to say, "I do." There was silence.

"Do you intend to swear, sir?" Byrnes asked.

Burley had had enough. From his standpoint, the case had gone too far already, with the verdict going against him despite his not having any say. Now he was still unrepresented, and a judge was telling him to swear to an oath that could bring more penalties. Burley searched for something to say that might bring the proceedings to a halt.

"I plead the Fifth," Burley said.

"Pardon me?" the judge said, leaning forward.

"I plead my Fifth Amendment rights."

"Okay," Byrnes said. "Officer, you can take him back then. Good luck to you, sir."

With that, Burley stood up, mumbling under his breath, and was led out of the room so that the Davis family and their attorneys could discuss with Byrnes how much money Burley would owe them for the rest of his life.

There had been a dispute within the family about how to proceed—the executor of the estate wanted to sue the police department for their role in a high-speed chase, but the other siblings wanted to proceed against Burley. The executor eventually stood down, and an amount to be assessed against Burley was reached: $1,092,500.

Burley remained in a prison cell the next day as Byrnes prepared an order memorializing the amount, and the clerk passed it around for each family member to sign. During the four years waiting to get to this point, the children had separated into factions. Byrnes said it was time to come together, for their father, and put the ordeal behind them.

"All I need you to do is sign your name under the second page and that'll bring happiness to all," Byrnes said.

MAYOR RAWLINGS-BLAKE DECIDED TO make another shift in the city's policing approach. With homicides and shootings maintaining a downward trend, she would move to slash hundreds of police officer positions—the first significant reduction in the ranks in decades. Though the Violent Crimes Impact Division (VCID) had been heralded as the key to driving down crime, the mayor continued to hear criticism during her rounds in community meetings about its detectives' aggressive tactics. Inevitably, when a resident raised a concern about being manhandled during an unjustified stop, they blamed the "knockers." When Bealefeld left in 2012, she saw a chance for a fresh start: She bypassed his deputy Barksdale and brought in Anthony Batts, who had led the Oakland, California, police department as it faced federally mandated reforms.

Somehow, the Baltimore police force had avoided such federal scrutiny while cities like Albuquerque, Cincinnati, Cleveland, New Orleans, Pittsburgh, Portland, and Seattle had entered into consent decree agreements that bound the departments to reform overseen by a judge. While Batts had branded himself as a reform-minded commissioner ("We must have a reverence for human life," he liked to say), he hadn't emerged from Oakland with a positive view of federal oversight. Batts had fled Oakland in part because he loathed the micromanaging involved with a federal judge having to approve decisions regarding the operations of the department. "Here in Oakland, I can't react as quickly," he said in an exit interview with *Oakland North*. "I have to ask, 'Mother, may I?' to make sure everyone is OK with what I'm doing. . . . So I really don't have control of all my resources and my numbers and my deployment." In Baltimore, Batts wanted to do whatever he could to demonstrate that the department was on the right track and to avoid going through that process again. But he retained a mostly homegrown leadership team, and institutional change would not come easy.

Within a few months of taking over, Batts slimmed down the VCID unit and renamed it the "Special Enforcement Section." It would now fall under the control of patrol districts, meaning that district majors were supposed to call the shots instead of a centralized plainclothes command. At least that was the plan. Many of the same hard-chargers remained in the new unit. Jenkins was freed from his patrol assignment and placed in the SES squad overseeing a team of officers.

Another one of Batts's efforts at reform was the creation of a new unit to take a close look at incidents in which officers used force, and one of their first cases involved Jenkins.

Demetric Simon had been driving through Northeast Baltimore in his Audi when he saw what appeared to be police in an unmarked car shadowing him. He parked and started walking. Jenkins pulled up and asked to speak with him. Simon said later he had thought the men in the car were officers, but "they looked up to something." Nervous, he took off running. Detective Ben Frieman jumped out of the car to pursue Simon on foot, while Jenkins followed in the vehicle. Frieman lost Simon around a corner, but Jenkins had him in his sights.

Simon was running down the street and through the front yard of a home when the vehicle hit him: He remembers looking back and seeing Jenkins's car go airborne, then landing on the steps of a home.

"I was under the car, and the wheel was spinning by my face," he said.

Simon, who was unarmed, said he looked up and saw Jenkins and Frieman standing over him. He said Frieman "looked at Jenkins like, 'Why'd you run him over?' Jenkins grabbed him by the wrist and was like, 'Don't freeze up on me.'"

Simon said he was unable to move, though he ultimately had no serious injuries. Jenkins "kept patting me down, kept asking, 'Why'd you run?'" Simon said.

Jenkins got onto the dispatch radio.

"Can I please have a medic? I got a number one male that was hit by my vehicle," he told the dispatcher, who asked whether the man was conscious. "Yes, ma'am, yes ma'am, he is. . . . He's moving around a little bit."

Officers heard Jenkins on the radio and responded to secure the scene. Among them was newly minted Sergeant Ryan Guinn, who had been promoted and was now assigned to Northeastern District patrol, where the incident had occurred. Jenkins was supposed to be working on the west side.

Guinn saw Jenkins's car parked on the street, and tire marks by the steps of the home.

"What the fuck did you do?" Guinn said he asked Jenkins.

"Yo dawg, we tried to stop this motherfucker. He ran across the street, then he pointed a gun at me, so I hit him with the car," Jenkins said, according to Guinn.

If true, that scenario was likely to be deemed an acceptable reason to use force, though that would be someone else's job to determine. Guinn asked where the gun was.

"I don't know, it's around here somewhere. He pointed it right at me," Jenkins said. Guinn told a patrolman to start canvassing the area looking for cameras that might show the incident. By this point, he said, Jenkins was charged up, "running back and forth like a psycho." Guinn asked Jenkins where his lieutenant was, and Jenkins walked away saying he was going to call Sergeant Keith Gladstone.

Gladstone was eating at a Peruvian chicken spot with an officer from his own squad when he got up from the table to take a phone call. A panicked Jenkins explained the situation—he confided that he had run over an unarmed man after a chase.

The officer Gladstone was eating with called another officer in the squad, and the pair went to that officer's home in South Baltimore and retrieved a BB gun, then drove up to the crash scene. Gladstone walked past Guinn and was out of view for what seemed like three to four minutes, according to Guinn.

"It's over by the truck," Gladstone told Jenkins, in earshot of Guinn.

Radio transmissions captured a patrol officer saying a firearm had been found. Jenkins then got on the radio: "You *do* have a firearm?" Jenkins said, sounding surprised. "Do not touch it, wait for crime lab!"

Frieman later took part in two interviews with the department's use-of-force investigators, telling them that Simon had grabbed his waistband area as if he might be securing a weapon but that Frieman had never seen one.

"I didn't see it until it was recovered. He didn't pull it out while he was running from me," Frieman said.

Simon was taken to a hospital for treatment, where police said hospital staff found drugs in his rectum. After he was taken to Central Booking and read the charging papers alleging he had a gun, he called Internal Affairs to complain but later stopped cooperating with the investigation. His attorney at the time, Paul Polansky, said that as a practical matter people in Simon's position had to make difficult choices out of fear that anything they conceded could be used against them in court.

"I tell my clients: Keep your damn mouth shut unless they're willing to offer you some kind of deal that's going to be to your advantage," Polansky said.

The case was supposed to be scrutinized closely by the detectives on Commissioner Batts's new Force Investigation Team. But in their subsequent investigation, which went on for months and spanned some five hundred pages of reports and scene photos, Gladstone's name never appeared as having been present. The Internal Affairs investigator wrote that she was "unable to gather any information which would contradict the sequence of events explained to me by the detectives." Jenkins was cleared of wrongdoing.

MOLLY WEBB, A THIRTY-ONE-YEAR-OLD assistant state's attorney, had questions. She had been assigned a drug case brought by Jenkins and Frieman in February 2014 against a twenty-nine-year-old man named Walter Price. In the statement of probable cause, Frieman said that while conducting surveillance of Price he'd watched him stuff an object into the inside roof of his van. Frieman wrote that when he and Jenkins approached the van with patrol officers and asked Price to get out they saw him reach back into the vehicle toward the ceiling. He said that Price then gave them permission to search the van and that Jenkins found a clear plastic bag containing seven grams of cocaine under the ceiling. During a subsequent raid on Price's home led by Sergeant Keith Gladstone, police said they found drugs throughout the residence.

Webb wondered about a reference to a "confidential reliable source" who'd tipped off Frieman about Price. When she followed up with him, Frieman told her the source had been arrested in a raid a few days prior and had given the detectives information on a number of dealers in the area. He had agreed to set up Price, calling him to purchase an eight-ball of cocaine, and Jenkins and Frieman had begun their surveillance.

Frieman's explanation gave Webb some pause: A "confidential reliable source" usually referred to someone who had established a relationship of trust with the police, rather than just a person officers had arrested a few days earlier. But she researched the issue and decided the case could move forward.

A few days later, however, she came across new evidence that would take her worries to another level: Price's defense attorney contacted her and said he had CCTV footage of the stop and arrest that he had obtained from the city. Webb hadn't been given the footage by police—a red flag. And Price's attorney said it showed the officers lied about the case.

The video showed Price being stopped, jostled around, and pulled out of his car, then taken into an unmarked police vehicle nearby.

Jenkins and other detectives were shown searching the car for about fifteen minutes, but at no point did any of them signal they'd found drugs. About an hour went by with Price being questioned inside the detectives' vehicle. There was no discovery of drugs seen on the tape after that either.

"When I saw the video," Webb recalled later, "it didn't corroborate what was in the statement of probable cause at all."

On dispatch recordings, Jenkins—not Frieman—could be heard telling patrol officers to pull Price over, falsely claiming it had to do with commercial burglaries in the area. They had also detained Price's girlfriend and infant child, who had arrived on the scene.

Webb showed the video to her supervisors, who instructed her not to contact Frieman and to forward everything to the Police Integrity Section, the prosecutors' unit that investigated police.

Those prosecutors started taking witnesses in front of a grand jury. In April 2014, Price sat down for a "proffer" session with prosecutors and Internal Affairs detectives. Though he was working in home improvement and trying to get a start-up tech company off the ground, Price admitted that he was still selling drugs—normally a half-ounce of coke, one-hundred-dollar and fifty-dollar amounts at a time. He claimed to hide the drugs in his pockets or his rectum. Price said he had left his home on February 19 when he saw a "knocker"— the street term for plainclothes officers—on his block. Concerned, he went back home and stuffed the half ounce of cocaine he was carrying into the arm of his couch.

For the hour he was in the car being questioned by the cops, Price said the officers tried to get him to give information on other dealers. He said that Jenkins left and then returned with a sandwich bag containing a half ounce of cocaine, which he claimed he'd found in Price's van. It "looked like what he put in his couch at his home," investigators said Price told them, adding that he "reported that he did not have any narcotics in his vehicle and does not know where the officer retrieved the narcotics."

On May 21, two of the police integrity prosecutors, Shelley Glenn and Jenifer Layman, met with Paul Pineau, the chief of staff to State's Attorney Gregg Bernstein, to discuss what to do with the case. They discussed their attempts to sway an unnamed officer—believed to be Frieman—to give up dirt on Jenkins.

"I think he's given us all he's going to give us, and we're not getting Jenkins," Layman said.

"Did we raise the possibility of a wire?" Pineau asked.

"We did not," Layman said.

Pineau wanted to know more about their conversation with the officer. "What did he say, how did it go," he said. "Tell me about it."

She said that Frieman claimed he didn't know where the drugs had come from. He told her that he was taking Jenkins's word for it but that he knew from working with the sergeant that he often had a knack for finding drugs. "He goes on and on gushing about Sergeant Jenkins," Layman said.

"Oh yeah, he idolizes the guy," Glenn said.

Again paraphrasing Frieman, Layman said, "'He's probably the best drug detective in the city. There's been plenty of times where . . . the suspect has said, 'The drugs are in the car,' and I go and can't find them, and Jenkins says, 'Did you look in the console' and pulls the rug back and boom. Plenty of times, he's gone behind me and found them.'"

"And he said, 'I've seen it, so I don't have any reason to believe it's a plant,'" Glenn said.

A few days later, the state's attorney's office formally declined to charge the officers with a crime after determining there was insufficient evidence.

But Jenkins and Frieman weren't in the clear yet. The police department's own Internal Affairs detectives would go on to interrogate them for violations of department rules in the Price case.

The two officers sat for separate interviews with their attorneys present and denied any wrongdoing. Jenkins, who had been given an opportunity to review the video ahead of time, asserted that the investigation had been done by the book and that the video didn't tell the whole story. Jenkins said they had taken Price into custody on a bluff, claiming that they had found the eight-ball already, and that he had eagerly agreed to cooperate. That was not what Frieman had told the prosecutor a year earlier, when he told Webb that Price "would not play." Jenkins claimed that after gathering information from Price, he looked in the car again, in a spot Frieman had already checked, and found the cocaine. "I missed it, apparently," Frieman said in his own interview. This discovery wasn't captured on tape, though someone who had viewed the video would know that there was a fifteen-minute period where the camera was pointed away from the van.

Investigators weren't buying it. On March 17, 2015, Jenkins was charged with several internal misconduct counts, as was Frieman.

During his twelve-year career, Jenkins had avoided punishment as his star rose. Now he was facing administrative charges with potential consequences.

The Baltimore Police Department as a whole had also dodged accountability over the years, often using its own dysfunction as a crutch. Too few resources, too much crime; the beat went on. But less than a month after Jenkins was charged, the city would erupt. A reckoning was coming, one that would bring unprecedented scrutiny to the BPD but also upend the case against Jenkins.

CHAPTER SIX
GROUND SHIFT

THE 2014 RACE FOR Baltimore's top prosecutor position had been fought over who was tougher on crime and would work better with police. Though homicides in Baltimore had reached a three-decade low in 2011, the number had crept upward since. Marilyn Mosby, a young former local prosecutor whose husband was an up-and-coming city councilman representing West Baltimore, hammered away on the incumbent state's attorney, Gregg Bernstein, saying the crime rate remained too high and the blame should fall on the first-term chief prosecutor.

In her campaign kickoff speech, Mosby spoke of the dangers lurking on the streets of Baltimore, with only the faintest undertones of a need to change the criminal justice system.

"I've been in your shoes. I've locked my doors. I've clutched my purse," she said. Baltimore was the "home of witness intimidation" and the "stop snitching mentality," she added.

She marched the streets with a bullhorn for weekly "Enough Is Enough" antiviolence rallies. During one radio appearance, a caller said that her comments sounded "like Republican rhetoric."

Bernstein had eliminated his predecessor's "do not call" list of problem cops and had declined to prosecute two recent high-profile

Baltimore police custody deaths: In 2013, forty-four-year-old Tyrone West died after he tried to get away from police during a traffic stop in Northeast Baltimore; onlookers said police had beaten him, while an autopsy concluded that his heart merely gave out. Activists and family members passionately took up the cause, with West's family leading a weekly "West Wednesday" protest. Before that, in 2012, Anthony Anderson, forty-six, was bear-hugged and thrown to the ground by drug cops in East Baltimore, breaking eight ribs, one of which punctured his spleen. Anderson had been walking through a lot when the officers stopped him and, saying they feared he was about to swallow drugs, took him down. In explaining why the officers would not face criminal charges, Bernstein said that there were different standards for dealing with law enforcement officers because force was often part of their job. "In point of fact, when you're dealing with investigations involving excessive force with police officers," he said, "it's a completely different paradigm."

His decisions on those cases and his decision to nix the list were not made into campaign issues. Mosby expressly praised police and said they were not the problem in Baltimore's war on crime. Raised in Boston, she came from a line of police officers, which she highlighted to beef up the idea that she understood law enforcement and would work with police to solve cases and drive down crime.

"It is my genuine belief that despite what we all might want to think, and we all might want to believe, the police officers in our city are doing their jobs. I repeat: The police officers in Baltimore City are doing their jobs," she said.

She said her motivation to fight crime was personal, sparked by the 1994 murder of her seventeen-year-old cousin, who had been sitting on a bicycle when another teen demanded money from him. She wondered aloud how the teenage suspect who killed her cousin could have been deterred from picking up a gun and ending up serving a life term in prison.

Mosby's campaign otherwise obscured, however, her experiences with injustice and activism. At the age of six, she had enrolled in a desegregation program that bused minority students from Boston to high schools in wealthier suburban areas. She was co-editor of the student newspaper and became involved in a program run under the auspices of the Massachusetts ACLU that took high school–aged youth on civil rights tours through the South, visiting important sites and meeting with movement veterans. In her 1998 high school yearbook, members of the senior class were asked to predict where they would be in the future. Mosby wrote that she would be "the next Malcolm X, MLK and Farrakhan all wrapped into one, with dreads, and preaching so the whole world can hear." Mosby was the first in her family to attend college, earning a scholarship at Tuskegee University, the private historically Black college in Alabama established by Booker T. Washington. She excelled, graduating magna cum laude and eventually being accepted into Boston College Law School.

She was a more complex person than the "crime fighter from a family of cops" she was portraying, but there was an election to win and she was courting the Fraternal Order of Police's endorsement.

Mosby had a commanding presence, though her résumé was on the thin side: She had been working as an insurance company litigator, following six years as a line prosecutor. As she mounted her run for state's attorney, Mosby collected endorsements from most of the city council, former NAACP president and congressman Kweisi Mfume, and powerful unions like the Service Employees International Union (SEIU) and the AFL-CIO, though she was significantly out-fundraised by Bernstein and would later say that some people had encouraged her not to run—that it was not her time.

She came up with a defiant campaign slogan: "Our Time Is Now."

On primary election day in June 2014, she defeated Bernstein by nearly 9 percentage points and became the youngest top prosecutor in the country. With no general election opponent, she would have the next six months to assemble a leadership team and map plans for her administration. Many veterans of the prosecutor's office couldn't believe that someone who had risen to only the lower rungs of the office was now returning as the boss; meanwhile, she was ready to inject new blood into the office and purged several career prosecutors.

But starting that July, the issue of police brutality seized national attention. In New York City, a video recorded on a bystander's cellphone showed the last moments of a man named Eric Garner, who was put into an illegal choke hold by a plainclothes officer in Staten Island.

"Every time you see me, you want to mess with me. I'm tired of it. It stops today," Garner had said. "Everyone standing here will tell you I didn't do nothing. I did not sell nothing. Because every time you see me, you want to harass me. You want to stop me [from] selling cigarettes. I'm minding my business, officer, I'm minding my business. Please just leave me alone. I told you the last time, please just leave me alone."

Officer Daniel Pantaleo grabbed Garner from behind and took him to the ground. As other officers joined in, Garner could be heard saying "I can't breathe" eleven times.

The next month, in August 2014, an unarmed eighteen-year-old named Michael Brown was shot six times and killed by a police officer in Ferguson, Missouri. Officer Darren Wilson had been called for a report of a robbery and had tried to stop Brown, whom he gunned down in the street. The officer said Brown had charged him, but a friend who was with Brown gave interviews saying Brown's hands had been raised in the air. Though a Justice Department report would later discount that account, Brown's death and its handling by authorities ignited national outrage and galvanized the Black Lives Matter movement—led by a new generation of activists taking on police abuses across the country, through social media and direct action.

Baltimore had seen more than its share of police shootings of Black men. Jenkins himself had been involved in a fatal shooting in 2013, though he did not pull the trigger: He and a partner said they had chased a man believed to be armed through a housing project. Jenkins eventually caught the man and wrapped him in a bear hug. Officers arriving as backup later said they saw the man reach for a gun. Jenkins shoved him away and the other officers opened fire. Witnesses disputed some of the police account: "They were pounding on him, trying to get him down" from the fence, a twenty-nine-year-old woman said. "Next thing I know, I see his hands go up, like he was trying to surrender. . . . He died with his hands still up." Others said they saw a cellphone, not a gun, in his hand. The case faded from the headlines after a couple of days.

Garner's death in New York occurred just a few weeks after Mosby won the election, and police accountability—an afterthought in the campaign—was becoming the central topic across the country and mobilizing young people to action. In Baltimore, hundreds marched when prosecutors in Ferguson declined to file charges against the officer who shot Michael Brown, weaving through downtown streets and shutting down the entrance to a major downtown highway. The city's annual holiday lighting of a downtown monument was cut short by demonstrations. "This is what democracy looks like!" protesters chanted at one point, while lying on the ground. New supporters joined in the calls for justice in the death of Tyrone West.

Meanwhile, *The Baltimore Sun* published a series of articles highlighting the millions of dollars the city had paid to settle lawsuits against officers for allegations of brutality. Pictures of people with black eyes and battered faces ran on the front page.

Since his arrival in late 2012, Police Commissioner Anthony Batts had been trying to strike a different tone in commanders' meetings. It wasn't uncommon for him to lead a discussion in which he asked others if they saw themselves as "warriors or guardians." He pushed back when homegrown officers said the city *wanted* them to be warriors. He began to speak more openly about systemic issues that drive crime—he discussed literacy, mentoring, mental illness, character building—and about rethinking the role of police. "People kept telling me as I toured the city that kids have nothing to do in the summertime. They don't even have food. They don't even have anything to eat. How can you address that?" One of the city's biggest challenges, he said, was racism.

"On the West Coast, I dealt with a lot of issues on diversity, and that was the discussion," he said at a panel on policing in early 2015. "When I go to Baltimore on the East Coast, I'm dealing with 1950s-levels black-and-white racism. It's taken a step backwards—everything is either black, or everything is white. We're dealing with that as a community, and I'm stirring that pot. I can bring those issues up in the bully pulpit and get those conversations started."

Batts didn't know it, but his time to highlight such issues was running out.

At Mosby's swearing-in ceremony on January 8, 2015, at Baltimore's cavernous War Memorial Building, her remarks were notably different from her campaign rhetoric. Gone was much of the populist bravado about out-of-control crime rates and support for police. While she talked about crime victims, she also invoked the innocent and the people of color who were affected disproportionately by the legal system. After leaning on her conviction rate to bolster her résumé during the campaign, Mosby repeatedly emphasized during her swearing-in the importance of "justice."

CHAPTER SEVEN

LET'S STAND TOGETHER

ON THE MORNING OF April 11, 2015, a twenty-five-year-old named Freddie Gray made his way through West Baltimore's Gilmor Homes housing project with two friends. Garrett Miller and Edward Nero, bicycle patrol officers wearing yellow vests and helmets, were riding around the area as part of a directive from city prosecutors to step up efforts and engagement in the neighborhood.

As things go in Baltimore's Western District, the area was coming off one of its safest years ever: Twenty-one people had lost their lives in the district in 2014—nothing to boast about in most cities, but it represented a big improvement over the previous year, when forty-three people had been murdered. Still, the social ills and other conditions that foment violence—vacant homes, drug addiction, unemployment—remained prevalent. About half the children in the area around Gilmor Homes were living below the poverty line, and nearly a quarter of adults were out of work; a study found that more people held in the state's prisons came from the neighborhood than from any other census tract. The development's history was rooted in racism: It shares a name with a Confederate cavalry officer (who later served as Baltimore police commissioner), and it was built during

World War II for Black defense workers and placed in the Sandtown-Winchester neighborhood to reinforce segregation.

That spring a constituent had contacted newly elected state's attorney Marilyn Mosby complaining about drug dealing in the area, and the head of her new "criminal strategies unit" brought the concerns to police.

"I've included some of the photos that a community member sent to Mrs. Mosby," the unit chief wrote, referring to several photos of young men congregating on the streets outside a mentoring office. "I realize that resources are thin for a long-term investigation, but hopefully we can combine community involvement with SAO/BPD cooperation to make something happen."

Police forwarded the email to shift lieutenants, instructing officers to begin a "daily narcotics initiative" in the area, saying they would monitor their "daily measurables."

In the tool kit of a police officer, such "measurables" are field interviews, car stops, and use of any violation of the law to try to flip people for information. The more people you make contact with, the more chances to squeeze someone. This is considered good police work, and there are countless examples of it leading to a break in a case. But in hyperpoliced areas it also promotes harassment and profiling, and when people are scared of police every interaction has the potential to combust.

When Officers Miller and Nero saw Gray and his friends that Sunday morning, they had committed no crime. But the instincts of both parties kicked in: for Gray and his friends, to flee at the sight of officers; for the officers, to give chase to find out why someone would be running from them.

Miller caught Gray first, taking him down to the ground and handcuffing him even though at that point there was no apparent reason to do so. While searching Gray, the officers found a folding knife that was commonly sold in area convenience stores but also appeared to violate an outdated local ordinance on switchblades. Gray, who had asthma, asked for an inhaler.

Brandon Ross, Gray's friend, made his way to where Gray was being taken into custody. Ross paced back and forth and asked a neighbor to get the badge numbers of the officers. "Why the [expletive] are you twisting his leg like that?" he asked. Another resident, Kevin Moore, later said it looked as if police had Gray "folded up like a crab, like a piece of origami." Moore started filming, and his video showed Gray groaning in agony; as the officers carried him to a van, his legs appeared to be dragging behind him.

"I got the whole thing on tape!" Ross said.

"Take it to the media," said one of the officers who had arrived on scene, William Porter.

The van drove off but stopped a block away at the intersection of Baker and Mount streets. The officers would later say Gray had been enraged and out of control, kicking the inside of the van, and the van driver wanted to shackle his legs. Jacqueline Jackson, fifty-three, was washing dishes when she heard a commotion, and then lifted her blinds and peered out the window. She said that Gray looked unresponsive and officers were moving quickly to get him back in the van as a group that included Ross ran down the street. "They lifted him up by his pants, and he wasn't responding, and they threw him in that paddy wagon," Jackson said. Ross borrowed a cellphone to record what he saw. It would turn out to be the last footage of Gray. In that video, Gray lay face down and motionless in the van, his legs hanging out the back. Ross can be heard yelling at Porter, whom he knew from seeing him around the neighborhood: "Porter, can we get help from a supervisor up here, please?" Those watching were convinced Gray had been beaten by the officers and was suffering from some type of spinal injury that had caused his legs to stop working. The officers would later say they believed Gray was demonstrating "jailitis," when an arrestee feigned injury to try to avoid being taken to Central Booking.

When the van arrived at the Western District station about forty-five minutes after the initial encounter, Gray wasn't breathing and was taken to the University of Maryland Shock Trauma Center and induced into a coma. The initial police report submitted in court reported that Gray had been arrested "without incident."

THE VIDEO OF GRAY screaming while being subdued and dragged by police surfaced online, followed by still images of Gray clinging to life, hooked up to tubes and machines at a hospital.

Police held a news conference the day after the arrest, declining to name Gray or to say why he had been arrested but telling reporters they were investigating. He was referred to by police and in media reports as a suspect. Officials pledged to get to the bottom of what happened and to be transparent throughout.

"During that arrest, the video, which we believe captures only a portion of it, shows the officers attempting to detain this individual, keep him on the ground," Deputy Commissioner Jerry Rodriguez said. "There's a lot of screaming and yelling; there's a lot of folks in the background. At no time—and I've seen the video a number of times—did I see the use of force at that moment, but again the video is a portion of the incident."

To many, the details were subject to spin, and ultimately not important: Gray had been killed while in custody of police, who are sworn to protect and serve, and people wanted to see the officers involved held accountable. They were wary that the longer the investigation was drawn out, the more likely that authorities would find ways to equivocate and absolve the officers of responsibility. The increased awareness from the series of killings across the country had ignited an urgent demand for justice.

Gray had grown up like many impoverished children in Baltimore. He had lived in a series of homes with peeling lead paint in the windows and walls, causing him and two of his sisters—one of them his twin—to register levels of lead in their blood nearly double what Maryland considered the minimum for lead poisoning. At home, his mother, who had dropped out of middle school, struggled with drugs and was unable to read. "I can't help him with nothing else but raise him," she said in a deposition. At one point, Child Protective Services was notified that the children were living in a home without food or electricity.

Gray dropped out of school in the ninth grade. A few years later, in 2010, he and his sisters won a $435,000 settlement after suing the owner of one of the lead paint homes. Because lead paint victims can have trouble with impulse control or be considered mentally disabled, such settlements are structured into monthly payments so they are doled out over time, preventing recipients from splurging. He would receive $605 a month.

A week after his eighteenth birthday, Gray was arrested for the first time as an adult. According to the officers who made the arrest, Gray made a hand-to-hand drug transaction, then fled at the sight of the police, tossing the drugs under a nearby vehicle. He was charged with felony possession with intent to distribute. Six days later he was back on the streets and arrested again under similar circumstances. He was held on $75,000 bail that his family was unable to pay and four months later was offered a hopeful plea deal from a judge: a three-year sentence, fully suspended, on the condition that he finish school and get a job. If he complied with those terms, his conviction would be purged. Instead, Gray would be arrested ten times within the first year of his probation and would end up serving a total of about two years behind bars.

Around this time, Gray and his sisters sought to cash out their lead paint settlement, against the advice of their stepfather. They wanted the money now, and there were predatory lending companies willing to help that happen by offering pennies on the dollar in exchange for a lump sum. The Gray siblings' $430,000 structured settlement, valued at $280,000 at the time, was relinquished for just $54,000, or less than 20 percent of its eventual value.

Over and over again, Gray was arrested with drugs, a futile revolving door that did nothing to satisfy the residents calling police about drug dealers or to help Gray.

That was the Freddie Gray of the court systems, the Freddie Gray who would be judged after his death even though he wasn't accused of a serious crime on the day he was fatally injured. Gray was well known and well liked in his community. They called him "Pepper," and everyone seemed to have a story at the ready that recalled him as charismatic and generous. There was a sense, as protests over police brutality played out locally and across the country, that Baltimore was ready to erupt at the next controversial police encounter. Yet that wasn't true—four people were shot by Baltimore cops, one of them fatally, between December 2014 and February 2015 without much public response. The reaction to Gray's death wasn't simply about timing.

ON APRIL 18, SIX DAYS after Gray was hospitalized, local megachurch pastor Jamal Bryant, who had thrust himself onto the national scene after traveling to Sanford, Florida, to help lead demonstrations following the death of Trayvon Martin, led the first large-scale rally for Freddie Gray. Hundreds of protesters gathered at Gilmor Homes, then marched down Mount Street to the nearby Western District police station. Police were ready, with metal gates set up and a line of officers fortifying the building. The first wave of demonstrators immediately breached the gates, jumping over them and climbing onto a concrete wall that lined the steps leading to the station's front door. Atop the wall they chanted and danced and taunted the officers. "What happened to Freddie was unnecessary and uncalled for," Bryant told the crowd. "All of those police officers involved need to be held accountable and answer for what they did, and need to be terminated from their positions."

"If this happens to him, it could happen to any of you," Gray's stepfather, Richard Shipley, told the crowd.

One woman said that in the days since the incident, police had been driving around the neighborhood but not stopping. When people saw officers, they put their hands up in the "Don't Shoot" pose popularized by protests in Ferguson, Missouri, and other incidents.

On April 19, 2015, Gray succumbed to his injuries at the hospital.

Demonstrations quickly grew, with protesters seeking to ratchet up pressure on authorities. "We believe the power is returning to the people in the city of Baltimore," Bryant said outside City Hall on April 23. "Indict! Indict! Indict!" marchers shouted as Gray's friend Brandon Ross and local pastor Westley West led a protest that began at City Hall, made its way through the Inner Harbor, touched into the city's posh Federal Hill neighborhood, then wound back up Pennsylvania Avenue to the Western District police station.

Jenkins, who just a month earlier had been charged by Internal Affairs for misconduct, can be seen in citizen videos and pictures riding shotgun in a police car with high-ranking Lieutenant Colonel Sean Miller as it was surrounded by chanting protesters. Gray's friend Ross stood at the base of their vehicle's hood, placing the megaphone down on the car and taking off his hat, yelling "Freddie, Freddie, Freddie!" into the vehicle, surrounded by others with their fists raised. Officers like Jenkins, who were used to running the streets, were now back on their heels.

Inside police headquarters that night, April 23, 2015, a task force of thirty officers and commanders who had convened to try to uncover the truth about Freddie Gray's death had so far gained little insight. The blinds were pulled shut, and a time line that included still pictures of Gray's arrest, notes, mug shots, and photos of the police transport wagon were taped to one wall. On another wall were graphic autopsy photos of Gray's head. By assembling video clips and statements from witnesses, police had produced a minute-by-minute account of what they knew about Gray's arrest and transport. Much of the chronology relied on statements from the officers involved in Gray's arrest who had agreed to cooperate with the investigation—which was all of them except Caesar Goodson, the van driver. Gray's injuries did not appear to have occurred during his arrest, and it was more likely that they occurred inside the van. There were still gaps in what they knew, and Commissioner Batts had set a May 1 deadline to turn their investigation over to prosecutors.

A *Baltimore Sun* reporter, Justin George, was embedded in the investigation and watched what transpired.

"We have to go through this chronology again," Deputy Commissioner Kevin Davis said. "Every time we do this, we're going to learn more, we're going to get better in explaining and articulating what we know."

A homicide sergeant announced that his team had checked the closed-circuit cameras of twenty-seven businesses in West Baltimore and found footage showing an undocumented stop of the van carrying Gray. It showed Goodson emerging from the van, opening both rear doors, and appearing to speak to Gray for about two minutes. The stop had not been announced on the police radio; it was also unknown what had caused Goodson to stop and what had occurred when he looked in the back.

"Does he go into the wagon?" Davis asked.

"No," the homicide sergeant said. "He just opens the door. He's on the outside of the wagon, and it appears that he's having a conversation with a person inside the wagon."

As they spoke, someone yelled, "Attention!" and everyone in the room jumped to their feet.

In walked Commissioner Batts wearing a dark suit. He asked everyone to sit and took a seat in the corner of the room. Backs stiffened in their chairs. The lead investigator was asked to go over the chronology as if it were being laid out for the first time. She did: The bike cops Nero and Miller had made eye contact with Gray, who took off running. When they caught up, Miller had yelled, "Taser, taser, get down," and Gray did. Gray was handcuffed by Miller, and he asked for an inhaler. Gray began to yell, and the officers searched him and found a pocketknife. Miller used a "leg lace" hold to keep Gray from moving and called for a transport wagon.

"So we've gone from eye contact to apprehension," Davis said.

As the officers discussed what happened next, including the loading of Gray into a transport van, Batts spoke up from the corner of the room. He wanted to know on what basis the officers had justified arresting Gray at all.

"What kind of probable cause do you have?" asked Batts.

"We got the knife," Davis responded. "The knife was found."

"What probable cause do you have?" Batts said again.

Gray had run when the bike cops made eye contact, a detective said, noting that a so-called Terry stop allows officers to pursue someone who flees in a high-crime area and to detain that person on the basis of reasonable suspicion. An arrest requires probable cause, a higher threshold, and Batts noted the detectives had handcuffed Gray prior to finding the knife.

Did detectives suspect Gray had a gun? "Bulges or anything?" the commissioner asked. "Do we actually have that at this point?"

"No," a colonel responded. "We do not."

Batts again asked what justified the search of Gray's pockets and subsequent arrest. No one from the task force knew the answer.

Hours later, after most task force members had gone home for the night, Batts sat with his commanders to discuss another thorny issue: compelling the police van's driver, Goodson, to give a statement to investigators. Evidence indicated that Gray had sustained his fatal injury in the van, but investigators didn't know how it had happened.

Of the officers questioned after Gray's arrest and death, only Goodson had declined to provide a statement. To Batts, it was imperative to know Goodson's version of events. But his commanders warned him that this was a legal minefield—anyone, even police officers, under criminal investigation has the constitutional right to remain silent. Under state law, however, police officers could be forced to give a statement as part of an internal investigation. But whatever he said there couldn't be used except in those administrative proceedings. Compelling him to talk might provide clarity, but it couldn't be used in the criminal case and could even imperil that process by raising issues of cross-contamination.

"So what do we tell to this community that's setting this city on fire right now?" Batts asked, referring to the increasingly tense protests. "Do we go out there and [say], 'I don't know'? Or do I compel him and get another statement or get an understanding, and say there is misconduct or there is not misconduct there? At some point in time, beyond this case, we have the responsibility of the public trust."

One commander noted that investigators had already uncovered enough evidence to establish that an "atmosphere" of negligence had caused Gray's death. Another thought up to four or five officers could face criminal charges. "We didn't seat belt the guy in. We drove this guy around for a half-hour after he said he couldn't breathe and needed a medic."

The commanders suggested Batts tell the public that investigators had uncovered police misconduct.

Batts was frustrated that so many questions remained about Gray's injury. "Can you definitively tell me that [officers] did not beat him before they put him in that van?" he asked.

The commanders said they could not.

"They're not going to believe us," Batts said. "The public will hear me and think: 'It's a conspiracy. We're hiding everything. We're trying to make those police officers innocent.'"

ON FRIDAY, THE DAY after Batts huddled with his commanders, he held a news conference and said officers had violated department policies while Gray was in custody. Police were now investigating whether Gray's injuries resulted from his arrest or from a "rough ride" in the van, Batts said.

A "rough ride" was when police intentionally drove in a way that would cause an unbuckled, handcuffed prisoner to be thrown about in the back of a van. A decade earlier, Baltimore juries had awarded $39 million to a man who was paralyzed from the neck down after a van ride, and $7.4 million to relatives of a man who became a paraplegic and died two weeks later.

The city was simmering the day after Batts's news conference. It was Saturday, April 25, and the weekend afforded protesters time to mount their largest crowds yet. At City Hall hundreds gathered as protesters listened to speakers who wanted them to "shut it down" or take control of the city. Police had been told that "anarchists" were traveling to Baltimore to cause chaos. There were later clashes in the downtown area, outside of Oriole Park at Camden Yards. Two youths climbed atop a police car and kicked in the windshield; the images of it were widely spread. Storefronts were smashed. Police arrested thirty-five people, including four juveniles. Six officers suffered minor injuries. Two journalists were detained, one of whom said he had been beaten. Police called it "inadvertent."

Gray's twin sister, Fredericka Gray, called for peace. "My family wants to say, 'Can y'all please, please stop the violence?'" she said. "Freddie Gray would not want this. Freddie's father and mother do not want any violence. Violence does not get justice."

The next day, Deputy Commissioner Kevin Davis's cellphone vibrated with an incoming message.

"I just got a text," he said. "The high schoolers are being urged to skip school and protest."

A group of students at Frederick Douglass High School were discussing an afternoon walk-out on Monday, April 27, while police intelligence analysts said they also found a flyer on social media supposedly calling for a "Purge," after a movie in which crimes are legal for a twelve-hour period. Davis said the students were being told to march from Mondawmin Mall to the Inner Harbor.

"Tomorrow might not be good," Davis said.

BATTS'S EYES WERE BLOODSHOT and blurry as he sat with his staff for the first time in the early hours on the day of the supposed "Purge." The commissioner was in a white starched uniform that belied the numbing amount of time he had spent at police headquarters since Gray's death.

He could sense that Baltimore was on the brink, and he feared he didn't have the manpower to handle a riot. He had reached out to police chiefs as far as Philadelphia requesting help but said no one had offered to send resources except a few agencies extending a handful of officers. The agency also had limited and outdated equipment.

Suddenly, Deputy Commissioner Dean Palmere and Lieutenant Colonel Melissa Hyatt burst in, saying they urgently needed to speak to him. When they emerged, the chief spokesman, Captain Eric Kowalczyk, sat down and began typing a press release about a "credible threat" of gangs "teaming up" to "take out" law enforcement officers. Kowalczyk later said authorities had an informant who said he had been present in a gang meeting and had directly heard the threat, which included the detail that guns were being stashed on rooftops, though the FBI would later say the information was deemed "noncredible."

Gray's funeral was to take place later in the day. The alleged threat, disseminated without citing specific information but coming from an untrusted authority, was stirring up emotions at the wrong time.

At the funeral, thousands of people listened as the Gray family attorney Billy Murphy denounced a police culture that he said protected officers from accountability.

"Let's don't kid ourselves. We wouldn't be here today if it wasn't for video cameras," Murphy told the mourners. "Instead of one cover-up behind that blue wall after another cover-up behind that blue wall . . . and one lie after another lie, now we see the truth as never before. It's not a pretty picture."

The "Purge" flyer said to be posted to social media called for an uprising starting at Mondawmin Mall on the west side. Years later, its origins—as well as whether it carried any real influence among youth—remain unclear, but its existence put officials on edge.

Around 1:30 P.M., police asked city schools to stagger dismissal times, but school officials said it was too late. Police from three agencies next gathered at the metro station on the edge of the mall for a roll call, with the city officers in riot gear. The first rock was reported thrown around 2:46 P.M., and within minutes police formed a skirmish line across the Mondawmin bus loop, blocking access to buses as teenagers arrived on the subway line, which was used by five thousand youth each day to get home from school. "Let's start corralling these kids and let's start making arrests," an officer said over the radio. At 3 P.M., the metro station was ordered shut down, a move that years later no one has taken responsibility for and that community members maintain was the real spark to what came next.

Teens who wanted to get home couldn't. Others appeared to be arriving with rocks in backpacks. Officers were told to stand in lines and not to engage. Rocks were flying, and officers, with outdated gear and little training for such a situation, were getting hurt. "We're getting creamed!" one yelled. At least one could be seen lobbing a rock back at the youth. "Do not go forward and chase them!" a supervisor said over the radio. "Hold that line, hold that line. Do not advance; hold the line."

WAYNE JENKINS STOOD IN the dim light of the department's sixth-floor surveillance camera nerve center, taking in the images on the screens. Regarded by some as one of the agency's best street cops, he'd made only four arrests all year after being put in timeout as he was investigated for allegedly planting drugs on Walter Price the previous spring. Then, just a month before Gray's death, Jenkins had been hit with internal misconduct charges that could bring serious punishment. Despite that, he'd been on the streets during the bubbling unrest, and now, as he watched the images of outnumbered officers getting hurt, he decided to head into the fray.

Officers were being asked to go to the edge of Druid Hill Park, at the entrance to the state's zoo, just a few blocks from the mall and metro station, to provide help for injured officers. Jenkins ran down the hall and found another sergeant, Lavern Ellis, and told her what was happening. They hopped in a car and navigated their way through gridlocked traffic to the park, where a Division of Correction van being used to drive officers around in platoons was parked. In a report to his supervisors, the prison corporal in charge of the van said he was climbing out when Jenkins jumped in with five others, saying it was an emergency, and took off, leaving the corporal behind. Video from a news helicopter and from the ground shows the van—with a broken side window—arrive at the mall around 4 P.M.

Jenkins would later write up his own account of what happened, saying the van had been pelted with objects as he made his way to injured officers and loaded them into the van. He then ordered another officer at the scene to drive them to safety and took that officer's place on the front of the police line, he said. His supervisors would nominate him for a special commendation for his actions.

A supervisor on the ground later recalled Jenkins lobbying to take on a group of rock-throwing youngsters about fifty yards away and drag them behind the skirmish line. The answer was no, and Jenkins argued with the supervisor about not being allowed to be more aggressive.

Other officers remember how Jenkins also dug into his own pocket at one point and paid $600 to feed hungry officers, making runs to Royal Farms and coming back with bags of fried chicken. "He pretty much fed the department for a day," one officer recalled. "It was a huge morale booster."

At Mondawmin, clashes were pushing into residential side streets, while a throng of young people pushed their way a half mile south to the intersection of Pennsylvania and North avenues, another busy area and transit hub.

The officers hung back as a CVS drugstore—one of the few reliable places in the community for residents to get affordable prescription drugs and supplies—was breached and looted. "Looting expected, let it happen," commanders had said over the radio, worried about the optics of officers getting into a street battle. People emerged from the store with armfuls of Tastykakes, detergent, and other goods; cars even arrived to drop people off to run inside. Once the shelves were bare, fires were lit inside and the store began burning. On North Avenue, an abandoned city police car was ransacked; a transportation police vehicle across the intersection was set on fire. When firefighters moved in to extinguish the blaze at the CVS, a young man wearing a gas mask punctured the hose.

As officers deliberated whether to move in and attempt to restore order, a twenty-year-old man named Donta Betts stood in the street lighting propane cylinders using charcoal and toilet paper, creating a barrier. Betts also looted three stores that day. Asked after his arrest about his motivation, he told federal authorities: "I figured I did all this because it was my period of time to go wild on the police."

Police eventually took control of the intersection, but looting continued throughout the night, with several drugstores and pharmacies hit. Nearly 315,000 doses of drugs were stolen, more than 40 percent of which were Schedule II opioids, a class that includes methadone, oxycodone, and fentanyl. It was "enough narcotics on the streets of Baltimore to keep it intoxicated for a year," Commissioner Batts would say. The DEA, meanwhile, later reported that none of the stolen prescription drugs were recovered by law enforcement.

They didn't know it, but that wasn't entirely true.

Later that night, in a quiet waterfront neighborhood in the suburbs twenty miles east of downtown, Donald Stepp was rousted from his sleep to meet a visitor outside his garage. It was Jenkins, fresh off his heroics in West Baltimore. From inside the trunk of his unmarked police car, he pulled out two garbage bags that contained thousands of pills.

"What's this?" Stepp asked.

Jenkins said he had stopped people with looted drugs and was bringing the intercepted goods to Stepp.

"I've got an entire pharmacy. I don't even know what it is."

THERE WERE STILL FOUR days until the deadline for police to turn over their investigation to prosecutors. Governor Larry Hogan declared a state of emergency, and a citywide curfew was instituted. The National Guard was deployed, with Hogan calling for one thousand troops and later doubling that number.

The investigation into Freddie Gray's death had taken on a new dynamic. Previously there had been the threat of a civil disturbance, but now that scenario had played out. The media were stoking tensions, and there was every reason to think another riot could break out.

Mosby's office was already getting ready to move on criminal charges. On April 23, four days before the riots, prosecutors reached out to Sheriff John Anderson and his deputy, Samuel Cogen, about bringing their office—which provides courthouse security and helps serve domestic violence warrants—into the fold. They said the public had lost confidence in the police department, and prosecutors wanted the sheriffs to look over their materials and help them finish and file the statement of probable cause. The sheriff's office was not asked to perform any investigative tasks, only review what had been compiled already. Cogen was a past president of the sheriff's Fraternal Order of Police lodge but also had a college sociology degree and had taken part in use-of-force studies with a police think tank. He reached a conclusion much different from many others in law enforcement: He agreed there was probable cause to charge the officers with crimes. "My gut inclination was, 'I don't want to charge other police officers,'" Cogen explained later. "But as I'm looking at everything, to me, it was very apparent that we had to charge, and to not do so would be a cover-up and dereliction of duty."

The police department task force was briefing prosecutors every few days, but the prosecutors shared little about their own process. Police worried that Mosby would charge the officers before receiving results of the police investigation. With such a move, some commanders believed, she could claim that her office had taken action at a time when the city needed answers, while the Baltimore Police Department had not.

Meanwhile, Mosby felt that Batts's plan to hold a news conference on Friday, May 1, was an attempt to pressure her to take action. She recounted to *The New York Times* a tense phone call with the mayor, Rawlings-Blake, in which she had chafed at the time line. "There are protesters outside; they are burning stuff down," Mosby recalled saying. "I had told them that was going to happen, because they were exacerbating distrust. So I called the mayor, and I was livid. I was like: 'You know, this is ridiculous. You all have single-handedly caused what's happening in this city right now.' I just screamed on her. But she was like: 'Oh, no, I'm getting phone calls from the attorney general and the president's office. They want to know—where's the state's attorney?' I said: 'That's because you and your commissioner have set false expectations. You did this, not me. Not me.' And I was like, 'You know what else?' I can't remember what I said, but I hung up on her. And that was it."

She told Batts to stop releasing information about the investigation. There would be no police news conference.

On Wednesday evening, Batts called Chief Stanley Brandford, who was leading the police investigation, to ask about its status. Brandford said the task force still had much to do but members were confident of one thing: Freddie Gray had been injured in the van and not beaten. The case file was turned over to Mosby's office on Thursday morning, a day before the deadline.

The autopsy would be finalized the following morning, Friday, May 1. The medical examiner's office was certain that Gray had suffered a "high-energy" impact to his neck, akin to a diving injury, that he would have had to have suffered from falling inside the moving van and being unable to brace himself. Most deaths involving motor vehicles and caused by someone else are ruled "accidents"—a passenger who is killed because the driver blows through a stop sign, or a child who dies because of not being strapped into a car seat, for example—but the medical examiner's office determined that police had a special duty to care for someone in their custody. And that made Gray's death a homicide.

The task force convened again early Friday to continue their work and learned Mosby was holding a news conference. About five minutes before the news conference started, Mosby called Rawlings-Blake to tell her what was about to happen.

HER STAFF HAD DRIVEN to the War Memorial Building with a lectern and flags covered by a blanket in the back of a pickup truck so no one at City Hall could see it. As the media assembled, her staff gathered and prayed, then descended down the stone steps of the War Memorial, a neoclassical fortress across the street from police headquarters and City Hall. Mosby stepped to the lectern, with her executive team fanned out behind her. Cogen, from the sheriff's office, declined to attend, instead staying in his office.

Mosby said her office had conducted an independent investigation, working around the clock, canvassing for witnesses and reviewing available information.

"The findings of our comprehensive, thorough and independent investigation, coupled with the medical examiner's determination that Mr. Gray's death was a homicide, which we received today, has led us to believe that we have probable cause to file criminal charges."

Mosby then read a lengthy account of the arrest and Gray's death.

"Despite Mr. Gray's seriously deteriorating medical condition, no medical assistance was rendered or summoned for Mr. Gray at that time by any officer."

Mosby listed the charges: Six officers were being charged. The van driver, Goodson, was facing second-degree murder. Three others were being charged with manslaughter.

"To the people of Baltimore and the demonstrators across America: I heard your call for 'No justice, no peace.' Your peace is sincerely needed as I work to deliver justice on behalf of this young man," she said.

"To the rank and file officers of the Baltimore Police Department, please know that these accusations of these six officers are not an indictment on the entire force. . . . The actions of these officers will not and should not, in any way, damage the important working relationships between police and prosecutors as we continue to fight together to reduce crime in Baltimore.

"Last but certainly not least, to the youth of the city: I will seek justice on your behalf. This is a moment. This is your moment. Let's ensure we have peaceful and productive rallies that will develop structural and systemic changes for generations to come."

She closed with her campaign slogan: "You're at the forefront of this cause and as young people, 'Our time is now.'"

There were cheers in the crowd.

Back at police headquarters, commanders and members of the task force were stunned; one dropped a file she was holding. They felt there were still too many unanswered questions; prosecutors couldn't have taken the task force's work into account if they had made their decision so quickly.

"How are they going to prove it?" one official asked. Michael Boyd, one of the lead investigators, reflected on his work and the quick action by prosecutors: "It was almost like being at a wake."

"Well, we are all fucked," Miller, one of the arresting officers, texted the others.

"Yup," Porter replied.

WITHIN A HALF HOUR of the news conference's conclusion, every Baltimore Police Department employee's email inbox lit up with a message. It was from Wayne Jenkins.

"HELP OUR BROTHERS AND SISTERS NOW" read the subject line.

> To all BPD members, every unit, retired or active. Now is that time that we ALL donate to our brothers and sisters in blue. Every member should donate without being selfish nor judgmental. I believe that all active members should donate $500. This tragic terrible situation could have effected anyone of us at anytime. Please I beg for you not to say "I have bills or I can't afford it." . . . Lets finally stand together and help one another without worry about self preservation.
>
> I, Sergeant Wayne Jenkins will collect all donations from the SES [Special Enforcement Section] unit. Could someone please step up and support each and every unit in our department and ensure that everyone, everyone, everyone donates. No more greediness or excuses, now is the time to prove we are a family. Remember, this absolute terrible situation could have effected anyone of us. Hold each of our brothers and sisters accountable for these donations ASAP.
>
> EVERY SINGLE MEMBER

Jenkins next organized a fundraiser at Silk's bar, owned by Stepp's associate Dennis Danielczyk, and sent out another email blast asking that notice of the event be read out at all roll calls. An email came back from a higher-ranking supervisor in the Operations Intelligence

Section, Byron Conaway: "You're [a] leader Wayne. . . . Much respect bro."

The decision to file criminal charges was instantly controversial. Mosby was widely praised for taking rare and decisive action—the high-profile cases over the previous months had shown that when it came to police, authorities too often dragged their feet, looking for ways to absolve officers rather than taking the kind of swift action regular citizens might face in similar circumstances.

To many others, Mosby had acted hastily; the phrase "rush to judgment" was repeatedly lobbed, and she was attacked by right-wing outlets and pundits. A magazine produced by a New York police union put her image on the cover with the headline "The Wolf That Lurks." Mosby drew more ire when she seemed to bask in the positive attention, sitting on stage at a Prince concert in Baltimore and being photographed by Annie Leibovitz for *Vanity Fair*.

One prosecutor, who eventually came to believe the case against the officers was just, nevertheless acknowledged that at the time most within the office viewed the case as overcharged at best and assuredly delivered for political purposes.

The city council and later Rawlings-Blake called on the Justice Department to conduct a civil rights investigation of the police department, a precursor to a consent decree in which a monitoring team and a federal judge would provide oversight of the department. As part of the civil rights investigation, the Justice Department dispatched a team of investigators to comb through internal files and hold listening sessions with residents. They would do ride-alongs and analyze data.

Officers reported being surrounded by angry people and cellphone cameras, even on routine calls. Arrests made by police fell sharply, as much as 90 percent from April to May. Officers working in the plainclothes unit recalled showing up for work and doing nothing. "All we heard was how horrible police were. We legitimately had conversations: Are we going to [do] work today?" said one officer who worked plainclothes at the time. "The public wants to police themselves? Let's see how they do."

No one was killed during the riots or during any actions related to the civil disturbances. But away from the demonstrations, violence exploded across the city.

Forty-two people were killed in May, the most in a single month in Baltimore since August 1990, when Baltimore's population was one hundred thousand higher. The shootings happened all over, but especially on the city's west side. Andre Hunt, twenty-eight, was a well-liked barber who mentored children and volunteered with the local NAACP. He had also been arrested by Jenkins eighteen months earlier and had become a DEA cooperator. He was ambushed and killed at his barbershop less than three weeks before he was set to report for sentencing. A thirty-one-year-old woman and her seven-year-old boy were gunned down in their home. The twenty-two-year-old son of the incarcerated producer of the *Stop Fucking Snitching* video from the mid-2000s was killed on the east side. One night, a man was shot to death in Northwest Baltimore; thirty minutes later, another man was fatally shot a block away. Police would later determine the second man had killed the first man, then been gunned down by somebody else—who himself would also be killed years later.

Commissioner Batts had lost the rank and file. He met with officers in a closed-door meeting at the union hall in late May, apologizing to them for putting them in harm's way during the riots. He urged them to stay focused on fighting crime.

"We had a nine-year-old kid shot yesterday by these knuckleheads, gangsters, thugs, whatever you want to call them," he said. "We have innocent people getting shot on the streets of Baltimore. People think we're down. People are giving up on us. I mean this with all my heart: We need to show how fucking good we are. . . . I stand ready to lead you out of this."

Batts was in a meeting on July 8 at a downtown hotel, participating in a review of how the police department handled the riots, when his cellphone rang. Pressure had been mounting; Mayor Rawlings-Blake felt Batts couldn't lead the city anymore, and she had been exploring options. She couldn't go with an insider, and the city couldn't endure a long search for another outside commissioner—besides, who in their right mind would want the job? Deputy Commissioner Kevin Davis seemed to fit the bill: He was an outsider, having spent his career in nearby Prince George's and Anne Arundel counties, yet with six months on the job also knew the city police department. Rawlings-Blake liked his cool disposition. She still hadn't made up her mind about Batts when she met with the president of Johns Hopkins University Ronald Daniels and Under Armour founder Kevin Plank, who both urged her that the only option was to fire him. Davis was put in charge.

The month of July would end with an unimaginable forty-five homicides, a record for a single month in the city. Officials announced a new "war room" effort where they would draw up a list of targets and collaborate among agencies to build cases against them.

"We are pushing for an all-hands-on-deck approach to this current surge in violence," Rawlings-Blake said at a news conference. "We know that crime is not static. Neither can we be. It is important for us to work together and recommit ourselves to that collaboration every single day in order for us to get on top of this crime spike."

As the new commissioner, Davis sought feedback on what he needed to do to turn the police department around and win back public trust. Community members and officers alike warned him "right away" that the plainclothes units were a problem he should address, though he said he lacked actionable specifics. "These were strong cautionary tales, without the benefit of real details," he recalled later. "It was kind of generally, hey, be aware that these guys work in the gray area and kind of do their own thing."

But he also believed plainclothes units were necessary to bringing down crime. "You have to identify people who carry guns and hurt people. Your patrol officers will stumble upon that guy once in awhile, but really, the short-term investigative strategies, the street activity that generates those types of arrests and seizures—that's not done by patrol," Davis said.

In mid-July, Davis and some of his senior commanders summoned the department's plainclothes units into the headquarters auditorium, a drab room with wooden chairs that resembles a high school auditorium. According to multiple people in attendance, the leadership urged the officers to get back to work. Deputy Commissioner Dean Palmere, who led the VCID unit in its heyday, told them the Batts era was over: "It's time to get out there and do what you know how to do."

"The message was: Show them [the public] that they need police," said one of several officers in attendance who recounted the meeting.

One of Batts's most trusted advisers, Captain Eric Kowalczyk, was present at the meeting and was so disappointed in the tone in the room that he said he decided that day to retire, short of his pension.

"Any hope I had of continuing to move forward with our efforts to reform the organization died in that moment. Here was one of the most senior people in the organization telling plain clothes officers to go out and do whatever it took to reduce crime. Whatever it took," Kowalczyk wrote in his book. "That mentality and operating modality were the exact reasons we had just gone through a riot, the reasons people had protested the department for weeks on end, the reasons nearly 200 officers were injured, millions of dollars in property had been destroyed, and lives were irrevocably changed. No lessons had been learned. Nothing was different."

CHAPTER EIGHT

CLEARED

THE OUTRAGE OVER FREDDIE GRAY'S death had shaken up the city and its police. Discussions with the Justice Department leading to a federal consent decree, a long-term agreement overseen by a federal judge, were finally under way. But crime had jumped to an astonishing rate overnight, and officers had largely drawn down, with street arrests plummeting. The crime rate had cost Commissioner Batts his job, and pressure was on the next administration to turn the tide.

Within days of leadership's pep talk for plainclothes officers in July, Wayne Jenkins was back on the streets making arrests for the first time since before the riots. Though still pending a disciplinary case for the Walter Price arrest, court records show he made six handgun arrests in four of his first days back.

Jenkins soon assembled a new squad within the Special Enforcement Section and tapped Maurice Ward, a thirty-five-year-old detective in another plainclothes unit. Jenkins told Ward he had been given permission to handpick his own squad of three detectives.

Ward considered it "an honor."

"I just got a call out the blue from Jenkins asking me would I like to come to his squad," Ward said in an interview years later. "Over the years, he was considered one of the best narcotic cops not [just] in the city but also the state. Everybody wanted to work for him."

One person, Ward remembered, warned him about Jenkins.

Sean Suiter "was the one person who actually told me to be careful with him [Jenkins]," Ward said. "He didn't go into detail, but he said, 'Learn what you can, then get out of his squad. If you look around, he do some crazy shit. They protect him and leave the guys who work for him to the wolves.'"

From the start, it was clear this squad had more flexibility and perks than Ward had been used to. The new team's schedule would be the day shift, 8 A.M. to 4 P.M., which was really a license to milk overtime, since their work would often involve hitting the streets at night. Ward said he was told there would be no weekends, and the overtime work would be unlimited.

"We never, from day one, came in on time. We always came in at least three hours late. Jenkins would always send a decoy text saying things like 'Break off from your target at such and such time and report here.' He did that to make it seem like we were at work. So if Internal Affairs were looking at us we could cover ourself."

Each day they would meet at police headquarters or in a field office on the grounds of the training academy—called "the Barn"—and review interdepartment emails to see where the latest shootings were so they could hit that area. They strove to stop as many people as possible. "On average we came in contact with thirty people a day," Ward said later. "We learned quickly it was a numbers game—the more people you come in contact with, the greater your chances of getting a gun."

When the squad roamed the streets, Jenkins always drove, and his penchant for swooping in on people often prompted chases. "We had several high-speed chases every day, sometimes the car would crash or Jenkins would ram cars with the ram he had specially built onto his car," Ward said. "When he chased cars, he always had tunnel vision, and we would have to physically shake him or hit him to make him come out of it."

Sometimes, when they came across groups of young men standing around, Jenkins would drive at them and do what Ward called "door-pops": Officers popped their car doors as if they were about to jump out so they could see who in the crowd took off running. Detective Marcus Taylor, the fastest of the squad's members, was the designated runner.

Aggressive police work and showing up to work late were one thing, but Ward soon got an up-close view of what Suiter might have been warning him about. Jenkins was pushing all sorts of tactics in pursuit of drugs and guns that went way beyond what was considered acceptable. They'd often take people's keys and search their cars or homes without warrants, Ward said, and they used GPS trackers without court authorization. Sometimes they would get warrants by creating their own evidence. When they stopped a suspected drug dealer, for example, Jenkins would go through the man's phone, reading text messages, and then would call Jenkins's own "burner phone," registered under a fake name. He or Taylor would then apply for a pen register to track that person's phone, Ward explained. "They would lie and say a confidential source had a phone conversation or text message [with] the person and talked about buying drugs. They would get the warrant signed—now they are tracking that person's phone.

"This was all stuff he literally teached us," Ward said, "like he would sit us down and have miniclasses, give us scenarios, see what we would do and show us how to do it and not get caught.

"Nobody could tell him nothing. He would not listen to anybody. There were times he wanted to do illegal things just too far and as a squad we said no, and he would get upset and leave us in Baltimore City with no ride. We would have to call patrol or another squad."

Ward said Jenkins would often collect and keep all the drugs they seized, saying he would submit them to Evidence Control before heading home.

"He lived in his office sometimes for a week before going home, so we believed him," Ward said.

A TWELVE-YEAR VETERAN OF the department when he joined Jenkins's squad, Ward does not allege that Jenkins corrupted him. By the time they started working together he had been skimming money from search scenes himself for years.

The oldest of three children, Ward was born into a military family and grew up on bases in California, New York, and North Carolina before settling in Baltimore in the 1990s when he was in middle school. He got good grades and ran track at Catonsville High School, in the suburbs just southwest of the city. He attended community college, worked for a while as a forklift operator, and then joined the department in 2003 at age twenty-three. "I was excited, because I felt like since this was my hometown, I could make a change better than an outsider from another state," he said. "I felt like I understood the people better."

But over time Ward said he came to feel that Black officers were discriminated against, with white officers more likely to gain placement in specialized units or to be rewarded for their work. "As a Black man, I had to work harder to prove myself," he said. "After about five years, it just became a job and I wanted to get the most out of the job, because I felt like they didn't care for my well-being—being underpaid, hard to get into specialized units, getting overlooked all the time."

Ward remembers the first time he realized he could get away with a lot in the Baltimore Police Department. Driving home from work one day, he remembered that he had forgotten to submit drug evidence in an arrest he'd made. "I was terrified because in the academy they teach that IAD knows everything, is always watching, to scare you," he said.

But no one noticed. No one asked.

"I knew there was no way to keep track of what we did on the street unless somebody was actually there with me," he said.

What else could an officer get away with?

Ward said he began stealing money when he finally joined the plainclothes units, around 2009. While it was "not a regular thing," he said, it was easy to do, because when money was being collected from a search scene, only one officer would be tasked with bagging the money up and counting it. "So nobody knows exactly how much money it is until the person who's submitting the money tells you," he said.

He recalled the first time he accepted stolen money from another officer. Without Ward or the other officers knowing it, the cop had kept money they'd found during a search, and at the end of the day he went around giving everyone a piece. "I didn't want them to think any less of me if I didn't accept it," Ward said. "The last thing I wanted was to be blackballed.

"I can say that I stole money before Jenkins not because I was poor, struggling—just because everybody else was doing it and I want to feel accepted and trusted to get into a specialized unit and out of patrol. To go from patrol to any specialized unit, it's not how qualified you are, it's can you be trusted and who you know. There's a lot of men and women in patrol who deserve a spot in drugs, shootings, and other divisions, but if you don't know somebody, you're stuck. The trust factor comes in knowing about extra overtime, witnessing police brutality, or working in the 'gray area.'"

With Jenkins, Ward was protected. Ward said that when Jenkins needed something—equipment, cars, help with Internal Affairs problems—he had a direct line to two deputy commissioners: Dean Palmere and Darryl De Sousa. In late 2015, after Jenkins had successfully asked his supervisors for a Chevy Impala rental car, he shot a message to Palmere. "Sir, I want to thank you personally for the Impala. It was the first time in 14 years that hard work was rewarded. My squad will continue to lead from the front but not for rewards. Because it's the right thing to do," Jenkins wrote.

"Your team is doing an exceptional job," Palmere responded. "Not the best car in the world but should keep you going. I'll keep my eye out for a new one when it comes in. Keep pushing and have a Merry Christmas."

"Sir I hate to call you for another favor when you always help out," Jenkins emailed De Sousa a few weeks later, asking for flashlights. "My squad gets guns every night when the sun goes down. . . . I just like my guys to get something new for what they've been doing."

"Wayne, will 30 flashlights work?" De Sousa responded.

"My guys only need 8 sir, thank u."

WARD HAD BEEN WORKING with Jenkins for two or three months when he discovered just how far Jenkins was willing to go. One night, the squad pulled over a car in East Baltimore and found two trash bags full of money in the trunk. No one stole anything that day, but Jenkins later mused about the possibilities. Jenkins explained that he'd already tracked the man to Essex in Baltimore County. They could stake out the home, go through the man's trash, and find something to parlay into a search warrant. Then they could enter the house and take money, leave, and call county officers, acting as if they had just arrived and needed assistance executing the warrant.

Jenkins then suggested another option.

"You guys willing to go kick in the dude's door and take the money?" Jenkins said, suggesting they drop the pretense of police work altogether.

The officers with him hesitated, Ward said. Nobody said yes or no, instead expressing ambivalence.

Later, Jenkins did more than talk about it. Jenkins told his officers that he'd heard over wiretaps that Belvedere Towers, the former name of a high-rise apartment complex in Roland Park, was "prime real estate where large drug deals" went down. So Jenkins and his officers drove over there and wound up stopping a drug deal in progress. They handcuffed two men, and Jenkins lied to them, saying he was a federal agent and was confiscating the cash and twenty pounds of marijuana. Jenkins released the men and told them he'd follow up with them later.

Ward wasn't sure what to make of it. It wasn't uncommon for the officers to take contraband and submit it to Evidence Control without arresting someone. Ward knew, of course, that the officers might take some cash for themselves and submit the rest as cover.

That day, however, Jenkins drove the squad toward the edge of town, bobbing in and out of traffic and running red lights, until he pulled over near a wooded area off Liberty Heights Avenue. He told the other officers to leave their cellphones and police vests in the car.

Ward and Taylor followed Jenkins into the woods. They walked far enough so they couldn't be seen from the street.

It was still daylight, Ward said, when Jenkins opened a black and red duffel bag taken from the car stop at Belvedere Towers. Inside was a stack of bills. He started counting the money, $20,000 in all. Jenkins doled out $5,000 to each of his officers and instructed them not to make any big purchases. He kept $10,000 for himself—a finder's fee—and said he planned to install a front-end crash bar so his department-issued vehicle wouldn't get damaged in his frequent collisions.

Then he said something that struck Ward as bizarre—Jenkins told them he was going to take the marijuana to his home and burn it all. "I just knew it was a lie," Ward recalled. Now he started to worry. The Belvedere Towers complex had a camera in the parking lot. What if one of the men they'd robbed filed a complaint? What if one of them who was robbed turned out to be a federal informant? What was Jenkins really going to do with the drugs? What had he gotten himself into?

But his worries passed quickly.

Had the officers done things by the book, the cash and drugs would be registered with Evidence Control. The dealers would be sitting in a jail cell.

Instead, the cash and drugs were gone, and the dealers were free men. It was unlikely they would report the incident to anyone and draw attention to themselves. For Ward and the other officers, the day's events served as another example that the chances of facing consequences for their crimes were slim.

IN NOVEMBER, JENKINS AND his wife were expecting another child, their third son. They had already picked out a name: Lucas Colton Jenkins.

But just days before the due date, the child was stillborn. Jenkins called his older sister Robin from the hospital a short time later. He asked if she would see the baby with him.

Robin arrived and accompanied Jenkins to the room where the baby's body lay inside a bassinet. He picked up Lucas and sat in a rocker, cradling the dead baby in his arms. She would later say the scene still recurred in her dreams.

Lucas was buried on November 10, 2015, the day he was supposed to be born, under a headstone inscribed with a Marine Corps symbol. A couple of hundred people attended the ceremony, many of them police officers.

Afterward, Robin said, Wayne would call her often seeking guidance. He "started asking me about God, and why bad things happen," she said. Years later, people close to Jenkins who had been unaware of his crimes would wonder if this was the turning point.

Jenkins took a short amount of time off to be with Kristy before returning to the job.

THOUGH HE'D RETURNED TO street enforcement months earlier, Jenkins was still pending charges from the Internal Affairs case stemming from Walter Price's arrest from 2014, in which video appeared to contradict Jenkins's account of finding drugs in Price's van. The case had been investigated by Internal Affairs and police misconduct prosecutors, with IAD recommending that he be demoted, transferred, and suspended for fifteen to twenty days. But nothing happened. Internal Affairs chief Rodney Hill would later say that the deputy commissioner De Sousa reduced Jenkins's punishment to verbal counseling—in effect, no punishment at all. Records show the decision was approved by De Sousa on November 25, 2015, following a recommendation from an administrative hearing board.

A few months prior, Jenkins had text-messaged Molly Webb, the prosecutor who reported him, with a message she found frightening: "States attorneys are informing me that you believe I'm a dirty cop that should be fired. It's slander and hurtful to me what is being said. This is not a promise, nor is it a threat to you in anyway shape or form this is just hurting me and my reputation."

Now with the case behind him, Jenkins still had to sign off on the verbal counseling in order to close out the case, and he was given the option of making a statement. It wasn't his style to stay silent. He chose to rip into Internal Affairs, saying the investigation was "conducted unprofessionally." "I'm only excepting [*sic*] this non-punitive counseling out of fear that if I don't except [*sic*] it our internal affairs division can continue to investigate recklessly and unprofessionally to target me and other dedicated members of our department who refuse to give up against the crime in Baltimore City."

Jenkins was acting as if he was invincible. Not content to avoid trouble of his own, he was also using the trust and support from commanders to look out for others. Jenkins set up a meeting with the new commissioner Kevin Davis to advocate that a fellow detective, Thomas Wilson, be promoted to sergeant, emails show. Wilson had been recommended for termination a decade earlier for falsifying information on a search warrant but stayed on the job. Then in 2013, he was criminally charged with perjury but acquitted by a jury. For nearly three years, while he was under investigation and continuing after his acquittal, Wilson didn't make an arrest. It was highly unusual for a sergeant like Jenkins to request—or for a commissioner to accept—such a meeting to discuss another officer's promotion, but Davis was new and trying to win over a skeptical force, and Jenkins was seen as one of the field generals.

Meanwhile, Jenkins was also lobbying commanders to reunite him with Ben Frieman, who had been reprimanded and reassigned as a result of the Walter Price case. "PLEASE FIGHT AND GET ME DETECTIVE FRIEMAN BACK ASAP," Jenkins wrote in an email to several of his bosses. "HE'S A GREAT DETECTIVE AND THE UNIT IS SUFFERING WITHOUT HIM."

"It's the holiday season and it tears me up to know he didn't do anything wrong. The evidence is all for him. The system is dysfunctional. He should be 10-8," Jenkins wrote in another message, using the code for "in-service." "I know it's out of your hands but he truly has talent and is a well-rounded investigator. Thanks Boss."

Every commissioner had cases they could point to to show they were taking police misconduct seriously. For Commissioner Davis, the firing of Detective Fabien Laronde in January 2016 was one such example. When he took over the top job, a community leader had warned him specifically about two officers: Daniel Hersl and Laronde. Laronde for years had been accused of stealing money and was even investigated by the FBI. When Laronde was brought up on internal charges of not properly securing a firearm, a guilty finding by the internal disciplinary panel would allow Davis to fire him, and he was able to do just that. Yet even that victory couldn't go without a cameo from Jenkins, who showed up trying to coach Laronde on what to say and offering to serve as a character witness. The trial board prosecutor and an Internal Affairs detective would both complain to

Davis that Jenkins tried to intimidate them in the hallway outside of the proceedings. The Internal Affairs chief looked for a way to charge Jenkins for his behavior but came up empty.

"He knew where that line was, and he stayed on that side of the fence. But he was definitely pressed up against it," the Internal Affairs chief said later.

LAUNCH OF AN INVESTIGATION

CHAPTER NINE

TRACKERS

AS A DRUG COP working across the city line in Baltimore County, Detective Scott Kilpatrick had heard of Wayne Jenkins, but it wasn't because of his prowess at getting guns and drugs. Instead, detectives there were warned to avoid Jenkins and Keith Gladstone.

"That was like lesson one when you came to Narcotics [in Baltimore County]," Kilpatrick said later. "Everyone thought they were dirty."

Higher-level drug dealers in Baltimore have been known to have homes in the suburbs, so it wasn't unusual for city cops to conduct an investigation that would lead them into Baltimore County. When that happened, they were required to alert county police to their presence and work together to execute a warrant. Kilpatrick said Jenkins's cases had raised concerns. "You'd read the search warrants, and the probable cause wouldn't make sense," he said.

Other times when working with city drug detectives, he said, county officers would search a room and clear it without finding anything. Then a city officer might go in behind them and claim to have found a gun or drugs somewhere obvious—like under the bed—that had already been checked. It was possible to miss something during a search, sure, but Kilpatrick said that county police, wary of getting dragged into questionable cases, began screening the city warrants before getting involved. Sometimes they would refuse to assist on the case, even if a judge had approved the warrant.

Kilpatrick worked drugs in the eastern section of Baltimore County, the jurisdiction where he was raised and where he now coached girls' soccer and served on the PTA. There he witnessed first-hand an explosion of heroin overdoses: In 2012, Baltimore County saw 104 opioid overdose deaths, and by 2015, that number would clear 300. As he and other county detectives pressed to find out who the big players were, one name kept coming up: "Brill."

"Brill" was a mysterious dealer. Kilpatrick wasn't sure if it was even a single person: when he pressed drug users who had purchased from "Brill" to describe him, they seemed to be identifying different people, almost as if it were a brand or a concept rather than an individual. "Brill's description was ever-changing, different each time," Kilpatrick said.

Eventually, when Kilpatrick and other county officers were able to monitor a drug deal at a grocery parking lot in Towson, they figured out that "Brill" was Antonio Shropshire, a twenty-eight-year-old from Northeast Baltimore. Shropshire's shifting description came from the fact that his associates passed around a "money phone": When buyers called "Brill," it might be other members of the crew who picked up and completed the sale. One of the other dealers even called himself "Lil Brill."

Still, Shropshire remained elusive. He had a knack for switching up cellphones just as it seemed law enforcement was making inroads, and few people would cooperate with police to make a case against him. Over and over again, Brill's customers told Kilpatrick they didn't want to burn him because he provided the highest-quality heroin and good customer service: if people didn't like his product, they could bring it back or he would make it up to them.

Shropshire may have also had some dirty cops looking out for him, Kilpatrick suspected: He came across a 2013 phone call that Shropshire had made from jail to an associate named Glen Kyle Wells, in which he seemed to mention getting help from a cop in the city.

"Your man Jenkins gave me an ear full. Said not to do anything 'heavy' no more," Wells told Shropshire on the call.

Wells said that Jenkins had given him the names of two people who were "the first ones screaming your name out"—indicating that Jenkins had given them the names of people who were snitching on them, the kind of thing that could get someone killed in Baltimore. Wells went on to say that Jenkins had complimented Wells and Shropshire on how they switched their vehicles—one way that police would often identify suspects. "People give us the make and model, and that's how we put it together to get people," Jenkins had explained, according to Wells.

ANTONIO SHROPSHIRE HAD GROWN up in Northeast Baltimore, raised by his single mother. She supported him, working hard and "providing me with the things I needed, but not my wants," he said. Kicked out of school for gambling in eleventh grade, he began selling drugs. "It seems like drugs are the only way to make money for a lot of Black people—it's not the only way, but that's what people see and know," he said later. Being able to make it out of a tough neighborhood, attend college, and get a good job was "movie stuff," he said. "Very few make it out of the hood that way. Most of them do what they see—either become a killer or drug dealer. Their uncle, cousin, or friend of the family sells drugs, and the son sees that money and says, 'I'm tired of living poor.'"

He told a story of driving his grandfather past a vocational school that the older man said he'd wanted to attend for its carpentry program—but he hadn't been able to, because it was for whites only. He'd learned the trade on his own but he'd been at a disadvantage from the start. If his grandfather had been able to attend the school, Shropshire said, he could have made a better living. Not only that, Shropshire's mother could have gone to college.

"I know people say slavery was one hundred, two hundred years ago, but the domino effect has Black people so far behind there's no catching up," Shropshire said.

He met his long-term girlfriend in 2003, and in 2007 they had a son, Antonio Junior. A few months later, Shropshire was shot for the first time, after shoving someone during an argument at a dice game. "The bullet went through my left leg, through both balls, and out my right leg," Shropshire recalled. "I had surgery and was told no more children." Within three months, he bought a BMW 750Li. Then he got shot again, this time leaving a Rick Ross performance at a local club. He was on probation for a crack charge at the time and was placed in an intensive supervision program. He was sent to jail for a year after failing to comply with the terms of the probation. When he returned to the streets, Shropshire said, police were on him hard. "They used to stop me often, asking was I a gang member and why I keep getting shot," he said. Among the officers who arrested him over the years—charges that rarely stuck in court—were Jemell Rayam, Daniel Hersl, and Sean Suiter, each at the time working in separate units. Shropshire said he knew it was their job to catch him and his job not to get caught.

He said he took the nickname of "Brill" in the twelfth grade when he decided to deal drugs for a living. The name belonged to Gene Hackman's character in the 1998 Tony Scott film *Enemy of the State*— "Brill" was a former spy living underground as a hired gun. "I said I was going to be smart like him . . . so I started to tell people my name [was] Brill, and I moved how I thought the character Brill would move," he said.

Once, explaining why his customers had such loyalty to him, he told his girlfriend, who owned a hair salon, that their businesses were not all that different: If customers didn't like the product they were paying for, you had to make sure they were satisfied and happy or lose them to someone else.

Drug dealing allowed Shropshire a comfortable lifestyle. He traveled the country and vacationed at various Caribbean islands. He frequently visited casinos. He even had a favorite Ruth's Chris Steak House location: "Sacramento, California, has the best 'Ruth's Chris [Steak House].' I love Ruth's Chris," he said. Then he was shot a third time, in 2014. The night began with Shropshire taking his son to a boxing match at the Baltimore arena, then dropping the boy off with his mother and heading to the Horseshoe Casino, where he said he won $4,000. He went on to a strip club on the Block, Baltimore's red-light district, and stayed there until the lights came up. On his way home, he stopped at a gas station and after filling up heard gunshots as he was pulling out. Then, a twinge of pain. The bullet came from behind, piercing the trunk, the back seat, and the driver's seat. He later saw surveillance footage showing he had been followed from the Block to the gas station. Shropshire believed it was a case of mistaken identity. But afterward he began regularly running red lights on purpose so no one—be it a shooter or a police officer trying to conduct surveillance—could catch him stopped in his car.

He and his girlfriend began talking about getting out of Baltimore.

"I always been a good man, always looked out for the streets, always been a family man," Shropshire said. "I went home every night. Me and Kelly lived together since 2005. All my son know[s] is us as a family."

But they ultimately stayed, and he continued to sell. Soon Kilpatrick was not the only detective on his trail.

OPIOID OVERDOSES HAD BEEN spiking in the Baltimore region since late 2013, a combination of an increase in doctors prescribing powerful medications that people became addicted to and the new availability of a substance called fentanyl, which is thirty to fifty times as potent as heroin. Law enforcement agencies in the city and neighboring counties started changing their approach to the epidemic, treating every overdose as a crime scene and sending officers out to gather information that could help trace drugs back to suppliers. Survivors were asked to reveal the people they'd bought from, while investigators talked to family and friends of those who died or went through their phones searching for clues. Prosecutors also wanted to start making more cases against dealers they could connect to overdoses. The charges of distributing drugs resulting in death brought punishment equivalent to manslaughter convictions.

Corporal David McDougall, a drug cop working in nearby Harford County, was trying to make such a case. As he debriefed overdose victims in his jurisdiction, he repeatedly heard the names of members of a crew operating out of an area around Northeast Baltimore's Alameda Shopping Center. Shropshire was one of the names he heard frequently, as well as the nicknames "Black" and "Twan." Black had been identified as Aaron Anderson, and Twan was Antoine Washington. McDougall suspected they were working together.

McDougall, working as part of a federal drug task force, started digging through old cases to see if he could find ties to the dealers that might already be documented in their files.

He found Jaime. A nineteen-year-old from a beach town in New Jersey, she had come to Harford County in 2011 for rehab. Growing up, she liked gymnastics, had an after-school job at a pizza place, and enjoyed skiing on weekends in the Catskills, but those interests gave way to marijuana and later a pill addiction. She twice enrolled in rehab before counselors pushed to get her into Maryland Recovery in Bel Air, where she attended sobriety meetings and took a job at the mall. By the fall of 2011, she had relapsed.

In late December, Jaime texted a man named Kenneth Diggins whom she'd met through a friend at the rehab. "Got any boy?" she wrote, using slang for heroin. "Let me get some boy off you."

"I can do a little something to help you out," Diggins replied.

"Oh my god, thank you so much," Jaime texted back.

Diggins was nearly twice Jaime's age, divorced, and laid off from his job as an insurance adjuster at a fleet management company. In his twenties he had started taking cocaine and Ecstasy, then moved to opiates: first OxyContin that he purchased illegally, then heroin.

"The supply of OxyContin dried up," Diggins explained later. "It was getting more expensive, harder to obtain. And at the time someone that I knew said, you know, you can just go down to Baltimore and get some heroin. It's basically the same thing but cheaper."

Describing himself as a "full-blown addict," Diggins was getting money from his family while maxing out credit cards and taking cash advances to support his habit. He'd begun buying heroin directly from Antoine Washington earlier that month. The cost was $120 per gram.

"Got da fire," Washington had texted him, referring to a particularly potent batch of heroin.

Diggins repeatedly reached out to Jaime, offering her drugs. "I'm trying to have a good time tonight," he wrote to her. "If you want to join in on the Christmas party, it's on me. I got you covered." She mostly ignored him. "If you're trying to be good, sorry. But no BS—it's definitely top shelf. Haven't had anything much better," he wrote another time. "Get anything good for Christmas? I'm still waiting for my best present. It's coming later from Twan."

After days of goading, she came to his house on December 28, 2011. They watched TV, then used heroin and had sex.

They resumed watching TV, and Jaime appeared to doze off. Diggins took out his cellphone and took a picture of her, lifting up her shirt to expose her breasts. He said later he'd intended to show her the next day to goof on her.

She never woke up.

Diggins was interviewed for hours that day by police, initially lying about the circumstances around Jamie's death before coming clean and giving the investigators Antoine Washington's name as his supplier. The information sat in the case file for four years before McDougall came across it in search of information he could use to build a significant case against the Northeast Baltimore crew whose drugs were ending up in Harford County. It was a solid start, but he knew he needed more.

McDougall checked "deconfliction" databases to see if anyone else in law enforcement was looking into this group of dealers. Oddly, city police were not. But Baltimore County authorities were—so McDougall set up a meeting with Kilpatrick to compare notes and discuss the possibility of working together.

Kilpatrick was game, but he wanted McDougall to know about his concerns that dirty cops could be involved. He shared the 2013 jail call in which Shropshire spoke of Jenkins. McDougall agreed that it sounded as if Jenkins was protecting the dealers and even revealing who had been giving information about them to the police.

"It was a really concerning call," McDougall recalled.

At the same time, the call was years old, and it was unclear what exactly Jenkins's involvement might be. McDougall was a drug cop, not Internal Affairs; he'd never heard of Jenkins, and his job was to stop the dealers. McDougall and Kilpatrick decided to work together on building a case that could go federal, and they agreed that they would bypass city police in order to avoid potential problems.

OVER THE ENSUING MONTHS, the county officers conducted surveillance and controlled buys. The dealers were working in one specific area around a shopping center in the Woodbourne Heights neighborhood, in a relatively suburban part of the city not far from the Baltimore County line. On a map, McDougall had drawn out the boundaries of his investigation using a red pen.

McDougall and Kilpatrick were amazed at the brazenness of the open-air dealing in the city, unlike anything they'd seen in their jurisdictions.

"These guys would be dealing all day long in the Alameda Shopping Center, and nobody would say a word," Kilpatrick recalled later. "We'd do buys—[there were] no patrol cars in sight. We'd take pictures and they didn't even care we were there."

The new opioid crisis had spread quickly across the country, disproportionately fueled by a rise in white middle-class people whose addictions began through the misuse of pharmaceutical drugs. In Baltimore, the people streaming to the shopping center at the intersection of Loch Raven and the Alameda reflected those demographics. A widow who had started using after her husband passed away made the two-hour round trip to Baltimore each day to buy $120 worth of heroin. A man who had a mechanical engineering degree from Johns Hopkins University had started using while he was a student. One college student studying business administration at a local community college was prescribed oxycodone for a herniated disc issue that stemmed from doing gymnastics. "When I was decreased off my milligram, I ended up using heroin instead," she recalled. A wheelchair-bound operating engineer was prescribed painkillers after being diagnosed with multiple sclerosis, but "it was never enough," so he started using between one and ten grams of heroin every day. He bought daily from Shropshire's crew. Messages would come to his cellphone saying "fire" or "missile." He recalled seeing customers lined up in their vehicles. "There would be anywhere from five to ten or more cars just lined up waitin' to be hit."

A thirty-year-old handyman said he had first started buying from Shropshire after Shropshire himself pulled up next to him at a stoplight, rolled down the window, and asked him if he liked to party. He threw a half gram of heroin into his vehicle as a "tester" and gave the handyman his phone number. "I called him ever since," the man said. "It was good."

In July 2015, the detectives used a confidential source to introduce an undercover officer from the state police to Shropshire. McDougall watched over a live feed from a camera hidden in the car as Shropshire climbed into the passenger seat, next to the undercover officer. Immediately, Shropshire seemed to know he was being watched. "The police, man," Shropshire said to the undercover officer. "That car right there; that car right there. That Cherokee; that's probably them too. That's definitely them. . . . You not no cop, is you?"

"Nah, dude," the officer said.

"I don't know who you are, know what I mean?"

"Nah, I feel you dude. I feel you."

"Them motherfuckers just in the area, so I don't know what the fuck is going on."

"You got a lot of heat on you?" the undercover asked.

"No, just the area—so many people around here doing shit. You know what I'm saying? You don't mind showing me ID, do you? I'm sorry to put you through this, man, but like I said, I never done business with you in my life, know what I mean?"

The officer handed him a fake ID with his assumed name on it. Shropshire studied it. McDougall watched nervously over the feed.

Just then, one of Shropshire's two cellphones rang. He chatted briefly. When he hung up, the officer tried to steer the conversation from scrutiny of the license. As they spoke, Shropshire reached toward the hidden camera and turned it away from him. Did he know he was being recorded? What was about to happen? McDougall's heart raced.

But Shropshire continued chitchatting as he directed the undercover officer where to drive. The officer pulled to a stop, and Shropshire climbed out before returning with a bag of heroin. The officer handed Shropshire a tight roll of cash, which Shropshire shuffled through so expertly it made the sound of a money counter.

Shropshire could have been arrested and charged on the spot, but the detectives wanted to make a comprehensive case. That would mean more surveillance, more buys, more evidence.

The undercover cop set up a second buy, but this time Shropshire followed his intuition: He took off when the officer arrived and then changed the phone numbers he had been using. He later asked the source who made the connection whether the buyer was a police officer. In court papers later, authorities would write: "Law enforcement has encountered unusually high occurrence of setbacks in these ... endeavors." They continued: "Investigators believe that Shropshire conducts himself in a way that suggests he receives information from someone who has knowledge of law enforcement techniques."

BY THE FALL OF 2015, McDougall decided the time was right to push forward with charges against a dealer named Aaron Anderson and see if he might flip on the Shropshire crew. While authorities initially had reason to believe that Anderson and Shropshire were part of the same group, they learned as their investigations pressed on that there was a more complicated dynamic. Tensions between the two had flared in early 2015. Anderson had found a higher-quality heroin source than Shropshire, and some of Shropshire's customers had started to buy heroin from Anderson instead. The detectives now believed the two were only tolerating each other's presence as they dealt in the same area.

McDougall got a judge to sign off on a warrant, traveled to Anderson's apartment in western Baltimore County one night, and hid a GPS tracker on his new Jeep Cherokee.

He soon learned that Anderson had stopped going to his apartment and was staying at a Red Roof Inn. On October 19, 2015, McDougall obtained search warrants for both the apartment and the motel room. At the apartment, agents found a dent and a boot print on the front door. Inside, it had been ransacked, and looked as if it had already been raided. At the motel, as Anderson and his girlfriend walked down the steps from the second floor and climbed into his car, agents swarmed.

Federal prosecutors had already approved charges. Offered a

choice to cooperate and remain free or go straight to jail, Anderson agreed to talk with the officers. He had moved to the motel, he said, because a week earlier masked men had kicked in the door to his apartment while his girlfriend slept and had taken $12,000 cash and some jewelry. Nearly a kilogram of heroin and a gun were also taken, but he did not mention that on this day. Anderson said he suspected "Twan"—Antoine Washington—was behind the break-in.

The county officers asked Anderson about an interaction he had had with city police in the spring of 2015. Anderson had been caught with three hundred grams of heroin—a large amount, worth $30,000 wholesale, which likely would have led to federal drug charges if it had happened in Harford County. But the Baltimore officer, Avraham Tasher, had let Anderson go without charges. Anderson said it was because he had helped the officer catch one of his suppliers with drugs. That struck McDougall as odd; officers were at least supposed to work out a cooperation contract with prosecutors. Maybe they did things differently in the city, he thought.

Anderson was released by the county task force officers on the condition that he continue to work with the detectives.

The county officers started to wrap up the day's operation. When retrieving their GPS tracker from Anderson's car, they found a second device also affixed by a magnet underneath.

Someone else had been tracking Anderson too.

McDougall and Kilpatrick's team, representing officers from three different agencies, huddled and passed the contraption around. It was cheap, and not the kind their departments used. Throughout his investigation, McDougall had repeatedly checked the "deconfliction" databases and was certain no other investigators were on Anderson's trail. He guessed that it might instead have been the work of rival drug dealers. Whoever had put it there might have also been responsible for the home invasion at Anderson's apartment.

McDougall got a subpoena for the GPS company, and by the next day he received an email with a detailed history of the device. It had been purchased for $436.86 in September of that year and had been activated the next day. The buyer was named John Clewell, and his photo in the driver's license database showed a white man with a goatee and a patch of hair on top of his head.

McDougall searched Clewell's name in the state's online court database to see whether he had been arrested before. But instead of a few hits coming back, as he'd expected, McDougall got a red error message—there were too many records to display.

Clewell was a Baltimore cop.

Police officers can place a GPS tracker on a suspect's car only if given permission by a judge. This tracker, however, had been purchased over the Internet, with Clewell's personal credit card, and had been shipped to his home address. He was paying the monthly $45 service charges himself.

McDougall ran the information back through his chain of command. We've got a problem, he said.

The next day, the drug task force investigators and the federal prosecutors overseeing their case convened a meeting at the local FBI headquarters in Woodlawn. Members of the public corruption squad had done a workup on Clewell. They identified him as a member of a city police plainclothes unit called the Gun Trace Task Force. When created seven years earlier, it had been a signature initiative of then-commissioner Fred Bealefeld to combat gun violence from the source, but in the ensuing years it had been less prominent and was relatively unknown outside of the department.

McDougall had already checked the law enforcement databases to see who in the BPD had run Anderson's name—neither Clewell nor any other officers in the GTTF ever had. No one conducting an investigation would have failed to take the simple step of looking up his information. What was Clewell, or his squad, up to?

CHAPTER TEN

VALOR

AS DARKNESS FELL ONE night in June 2014, Baltimore police detective Jemell Rayam sat in a vehicle outside a duplex in an industrial area in Southwest Baltimore underneath Interstate 95, watching. Two other men wearing tactical vests marked "POLICE" sat with him. A day earlier, Rayam's squad had raided a business belonging to the residents of the home in question. Now he was back to finish what he'd started.

At midnight, Rayam was sitting in the car, listening over the police radio as his two associates crept past an aluminum front gate and up to the home. They knocked a security camera from its mount, then rapped on the door. Donna Curry, a white woman in her forties, answered, and the men showed her a search warrant. She invited them in. One gripped a gun and told her husband, Jeffrey Shore, to "sit still and be quiet." The man with the gun started moving through the house, making a lot of noise in the kitchen, as the other stood watch. The armed man emerged from the kitchen and said to Curry and her husband, "Today's your lucky day."

After they left, Curry noticed her pocketbook was missing from the dining room where she'd last seen it. She found it in the kitchen, tossed in the sink with cash missing. It wasn't just a few bucks, either—

Curry had $20,000 inside. It was all legal: cobbled together from sales at their pigeon store, a federal income tax refund, income from Shore's secondary business selling junk cars as scrap, and loans they had received from friends, including a pastor. The plan was to pay their property taxes at the city municipal building the following day.

Curry called 911 to report a home invasion. The robbers had never showed their badges and hadn't carried themselves like officers; they must have been police impersonators, she thought.

She was partially correct. The men who entered her home were certainly not police officers—but Rayam, the thirty-three-year-old detective who had recruited the two robbers and provided them with police vests, was part of the Gun Trace Task Force.

Rayam had been in Curry's pigeon-feed store in Baltimore's Brooklyn neighborhood just hours earlier with other members of the GTTF, executing a search warrant approved by a judge. The officers hadn't found anything illegal during their search. But Rayam had noticed the cash. He looked up Curry's address in law enforcement databases and had an idea. A friend named Thomas Finnegan, who worked as a plumber and occasionally received drugs from Rayam, had told Rayam that he needed cash. "I called Jemell asking him to borrow money. He said he had an opportunity for me," Finnegan said later. Rayam had contacted him "seven or eight" previous times with such an offer, and Finnegan had always declined, but now he was facing eviction.

They cased the home during the day but decided not to do anything just then. Rayam then brought his cousin David Rahim, who worked as an autopsy technician for the state medical examiner's office, into the fold for the robbery.

This wasn't unusual for Rayam. He had been stealing for years. Sometimes he just skimmed money from people he stopped or arrested. But he also carried out elaborate heists while off-duty.

He did not fear getting caught.

"I was law enforcement, so I wasn't too worried about it," Rayam would say a few years later.

Rayam was born in Newark, New Jersey, where his father was a police officer and his mother was an elementary school teacher. He grew up in a Christian household—his grandfather was a Pentecostal pastor. His three siblings all went on to become educators like their mother, while Rayam went to college at DeSales University, a private Catholic university, where he earned a marketing degree.

His first job out of college was as a case worker at a juvenile detention center in Allentown, Pennsylvania. In 2005, at age twenty-four, he decided to join the Baltimore police force. He met his future wife, Cherelle, not long after graduating from the academy.

"For myself growing up in the inner city of Baltimore, back then I never understood why a bright individual from out of state would want to come here to tackle these stressful streets," Cherelle wrote in a character letter to a judge years later. "But Jemell had something to prove, and proved it through his hard work and dedication to Baltimore."

In June 2007, Rayam shot someone for the first time. His account was that he and other officers had rolled up on a group of men just after midnight and that as he approached one took off and fired at Rayam while running. Rayam fired back and continued giving chase. When he turned into an alley, he reported, he saw the man lying on the ground. Rayam said the man was still holding a weapon, so he fired again. The man survived.

Even while the shooting was still under investigation, Rayam was promoted into a plainclothes unit. He had been on the streets for only a year, but the department wanted to reward hungry, promising officers. Within three months, Rayam was involved in another shooting, this time after he said he got his arm caught in a fleeing vehicle that had dragged him until he pulled his gun and fired at the driver. Prosecutors ultimately found both shootings to be justified, and another promotion soon followed, this time to the Violent Crimes Impact Division.

Rayam left the Baltimore police force for the New York State Police but quickly returned after just two weeks.

In March 2009, Rayam shot another person, this time fatally. Rayam and another officer told homicide investigators that they had seen a man walking with his hand in his waistband, who then climbed into a vehicle sitting on a parking pad in a rear alley. As the officers walked up, they said, they yelled for the driver to show his hands, but the car pulled forward and made contact with the leg of Rayam's partner, Jason Giordano. Rayam fired one bullet into the temple of the driver, thirty-year-old Shawn Cannady.

The observation that Cannady's hand was in his waistband was unverifiable, but it gave the officers justification to say they had been worried that Cannady was armed. It turned out he had no gun. The other passenger, Keith Hill, told homicide detectives that he had been asleep in the car until being awoken by the gunshot.

It was the third time in less than two years that Rayam had shot someone, and some elected officials and the NAACP called for an outside review. "There are officers who go their entire career and never find it necessary to shoot or kill anyone," said Delegate Jill Carter. Cannady was unarmed, and there was no evidence he had committed a crime. "It definitely calls for further investigation," she said. A police spokesman at the time said officers had been tasked to go after bad guys with guns and that "bad guys fight back." The police union backed Rayam too. The pleas for an independent review went unfulfilled.

A week later, the police department held its annual awards ceremony. All but six of the twenty-four officers honored were recognized for incidents in which they had shot someone. Rayam received a Citation of Valor and a Silver Star for one of the 2007 shootings.

It would take years before it emerged that during this period Rayam was engaged in a series of robberies, some of them highly orchestrated. At one point, he teamed up with a woman who socialized with drug dealers. She helped Rayam track dealers as they came out of clubs or to break into their homes when they were away. An officer from his police academy class, Michael Sylvester, sometimes took part and also collaborated on a scheme to finance drug dealing using Workers' Compensation money Rayam was receiving. At one point Sylvester stole more than ten pounds of marijuana; he and Rayam funneled it to Eric Snell, another Baltimore Police Academy classmate who had since left the city for Philadelphia and had relatives in the drug business.

It is not clear when the robberies started, or how many occurred, but in June 2009 one such robbery came to the attention of Internal Affairs.

Rayam and Giordano pulled over a driver on the west side of downtown near the State Center office complex. Near them in a separate vehicle was Sylvester, who wasn't on duty at all. The driver, Gary Brown, was told he was stopped for not wearing a seatbelt. He was placed in plastic flex-cuffs and asked to sit on the curb. Rayam and Giordano searched Brown's vehicle and found nothing illegal. In his trunk, however, they found $11,000 in rolled-up bundles inside a paper bag. The officers asked Brown who the money belonged to, where he was headed, and where he lived. "They was telling me they could get a search warrant to search my address," Brown later recalled. Rayam asked him if he had any information about illegal activity in the area. Then he asked if Brown could get him a gun that could be reported as a seizure. Brown said no. After that, one of the officers pulled out a knife and cut the flex-cuffs off. Sylvester picked up the money and put it in the back seat of his vehicle.

"You can pick this up from [Evidence Control]," Sylvester said, as he and the other officers drove off.

Brown did something dirty officers weren't used to seeing: he reported the incident to Internal Affairs. He couldn't be sure that the men were even police officers at all—they wore regular clothes and drove unmarked cars—but Brown had noticed their badges. Still, he didn't have names, and the incident hadn't been logged by anyone working that day. Brown wasn't given a "citizen contact" ticket to document the encounter, as required by department policy. The only evidence he had of the episode was the pair of plastic flex-cuffs, which the officers left behind.

During the investigation, Internal Affairs expended significant time trying to account for how Gary Brown had $11,000. They compiled his criminal history and asked him to submit to a lie detector test, which he passed.

Investigators determined that Rayam and Giordano were two of the officers involved in the stop, probably from Brown's description of their car. The detectives were interviewed separately on June 16, 2009, about a week after the incident. Both said they had stopped to back up an officer who was unknown to them, who was "pointing to his badge and pointing to the car and [asking them] to assist with it," Giordano said, according to a transcript of his interview.

Giordano said he followed the unknown officer's directions. He didn't know what, if anything, was recovered.

"When he said he was good . . . we went ahead and left," Giordano said. "Like, he was done with the car stop I guess."

Rayam also said he didn't know the officer.

"We observed another car pull next to ours and ask us if we could help. And we wound up pulling this car over," Rayam said.

"And who was operating it?" asked the Internal Affairs investigator, Detective Barbara Price.

"Another officer," Rayam said.

"He didn't really identify you or give you his name or anything?"

"Like I said, we really didn't ask. We just assumed or I just assumed that it was plainclothes drug work and we assisted," Rayam said.

"And you said you didn't know that officer's name?"

"No," Rayam said.

Rayam was shown a lineup of six officers, which included Sylvester's picture. He picked four of them, including Sylvester. He said they all looked like the officer he saw.

Investigators focused on Sylvester, who had received other complaints around this time. They asked Brown to wear a wire and participate in a sting against Sylvester.

"It was like movie shit," Brown said later. "They were going to stage some kind of big drug thing and have it so he was the one who came. They wanted me to get him to admit he took my money."

Brown said he declined, out of fear.

"If he robbed me like that in broad daylight, then he wouldn't have a problem shooting me in my face," Brown said.

Internal Affairs investigators decided to move forward with a sting operation using an undercover police academy cadet outfitted with a wire. They put $260 in the cadet's pockets and $135 in his vehicle's center console. The bills had been marked using ultraviolet light with the letters "IID," for the Internal Investigations Division.

The cadet was sent to a block in Northwest Baltimore, and dispatchers directed Sylvester to check out a suspicious person fitting the cadet's description. Sylvester found the cadet and told him to get out of the car, empty out his pockets, and place the contents on the passenger seat. Sylvester's partner that night, a rookie officer, shone her flashlight in the cadet's eyes as Sylvester rifled through the vehicle, including the trunk. After Sylvester had searched the car, investigators said, $70 was gone.

Investigators secured a warrant to search Sylvester's police station locker, where they said they recovered the cash and a Ziploc bag containing suspected rock cocaine.

Sylvester was arrested and criminally charged with theft and misconduct in office. But prosecutors dropped the charges just two months later, saying sloppy errors by the police investigators—an apparent incorrect time stamp on photos, and calculation mistakes regarding the amount of cash taken—had compromised the case. Sylvester remained on the job, with internal charges pending.

In March 2010, almost a year after Brown was robbed, Rayam sat for a second interview with Internal Affairs, this time with a lawyer. He was being compelled by the department to talk under the state Law Enforcement Officers' Bill of Rights, which meant that what he said couldn't be used against him in a criminal investigation.

Rayam was asked again to identify the officer involved in the car stop, whom he'd previously denied knowing.

"Michael Sylvester."

Phone records subpoenaed by investigators showed that Rayam had contacted Sylvester 474 times over a four-month period around the alleged theft. They'd also had five contacts, including one that lasted seven minutes, just two hours before Rayam first spoke with Internal Affairs.

"Did you know his name at the time?" Price now asked.

"Yes. Yes," Rayam said.

"Why didn't you provide his name to me if you knew it?" she said.

"I was answering the questions that were asked," Rayam said.

What about the photo lineup, where Rayam had picked out four of the six officers? He said that because the photos were black and white, it was hard to see.

But Rayam still maintained he knew nothing about the stop and what had occurred.

"I can speak for me personally, when I assist anyone . . . they're doing their job and I really—excuse me for saying it—but I really don't care," he said. "I care, but I respect them, I guess, that they're doing a job and nothing is going on."

The phone records also showed a common person who had been in touch with both Sylvester and Gary Brown. "Based on the sequence of calls it is believed that [the mutual contact] was setting Gary Brown up for the theft to occur," investigators wrote.

Questioned by Internal Affairs investigators, Sylvester conceded nothing.

"Why would Officer Rayam advise that he assisted you on a car stop on June 8, 2009?" Price asked.

"I can't tell you why," Sylvester said. "You should ask him."

"I did ask him, and that's what he said."

"That's fine. I'm not him."

Internal charges were brought against Sylvester, which he appealed to the state courts on procedural grounds. He ultimately resigned from the department in 2012 in lieu of termination.

Rayam took a lie detector test related to the Gary Brown case in July 2010. He failed with a 99 percent certainty of being untruthful and was suspended in the fall—a suspension that would last for two years. In a previous time, he likely would have landed on the State's Attorney's Office's "do not call" list and been prohibited from working the streets. But prosecutors, first with Bernstein and continuing with Marilyn Mosby, had abolished the list, saying they would evaluate each case on its merits and rely on other officers involved.

When Rayam came back, he remained in the GTTF.

And the GTTF was where he would be paired up with Momodu Gondo, who would be his partner for the next six years. Unlike Rayam, Gondo was from the city—he had grown up in North Baltimore, a couple of blocks from the Alameda Shopping Center, the son of a city high school teacher who had immigrated from Sierra Leone. As a rookie officer in 2006, Gondo had survived what was said to be an attempted carjacking outside of his home. A suspect whom Gondo picked out of a lineup was acquitted by a jury of all charges; some in the department said later they were privately skeptical about the circumstances of the shooting.

By the time they were working together on the GTTF, as Rayam described in an early 2013 deposition, the unit had become laid back and largely bureaucratic.

"We pretty much assist patrol units," Rayam said at the time. "If they get a gun, we investigate the serial number as far as where the gun came from, if it was stolen. . . . We run guns, straw purchases. It's not really proactive. We assist school police if they have a kid who says they have a gun in the house. We just assist in investigations. So it's more investigative work."

As part of his efforts to reform the department and stave off federal oversight, Commissioner Batts had hired legendary police chief Bill Bratton, who had led the police forces in Boston, New York, and Los Angeles, as a consultant to do an evaluation of the Baltimore police. His report, released in late 2013, laid out a slew of recommendations. Among them was activating the Gun Trace Task Force into a more operational role. "While tracing and registering guns are important, is the priority of these units targeting and arresting those individuals selling and buying guns illegally?" the report asked rhetorically. Units like the GTTF "should be evaluated using productivity measures, including arrests and successful investigations," with commanders asked to "display specific measures of productivity or success," the report said.

IN RAYAM'S 2014 HOME invasion of pigeon store owner Donna Curry, the detective assigned to investigate actually filed charges on an innocent man. A patrol officer said he thought he recognized one of the men in the security camera footage as someone he'd arrested before; the investigating detective agreed that there was a similarity and put the man's picture into a photo lineup for Curry to consider. Curry selected him, saying, "This is the guy I recognize that stood over me and my family." The detective issued an arrest warrant.

Two weeks later, a city prosecutor informed the detective that the man he had charged was in federal prison—where he had been for the previous three years. The case was dropped. But had he not had such an airtight alibi, the innocent man easily could have been convicted of the crime, which carries a twenty-five-year maximum penalty in Maryland.

After all, it was his word against theirs.

CHAPTER ELEVEN

STRAP IN

THE REVELATION THAT THE GPS tracker found under Aaron Anderson's car belonged to a cop meant it was time to hand the investigation from the DEA to the FBI. The FBI comes up with case code names at the outset of an investigation. This case was dubbed "Broken Boundaries."

Along with federal prosecutors, agents walked through the possible scenarios that might explain the GPS found under Anderson's car. Maybe, like a teacher who buys class supplies out of his own pocket, John Clewell had sought to cut through red tape and had just bought the GPS himself. And though it was unlawful for police to use the device without a warrant, it was possible Clewell or someone else on the Gun Trace Task Force had cut corners while conducting a legitimate investigation.

But these options also seemed unlikely. The GPS had ended up at the county police precinct station in Cockeysville, meaning whoever it belonged to should have known it was last in police custody.

"Frankly, if Clewell had called up and said, 'Hey, you've got my tracker,' we might not have ever thought another thing of it," recalled then–assistant U.S. attorney Andrea Smith.

Smith had been running the Shropshire and Anderson drug investigations, but she was also nearing retirement from a thirty-seven-year career as a federal prosecutor. The drug cases, and wherever the Clewell investigation was headed, would require prosecutors who could see it through.

Assistant U.S. Attorney Leo Wise, thirty-seven, a public corruption prosecutor with an inquisitive mind and an unmatched work ethic, had earlier in his career worked on the civil racketeering case brought against the tobacco industry. He typically didn't handle drug cases but had been involved from the start with the Shropshire case as well as a separate but related investigation—not because anyone had an inkling that corrupt police officers were involved but because he had sought more experience in handling fatal overdose cases.

Another eager assistant federal prosecutor brand-new to the office and assigned to drug cases, Derek Hines, would be brought in to help with the work. Wise was a wiry six-foot-four; Hines stood six-foot-six. Some started calling them "the Twin Towers."

The FBI's lead case agent would be Special Agent Erika Jensen, a New York native and former software engineer who after 9/11 joined the bureau and had since chased cartels and provided security for then–attorney general Eric Holder. Also part of the team was Baltimore police sergeant John Sieracki, a second-generation city cop assigned to the Public Corruption Task Force and working out of the FBI's office in Woodlawn. Sieracki provided key knowledge of the department's inner workings and access to its databases, but he reported directly to the FBI—a deliberate firewall set up years earlier to protect investigations of department personnel from interference and leaks.

They focused hard on Clewell, a former marine who'd joined the force in 2009, but didn't find any record of serious complaints or trouble on his record, let alone any connection to Shropshire and Anderson. The team's gaze turned to others in the squad—Detectives Momodu Gondo, Jemell Rayam, and the veteran sergeant in charge of the group, Thomas Allers.

One day, as Jensen was shuffling through personnel paperwork for Rayam, she saw something that sucked the air out of the room: Rayam had once lived in the same apartment complex on Marnat Road as

Aaron Anderson. The apartments were side by side. Rayam might have known Anderson, and assuredly he knew the layout of his apartment and other features that could have helped in a robbery.

Looking over the new information, McDougall wondered out loud: What if the officers themselves were the ones who had broken into Anderson's apartment?

As he asked the question, McDougall recalled later: "I wasn't even believing it as I was saying it."

Authorities combed through their files for any previous intelligence on the officers. Gondo, they noted, had grown up near the Alameda Shopping Center, where Kilpatrick and McDougall had spent so much time watching the Shropshire drug crew. They also found that two years earlier, in 2013, a Baltimore police officer had brought suspicions about Gondo to the FBI.

The officer was Ryan Guinn, one of the original members of the Gun Trace Task Force. Along with Jenkins and Sean Suiter, Guinn had been involved in the pursuit of Umar Burley in 2010 and had shown up at the scene of the Demetric Simon arrest in 2014. He was now off the streets, having settled in as a sergeant working in the training academy.

Guinn had worked with Gondo and Rayam on the Gun Trace Task Force from 2012 to 2013. Everything they did rubbed him the wrong way—especially Gondo.

Guinn remembered how when he was making a gun arrest in Northeast Baltimore, Gondo and Rayam were called to the scene to assist with a search warrant. When Gondo arrived, he warmly greeted the suspect. Guinn was unnerved. "That's my boy," Gondo told him. "We used to ball together."

On another night, while Guinn was eating at Mo's Seafood restaurant near the Inner Harbor in Little Italy, he bumped into Gondo and Shropshire together. There was tension—this was more than Gondo happening to know someone Guinn had arrested. Shropshire was, in Guinn's mind, a verified criminal, and Gondo was socializing with him. Gondo sought to vouch for Shropshire, saying they were "blood" and assuring Shropshire that Guinn was "cool." That made Guinn mad: What did Gondo mean that he was "cool"?

Guinn didn't know what to do. He sought advice from an officer he looked up to, who suggested Guinn reach out directly to the new deputy commissioner overseeing Internal Affairs, Jerry Rodriguez. Rodriguez wasn't a BPD guy—in fact, he was one of the only other outsiders Commissioner Batts had recruited for his leadership team. Rodriguez came from the LAPD, where he'd taken part in investigating corruption in the famous Rampart Division case. Rodriguez was already ruffling feathers by trying to make even incremental changes within the BPD. He agreed to take a meeting with Guinn.

After Rodriguez took in what Guinn had to say, he asked if Guinn would meet with some of his investigators. He directed Guinn to go stand outside the Walters Art Museum in the Mount Vernon neighborhood. "A couple guys will pick you up," Rodriguez told him.

Guinn waited there, smoking cigarettes and pacing back and forth. The scenario seemed so strange. "Where the fuck are these guys?" he wondered.

Then, a black van pulled up and the sliding door opened.

Inside were Internal Affairs detectives detailed to the FBI.

"Detective Guinn, can you get in?" one of them asked.

They never went to an office. As they drove around, Guinn told them what he knew—that Gondo appeared chummy with known drug dealers and seemed to have a lot of money. It fell well short of hard evidence of corruption, he knew, but he hoped it would spark something.

Guinn was also worried, he recalled later. He had snitched on a fellow officer and had no idea whether anyone was going to do anything with the information. He was aware of other cops who'd been flagged for suspicious behavior, only to wriggle free. And then you still had to work around these guys. A year earlier, a plainclothes officer who reported others had found a dead rat on his windshield.

Guinn decided to take matters into his own hands. He called his lieutenant and asked what time Gondo was getting off work. That night, he drove to Gondo's apartment complex, parked a distance away, and took out binoculars. Through his dark-tinted windows he watched cars pulling up and wrote down their tag numbers to see if he could get a lead, though he was really hoping he could catch someone like Shropshire arriving or leaving. Then he could take pictures. Hell, maybe he'd catch them in a full-blown drug deal.

"If I could get him dirty myself, I'll take him down myself," Guinn thought.

Guinn returned six or seven times over a three-week period but didn't get anything. He was up for promotion and soon left the Gun Trace Task Force. He never heard anything more about Gondo, except that he was still working the streets and still in the GTTF. Guinn's tip stayed buried in the FBI's files.

That was in 2013. Two years later, Jensen and the federal investigators sought Guinn out to learn more about what he had reported previously. Contacting anyone about the investigation was considered risky—the BPD had an active rumor mill, and there could be unseen alliances that could compromise the case. But Jensen decided that a limited conversation that could generate additional information was worth it.

Guinn was encouraged that the FBI was following up, even though he wasn't sure why. He gave the FBI two cellphone numbers for Gondo that he had saved and told them that Gondo and Antonio Shropshire partied at clubs together in D.C.

As Guinn sought to aid the inquiry, he thought of someone who might have additional information to pass along—a former squad member who had also worked with Gondo in the past and had also expressed concerns that Gondo was "dirty."

He reached out to Wayne Jenkins.

"The feds just called my office; I need more information on Gondo," Guinn said he told Jenkins.

Guinn said later that Jenkins had wanted to help and had provided him with the name of another Gondo associate, Glen Kyle Wells, as someone the investigators should be looking at too.

Meanwhile, an analysis of Gondo's phone records showed a high number of contacts with Shropshire and Wells: Between October 11, 2015, and January 1, 2016, Gondo and Shropshire exchanged 99 telephone calls—more than one per day. And between July 2, 2015, and January 1, 2016, there were 316 contacts between Gondo's phone and a number associated with Wells. While the nature of the calls was still unclear, Jensen confirmed that neither Shropshire nor Wells was registered as a confidential informant. The FBI decided to be patient and let the drug wiretaps running in the Shropshire investigation do the work.

"If we get a dirty call, strap in, it's going to be a ride," Jensen told her supervisor after a meeting in late December 2015.

In the meantime, they would not tell the BPD of their investigation; they had to keep a tight circle.

"The best way to keep a secret is to keep a secret," Wise, the federal prosecutor, would say.

IN THE MIDST OF the investigation, another officer joined the Gun Trace Task Force to work with Gondo, Rayam, and their sergeant, Allers. Daniel Hersl grew up in the white, working-class East Baltimore neighborhood Highlandtown and had earned a reputation among residents and defense attorneys as a brutal cop. A decade earlier, a defense attorney challenging Hersl's credibility revealed that he and another officer had already collected forty-six Internal Affairs complaints between them. Only one of the complaints had been "sustained," meaning the department had brought charges forward, but a judge agreed that that number of complaints was enough to warrant a mention at the trial of three East Baltimore men whom Hersl had arrested. "Misconduct, sometimes when it's frequent enough, it indicates a lack of desire to tell the truth," said a city judge.

The defense attorney in the case was so disturbed that he sent a letter to the police commissioner at the time, requesting an audit of personnel files. The city's chief legal counsel sent this snarky reply: "Your concern about the management of the Baltimore Police Department is commendable, as it is rare for an attorney representing members of violent drug organizations to be interested in strong, effective law enforcement. Please be assured that [the commissioner] is committed to enforcing strong, department-wide discipline." When prosecutors dropped the case rather than air Hersl's history, the chief lawyer groused: "Unsubstantiated complaints should not shut down the prosecution of bad guys. These officers could have explained to the jury the reality of being narcotics officers and that they receive a lot of spurious complaints from drug dealers."

Hersl repeatedly redeemed himself in the eyes of fellow officers, however, no more so than in 2010, when he took swift action to save a partner who had been shot. He was awarded the department's highest honor, the Medal of Honor, in 2011.

But trouble continued to follow. By 2014, the city had settled multiple lawsuits involving Hersl for $200,000. Young Moose, the city's top rapper at the time, publicly accused Hersl of harassment and said the officer had stolen money from him. He namechecked Hersl, among others, in a song called "Fuck Da Police."

None of these complaints had been enough for the department to sideline Hersl. Though commanders did take the extraordinary step in 2015 of banning him from patrolling the city's particularly crime-ridden east side because of excessive complaints, he was instead moved to the GTTF, a better assignment and one that had citywide jurisdiction. His supervisors continued to back him: after Hersl was flagged for discipline, his then-sergeant John Burns would tell higher-ranking commanders in an email that "criminals feared [Hersl] so much, they made false complaints and allegations."

"Hersl has always been a great detective and I never had any issues with him. He worked for me for almost 8 years and never saw him do or say anything inappropriate that I am aware of," Burns wrote. "We can't let criminals dictate the lives of our officers."

CHAPTER TWELVE

MONSTERS

THE GUN VIOLENCE THAT spiked in the wake of the Freddie Gray riots did not abate. The year 2015 ended with 342 homicides, the second-most in the city's history, and a per capita record. In the beleaguered homicide unit, caseloads rose and detectives struggled to solve the killings, with the closure rate sagging to three in ten, a rate so low that detectives groused that the year's statistics shouldn't even be counted. One likened it to baseball's steroid era, when players used performance-enhancing drugs to rewrite the record book. Mark 2015, they said, with an asterisk: "the Freddie Gray Era."

There was no real pattern to the violence. Some groups and even individuals were responsible for multiple killings, but most of the cases were the usual beefs and tit-for-tat shootings, now coming in at a higher volume. Detectives lamented that fewer and fewer tips from the community were coming in. At community meetings and city council hearings, citizens were demanding a stop to the violence. Detective Sean Suiter had since risen to the homicide unit and picked up one of the year's highest-profile cases: the slaying of a twenty-four-year-old truck driver and father of three, who was believed to have been targeted for building a fence to keep drug dealers from cutting through his Northwest Baltimore property.

Among those killed in the year to come was Walter Price, who had cooperated with authorities in their investigation of Jenkins in 2014 and 2015, to no avail. The thirty-two-year-old was found shot dead in an alley in South Baltimore, his hands bound behind his back and mouth covered. The investigation went nowhere.

Commanders desperate to stanch the bleeding knew who they could rely on: the department's plainclothes "knockers," who were willing to prowl the streets undeterred by the new scrutiny on officers. A "War Room" had been created in an effort to identify top targets in the city for officers like Jenkins and his team to go after. But often they found people like Malik McCaffity.

The twenty-year-old was walking home from a corner store on North Avenue and Pennsylvania on March 10, 2016, when he spotted plainclothes officers down the street who appeared to be searching someone. McCaffity had a bag of marijuana—and $1,300 fresh out of a bank machine in crisp hundred-dollar and twenty-dollar bills stuffed in his left pocket, which he says he was taking to Western Union for his girlfriend to pay her rent.

Now the officers were coming toward him. "I ran," McCaffity recounted later.

Prior to the encounter, McCaffity did not have the type of record that would land one on a "trigger puller" list. He had been arrested once for possession of marijuana and "riding a bicycle without lights at night," and again for possession of marijuana. He was struggling with substance abuse, which had begun after he was shot as a teenager.

McCaffity had lost his father at age six. Oliver McCaffity, who ran a clothing store on Eutaw Street for the former heavyweight boxing champ from Baltimore, Hasim Rahman, was found shot to death in February 2002 inside a car owned by the fighter. A woman he was dating at the time, the daughter of a city minister, was also killed. Oliver McCaffity had done more than sell clothes, however.

"His father was a hit man," Malik's mother, Lori Turner, recalled matter-of-factly.

Turner remembers living in East Baltimore and once confronting Bloods gang members who she believed were recruiting Malik at age ten. "He was looking for acceptance; he wanted to feel like he belonged," she said. She bought a PlayStation to keep him inside. He was enrolled in an alternative school, where he was identified as a student in need of specialized services.

Malik expressed a love of computers and a desire to go to college. He participated in extracurricular activities and a mentoring program. A male mentor would take him to the movies occasionally; the structure of the program meant he had to keep up with his homework.

"He was always in the house, playing games," older sister Leedra Turner recalled. "He was the one who fixed everything."

Malik was shot for the first time at age thirteen, after a friend got into a confrontation with other teens and someone pulled a gun. He was shot in the foot and prescribed pain medication.

At age fifteen, he spent three months learning how to develop a business plan for a clothing line, and he won a local entrepreneurship contest. A video of the award ceremony shows Malik, wearing a white dress shirt and tie, accepting a plaque as attendees clapped and snapped photos. He got to travel to New York and meet executives and designers of the FUBU clothing line.

Just two months after the awards ceremony, McCaffity was shot again, this time the victim of a robbery. He was treated at Johns Hopkins Hospital for an injury to his chest cavity and liver. He was again prescribed pain medication, but this time he became addicted.

"He almost lost his life," Lori Turner said of the shooting. "When he started taking them pills, I didn't realize he was addicted until one day I was having a conversation with him, he was mumbling. . . . He was never disrespectful, never had him lash out or anything. But those pills . . ."

He stopped going to school and moved from popping Percocets to taking Xanax bars and drinking "lean," a cough syrup mixture. His sister recalled he would black out.

"It's something explainable—it's something unimaginable," McCaffity said later of his addiction. "Your mind is hating it, your body is wanting it."

Lori Turner said the city took a turn for the worse in 2015. The violence, the drug use—it seemed to be out of control. "Everybody's children was getting killed," she said. "Everybody looked like zombies." In early 2016 she decided to move to Florida, and she wanted

Malik to come with her. He was now twenty years old, and he said he wanted a change too. "Just give me a few months to get myself together," he told her.

It was only a few months after his mother left Maryland that McCaffity encountered Jenkins while on his way through the neighborhood. He'd gotten food and something to drink at a corner store, and now the officers were driving toward him. The cash in his left sweatpants pocket was taken. He said Jenkins took out a cellphone and told him to admit to having marijuana and he'd get his money back. One of the officers hopped a nearby wall and found a loaded .45 caliber gun on the other side.

McCaffity insists the gun did not belong to him.

"The gun didn't come along till they got the money," he said.

McCaffity was booked on four counts of weapons charges. The statement of probable cause made no mention of any money being recovered. He was able to post bail and was released. At first, he was most concerned about the money that had been stolen.

"Because I knew I was innocent," he explained. "But after my first appearance in court, and I saw what the charge carried, I thought damn, I might really go to jail for five years. I was really more concerned about how was the outcome going to turn out. I ain't want the money, I just wanted to make sure I wasn't going to jail."

The experience changed his view of police.

"I started looking at police like all of them were crooked, which I know they're not," he said. "But that's how I started looking at them: like everybody is crooked."

LATER THAT SAME MONTH, Jenkins caught a bigger fish. He and his officers were barreling the wrong way down a one-way street in Northwest Baltimore, hoping to catch criminal suspects off guard, when they spotted a thirty-six-year-old man with a camouflage backpack duck into the passenger side of a Toyota minivan. For Jenkins, the backpack set off alarms. He was known within the department for having "the eye"—like an outdoorsman spotting a hawk in the trees, Jenkins was said to be able to register the smallest signs of possible criminal activity on the streets—things that others might never have noticed. A lot of the time, however, it was simple profiling. "Anytime a grown man had a book bag, he always thought it was concealed weapons or drugs," one of his officers, Maurice Ward, later recalled. "He always wanted to stop them and check it out."

Jenkins pulled his car in front of the minivan, and his squad stepped out and surrounded it. Jenkins peered in through the passenger side window. He could see a box at the man's feet. Detective Ward pulled open the sliding door on the other side and reached for another bag that had been tossed in the backseat. Ward pulled it open and could see more than a half kilogram of cocaine inside. The box at the other man's feet contained $21,500. The officers ordered the driver, Oreese Stevenson, and his passenger out of the vehicle, handcuffed them, and sat them on the curb.

The stop and discovery of drugs appeared to be a chance encounter, though Ward would later say that Jenkins had seemed eager to cruise that location beforehand, as if he had an expectation that he might find something interesting. Now Jenkins was going into his "federal agent thing," as those who worked with him called it: Jenkins told the two men that he was a federal drug agent and that he'd known of the drug deal in advance. He assured them they weren't the desired targets of the investigation but said they could help themselves by telling the officers where to find more drugs and who they were working with.

The men were separated, with Jenkins taking Stevenson into the back of the minivan to try to squeeze him for information. According to Jenkins's report at the time, Stevenson initially gave a false address, but the officers found a temporary registration permit in the van with his actual address. Jenkins lied to Stevenson again and said the officers had another team of cops already executing a search warrant there. "At this moment in time, Stevenson placed his head down and began breathing heavily. Sergeant Jenkins advised Stevenson that we observed him to and from this dwelling on several different occasions and we know he lives there," the officers wrote in court papers. "Stevenson then attempted to ask how he could get out of this situation."

Jenkins asked Stevenson how much more cocaine he had at his home. None, Stevenson said. Then suddenly, Jenkins would later claim, Stevenson pleaded for them not to arrest his child's mother and admitted that he had a "few keys" of cocaine at the home. Pressed for how many, he said, "Seven, maybe eight." And guns? "Yeah," Stevenson said.

Jenkins emerged from the van and turned to the officers: "We have a monster," he said.

Monster was Jenkins's term for the heavyweight dealers, the kind who trafficked in brick-shaped kilogram packages worth tens of thousands of dollars apiece. A dealer at that level was likely to have a fortune in money and drugs at home—wads of bills and stacks of powder tucked away in ceiling cavities, under mattresses, and in basement vaults. A decade earlier, Stevenson had been indicted as part of a drug organization that pumped $27 million worth of heroin into the city. He had spent eleven years in federal prison for his role, his second extended stint behind bars. Now he was a truck driver with kids, living in Northeast Baltimore.

The officers called the police department's intelligence analysts to pull whatever they could on Stevenson. They came back with several potential addresses. The first was at Fulton and Presstman streets, a small two-story home in the heart of West Baltimore. Though the officers had found drugs on Stevenson, the law dictated that they needed specific probable cause to connect the properties to Stevenson's drug activities in order to search those premises. But the detectives had something even better: Stevenson's house keys.

Jenkins stepped away from the others to make a phone call. He told them he was calling an officer from another unit to have him sit on the dealer's home until they could get there and to make sure nothing was disturbed.

Jenkins's bail bondsman friend Donny Stepp was at home when the phone rang. On the line was Jenkins, his voice characteristically measured but urgent.

"I need you to come to this address as quick as you can," Jenkins told him. "I just got a drug lord."

With Jenkins's squad headed to one of Stevenson's addresses on the west side of town, Jenkins wanted to get Stepp inside Stevenson's Northeast Baltimore home first. Jenkins would occasionally bring Stepp into police headquarters, slipping his friend in as if he was allowed to be there. Stepp took pictures of himself sitting next to Jenkins in a police department office, posing in a police vest and pointing a gun. Other times, as on this occasion, Jenkins discreetly summoned Stepp to show up undetected to help pilfer drugs without his officers knowing. The others did not know much about Stepp, only that Jenkins generally had a contact in the bail bonds world.

"He told me that if I hurried up and would get there, that his squad didn't realize what was really going on," Stepp recalled in court a few years later.

Jenkins also had a tendency to oversell Stepp on the bounty that awaited, hoping it would motivate him: "Wayne was telling me I could get—there was a quarter-of-a-million dollars on top of a small safe and that there was over a half-million dollars of cash in the safe. And 6 feet to the left of the safe, he told me there was a closet that contained 10 kilograms of cocaine. He said, 'Donny, you're looking at a total take of $1.75 million.' He says, 'If you get in, we can split it.'"

Stepp punched Heathfield Road into his GPS and started making his way there—the eighteen-mile drive would take about a half hour. He'd been told to go around to the back of the home, but when Stepp drove up to the house he saw someone nearby and got spooked.

Instead, he sat two blocks away and waited for Jenkins and his team to arrive.

Across the city, Stevenson's Presstman Street home seemed like a prime stash house. Stevenson had purchased the two-story property a few months earlier for just $16,500, the going rate for vacant or dilapidated homes in the area. Stevenson's wife registered a limited liability company called "Living Memories" at the address, apparently in hopes of starting a small residential care home. No one appeared to be inside the house that evening, but there was a mattress delivery man waiting outside. Not wanting to attract attention, Jenkins and his squad took off their police vests and acted as if they owned the property. Entering with no legal justification but using Stevenson's keys, they searched around and found nothing inside but adult diapers and other supplies related to the assisted living business.

Next the officers headed to Stevenson's actual home on Heathfield Road, in a residential neighborhood sandwiched between Morgan State University and Good Samaritan Hospital, where Stepp was waiting. The officers could see that one of Stevenson's neighbors was outside, so they devised a ruse in which Detective Marcus Taylor would pretend to chase someone from the rear. To anyone else on the block who might be paying attention, the apparent chase would provide the exigent circumstances allowing them to enter the home and "secure" it by making sure no one was inside destroying evidence.

Though the officers still didn't have a search warrant, they entered with keys and, after rummaging around, found cocaine, guns, and bags of money. Jenkins cradled a kilogram of white powder. "When was the last time one of y'all seen one of these?" he said. "It's been a while."

Stepp watched through binoculars as Jenkins emerged from the home just a few minutes after he'd entered.

"He come out the door looking like Santa Claus," Stepp said. His police vest was stuffed with something, and he tossed a sack into the back of his police vehicle. Jenkins called Stepp on his cellphone and asked where he was, then instructed him to drive down the street. Stepp recalled Jenkins flying up behind him.

"He opens the—the passenger door to my truck, throws two kilograms of cocaine in it and says, 'Donny, I'm going on vacation, can you get me $5,000 within this week? I'm leaving for vacation.' I said, 'Yes, I ain't got a problem.' He just threw me a couple hundred thousand dollars' worth of drugs in my truck. So, of course, I told him that I'd get him his $5,000 within a week. And he told me if I got pulled over, to give him a call, that he would come and fix it and told me to drive and do the speed limit and I left."

Ward was told to stay in the home while Jenkins and the other members of the squad drove back to headquarters to procure a search warrant for the home they'd already been inside. He wondered if they were cutting him out of splitting up the money taken from the traffic stop.

At Central Booking, Stevenson placed a phone call to his wife, who said she had stopped by the house and seen officers inside.

"Everything OK?" Stevenson asked.

"No, I mean no," Keona Holloway said.

"Who you with? You by yourself?" he said. "What happened? When you got there what happened?"

"They were in there," she said. "But they don't um . . . they don't have a search warrant."

"They seen you?"

"Mm-mm."

"They was there before you got there?"

"Yeah."

"You seen 'em when you roll by?"

"Yeah they must have went inside. . . . They must have used your key."

Jenkins and the squad had pulled Stevenson over just before 4 P.M. When they finally got a warrant and returned after midnight, Jenkins showed it to Stevenson's wife. She watched as one of the officers filmed Jenkins putting keys into the front door, as if for the first time, even though the officers had already been inside. He then recorded himself speaking to her in the living room.

"Do you know, in this house, if there's any firearms, narcotics, or money?" Jenkins asked on a video filmed by Taylor.

"No I don't," Holloway said.

"Do you think there's anything in here?" Jenkins asked.

"No I don't. I wouldn't be sitting here if I—"

"You wouldn't know? Okay. And, do you have any large sums of money in the house?"

"No, I don't."

"Anything? Do you believe your baby's father does? Would it be uncommon for him to have money hidden anywhere?"

"No."

"No? What about narcotics hidden in your house? What about firearms? No? Okay, ma'am, we're about to search your residence," Jenkins said.

Holloway was sent away. She stayed in her car outside for hours, waiting for the officers to wrap up, but eventually grew tired and left.

The officers had moved into the basement, where they went to work on a safe in the unfinished basement. Using a ram designed for breaking down doors, they beat the safe until it cracked open. Inside was more than $200,000.

They considered taking it all, but the group decided on what they deemed to be a safer route—it was easier to cover up a robbery by reporting some of what was taken rather than trying to pretend it never happened. If the drug dealer said he had more cash than was seized, the onus would be on him to prove it. That would likely require taking ownership of the drugs—a losing proposition all around.

"How much did he [Stevenson] say would be there? $100k?" Jenkins asked the others.

Jenkins put back what he estimated to be $100,000, took the balance, and closed it back up. He went upstairs, dropped the money into a black plastic bag, and told his officers to open the safe again but this time make a cellphone video recording. With the camera rolling, they pretended to open it up for the first time—except with half the original contents.

"Hey Sarge, come downstairs right quick. They about to get it open!" Taylor said on the cellphone recording.

When the safe opened on the tape, the officers acted impressed. "Whoo!" "Oh shit!"

Then Jenkins stepped in as the concerned supervisor.

"Stop, stop right fucking now," he can be heard saying on the tape. "Take a picture or record it right now. Nobody touches it, you understand me right now?"

"I'm keeping the camera rolling," Taylor assured him.

"How much you think it is? Yeah, keep the camera on. We're calling the feds," Jenkins said.

"I'd say 100," Taylor said.

"Don't touch it. We're not even gonna fucking touch it. Keep recording, no one is touching this money. Keep your fucking camera on that, so we don't get any bullshit," Jenkins said.

Jenkins called a federal drug task force agent he knew to collect the money the officers said they had found. It was a standard procedure when police came into a large amount of money to have the DEA collect it. The task force officer, Ethan Glover, just so happened to be conducting an active wiretap investigation on Stevenson at the time. And he and Jenkins had been in the same training academy class. Glover would later testify that it was a coincidence that Jenkins had come upon and robbed his target and called him to collect the money.

Jenkins told Glover that his squad hadn't touched the money and had taken pictures to prove it was undisturbed. Glover said he looked into the safe and said the earlier pictures looked the same.

After wrapping up at Stevenson's home, the four officers—Jenkins, Ward, Taylor, and Detective Evodio Hendrix—went to Taylor's house in Glen Burnie, south of the city. He didn't have a wife or children who would be disturbed by their late arrival. In Taylor's den, Jenkins dumped the money all over the floor.

Their take was about $20,000 each. Jenkins took about $40,000.

Jenkins was ready with pointers on what to do next: He instructed the officers not to deposit the money into a bank and not to make any big purchases that would attract attention or be traceable. That was easy for Hendrix, a thirty-one-year-old married father of five whose wife was going back to school. He could put the money to use on everyday expenses.

Taylor, meanwhile, wanted to add a deck to his new home, which he had purchased just a few months earlier. Jenkins recommended a contractor who could do the job and fudge the receipts to reflect a different price.

As Ward drove back to his home east of the city, he dwelled on what had just happened. He wondered what to do with the money.

In one sense, it was too late. Ward had taken part in the robbery and the cover-up and had accepted his cut just like the rest. If the officers were to somehow get caught, a guilty conscience wouldn't save him.

"For one, you don't want to be the one in the squad to be like, I'm not with that. Like, you [don't want to] make them feel that you would tell on them. You don't want to get blackballed," Ward said later. "Second, it's like drugs was missing, and it's like 20,000—between me, Hendrix, and Taylor, that's $60,000. That's a lot of money. Who won't make a complaint about that money? I think I was the only one still renting my house. I couldn't take $20,000 and get my whole house redone, countertops and all that stuff, 'cause I'm renting. So I didn't have the means to put the money to anything. I wasn't going to put that money . . . in my house, jeopardize [my family] and get them in trouble. So it's just too much. The bad outweighed the good." Mostly, he told the FBI, he was scared that his fiancée, also a BPD officer, would find out.

When he got home, Ward said he went to a wooded area nearby and ditched the $20,000.

JENKINS WASN'T THROUGH WITH STEVENSON. He listened obsessively to Stevenson's calls from jail, trying to anticipate whether he was going to make waves about what had happened. Stevenson was indeed concerned, asking his wife to check for a bag that contained coats and jackets. "There should be money in there," he said. Nope, she responded. The officers had taken everything, she said, including the drugs and cash from the basement, as well as one of his expensive watches, a Breitling Navitimer worth about $4,000.

Stevenson said he wanted to hire a good lawyer, which made Jenkins worried.

Jenkins came up with a plan: Stevenson's lifeline was his wife, who was taking care of his situation from the outside. If Jenkins could cut Holloway out of the picture, maybe Stevenson would be unable to arrange for a good lawyer. He'd have to go with a public defender, who, overworked and perhaps unmotivated, would likely tell Stevenson he had few options and urge him to take a plea.

Jenkins decided that the officers should write a note purporting to be from another woman, claiming she was pregnant with Stevenson's child, and stick it in the front door of Stevenson's home for his wife to find. But Holloway didn't fall for it, and she was able to connect her husband with prominent defense lawyer Ivan Bates, who had had plenty of previous run-ins with Jenkins and at the time was also representing one of the officers charged with killing Freddie Gray.

If the members of Jenkins's squad were reluctant co-conspirators, the sergeant was about to get reinforcements. He would soon add a new team of officers who had fewer qualms about using their badge to commit crimes.

CHAPTER THIRTEEN
THE WIRE

SERGEANT JOHN SIERACKI WAS in the Woodlawn FBI offices on the last day of March 2016 when an agent came to him with important news. He said he'd been sent a copy of a call from a wiretap the county drug detectives had placed on Shropshire. The agent sat listening over his headphones as Sieracki searched his face for a reaction. The agent unplugged his headphones, allowing everyone within earshot to hear through the speakers. It was the break they had been waiting for.

It had been months since federal investigators found Clewell's GPS device and talked to Guinn about Gondo's ties to Shropshire, but they had not yet gathered enough information to tap Gondo's phone. Wiretaps face a high judicial bar, with investigators having to show that incriminating information was likely being discussed over the phone and that it could not be obtained through other means.

Now the previously authorized wiretap on Shropshire's phone had picked him up calling Gondo to ask about a GPS tracker he'd found under his car. Gondo asked Shropshire to call him on FaceTime so he could see what Shropshire was talking about. On the screen, Shropshire showed him a black tracker, wrapped in aluminum foil. It was definitely the work of law enforcement, Gondo told him.

"Ain't no question," Shropshire said. "I'ma pop it on someone else's car."

Gondo realized he was talking to someone whose phone was possibly being tapped.

"Um, I ain't even know who I'm talking to, so whatever you do, be mindful," Gondo said before signing off.

When Sieracki played the tape for Special Agent Jensen, she was elated. They now had Gondo on the phone helping a drug dealer, and that combined with other contacts from Gondo's phone logs was enough to request a wiretap on Gondo himself.

"This is it," Jensen told other members of the public corruption squad. "We're going to write this wire. We're going to get up on this phone."

Once the wiretap went active on Gondo's phone at the end of April, it quickly paid off. Two days in, Gondo received a call from Glen Wells, an associate of Shropshire. Gondo's girlfriend answered the phone and asked Wells for some painkillers because Gondo had had some teeth pulled. It demonstrated a "longtime, personal relationship," authorities later wrote in court papers.

That same day, the agents were listening when Gondo told someone, "I don't make $1,200 in one day, you feel me, without me doing some other" stuff.

On May 4, another member of the GTTF, Rayam, called Gondo with a cryptic proposal.

"I may got something, um I may got somethin to where it may pan out," Rayam said. "The plan is, if I call you, then it's worth for you to come in."

"Okay," Gondo said.

"I know you got things going on, but feel what I'm saying."

"Right, I got you."

"Yeah, yeah and then I may just have it to where it just me, you, and [Sergeant Allers]. All right?"

"All right, I got you, yo."

"You just, you just, meet me, um, you come meet, and then you leave in 30 minutes. You know what I mean?"

Later, investigators would write, with some understatement, that they were "concerned about the tone and vagueness of the conversation and believe that if it was a legitimate activity, they would speak openly about the details."

Another recorded conversation bolstered the ties between Gondo and the Shropshire crew, with Gondo discussing setting up special access for himself, Wells, and Shropshire at an upscale club. Then, in an early-morning call where he was slurring his words after a night out drinking at a D.C. club, he bluntly told a woman over the phone: "I sell drugs. That's what I did today."

The case took a sharp turn on the afternoon of May 9.

Jensen was in the wire room in the FBI's Woodlawn field office, listening to Gondo's phone calls over headphones. Gondo made calls to an informant about busting a planned drug sale; it was one of Jensen's first chances to hear Gondo at work.

"We gonna be able to do that thing this week, yo? [With the] white boy?" Gondo asked the informant.

"Yeah, but the issue is I gotta get some [Xanax] bars first," the informant said, before correcting herself: "Oh, no I don't."

"Right," Gondo said, "because he ain't gonna make it to you."

They discussed how the informant was to "set up" a twenty-five-year-old Harford County man named Nicholas DeForge. Gondo said he wanted the informant to ensure that DeForge would come to the meeting with a gun so that the officers could arrest him with it. When the informant called back later, she said the plan was in motion.

Sieracki was out on the streets on another investigation around midday when Jensen asked him to make a pass-by and conduct surveillance. It was pouring rain, and Sieracki set up a couple of blocks away to watch. From his perch, the encounter looked like any normal traffic stop. But over the wiretap, Jensen was hearing a different sequence of events play out.

DeForge and his girlfriend drove his gray 2011 Scion through West Baltimore, following Gondo's informant to a meeting location. The informant worried that DeForge knew he was being followed by police. "You need to just get them," the informant told Gondo.

Gondo, along with Rayam, Daniel Hersl, and their sergeant Thomas Allers, finally pulled their car over near Coppin State University.

Gondo called the informant.

"It's a gun in his right pocket, his jacket," the informant said.

"You saw that shit?" Gondo said.

"Yeah, he carry it every time he come because they come with so much money and they be scared. Cause he should have like six or seven hundred dollars on 'em too," she said. "He be thinking he gonna get robbed, so that's why he comes every time with it [a gun]."

But as officers checked, Gondo said, they weren't seeing a gun in a jacket. He didn't even see a jacket; DeForge was wearing a T-shirt.

"It's in there," the informant insisted. "He's not gonna come without it."

"He's shaking his head, saying he ain't got nothing," Gondo said, referring to Hersl searching the car.

"It's in that car, he never comes without it."

"They searched him. It ain't in his pocket."

"Well, search the car, look under the seat."

The gun—a two-shot .22 caliber pistol—was eventually found in a backpack, and DeForge was arrested. The conversation between Gondo and the informant had sounded strange to Jensen, particularly how long they had gone back and forth about officers not being able to find the gun. She later pulled the statement of probable cause that accompanied the arrest. It didn't read anything like the encounter Jensen had listened to.

The officers said that they had conducted a traffic stop on DeForge for following another vehicle at an unsafe distance and that upon approaching DeForge's car Hersl had "observed DeForge reaching from his right pants pocket, placing a small caliber firearm into a camouflage backpack." As the wiretapped call showed, Hersl had made no such observation, as the officers had had great trouble locating the gun at all. What they had described in the statement of probable cause for the arrest on the gun charge was a clean sequence of events that justified the officers' actions.

For federal investigators, the encounter revealed not only that Gondo was working with drug dealers but that he and his squad were lying about their police work. But there was another twist to come.

The federal team next decided to pull phone calls DeForge had made from jail, including one between DeForge and his girlfriend not long after he was booked. They speculated that they had been set up by someone they knew and said the officers had lied about the traffic violation that had led to them being pulled over.

Then DeForge's girlfriend asked, "What happened to your money?"

"The police said they gave it to you," DeForge replied.

"No. That's a downright lie," she said. "They gave me my wallet with the money that was [already] in my wallet. Your wallet was completely ransacked. They never gave me anything."

"I don't keep it in my wallet, it was just in my pocket in a money clip."

"I didn't see any money clip."

DeForge had brought cash for the drug buy, as the informant had told Gondo he would, but it wasn't accounted for in the court paperwork. The informant told Gondo that DeForge would have $700 on him; DeForge's mother later said her son had at least $1,500. The court papers didn't mention any money being seized.

Jensen was in constant contact with Wise, the federal prosecutor who was now overseeing the investigation, and gave him the update. "You're not going to believe what I think is going on here," she told the prosecutor. "We believe money is being taken."

The case had now veered from an investigation into one officer's potential collusion with a drug crew, to potential civil rights violations when they lied on their arrest report about the traffic stop and gun seizure, to what appeared to be officers robbing people.

DeForge's mother, Laura Slater, remembers her son's girlfriend calling from the scene while the officers had them stopped. "I think they're going to arrest Nick," the girlfriend told her. They had a pit bull in the backseat with them, and the girlfriend said the officers were threatening to take the dog to animal control and impound the vehicle if DeForge didn't help the officers set up someone else that they could arrest. DeForge's mother says her son did as he was asked, but his efforts came up short of what the officers had expected, and they charged DeForge for the gun. His booking time for that arrest appears to confirm the account: though DeForge had been stopped at 1:15 P.M., he wasn't booked until 7:43 P.M.

Jensen, nicknamed "Honey Badger" by her FBI colleagues for her persistence in investigations, decided to take another chance. She asked a source within the department to obtain footage of the stop recorded by city surveillance cameras in the area of the arrest and spent the weekend scouring the tapes. The footage confirmed what she had heard: that the officers had spent a great deal of time trying to find DeForge's gun and had not made the quick observation relayed in the sworn court papers. She saw Rayam going through his pockets.

The FBI did not yet want to engage DeForge, since they were wary of their investigation somehow making it back to the officers. They would not get the chance to talk to him: eight months later, DeForge overdosed on fentanyl and cocaine.

Jensen knew they had stumbled onto a potentially deep pocket of corruption inside the GTTF. But she needed more—an isolated case of wrongdoing was never as powerful as demonstrating a pattern, and continued investigation could lead to more serious crimes and additional participants. She and her team weighed their options for moving the case forward. They could introduce a confidential informant of their own to the officers, but they decided Gondo and Rayam would be too guarded. "Even if a confidential informant was successfully introduced, it would be highly unlikely that Gondo or Rayam would trust them and they would have only a small window into Gondo and Rayam's activities," Jensen wrote at the time. The same problem would hold for an undercover agent: "In order to introduce an undercover employee into this investigation, a relationship would have to be established with Gondo and Rayam. There also exists a high probability that Gondo and Rayam are familiar with this technique, thereby jeopardizing the investigation and placing the employee in danger," she wrote.

Then they moved to another option: a sting operation.

The FBI rented a ten-year old, twenty-eight-foot Ford Yellowstone motor home and installed video and audio recording devices inside. They planted $4,500 in "bait money," along with some personal items that would make it appear someone had been traveling using the vehicle. The trailer was parked at a rest stop off of Interstate 95 in Southeast Baltimore.

A supervisor from McDougall's Harford County team would place a call to the GTTF requesting assistance securing and searching the trailer. The city officers were to be told that the county officers had taken someone into custody who was cooperating and had told them about the trailer and had said the vehicle's key was hidden under the bumper. The county officers would say they were busy with the debriefing and would remain offsite.

It would just be the GTTF and a motor home full of money. And the cameras would be rolling.

The obvious upside was catching the officers in the act, in an irrefutable way. There was a downside to consider too. For one, if the officers happened to play the case by the book, their defense attorneys could play the tape on a loop at an eventual trial as proof that the officers hadn't taken the bait after being set up by an overzealous government.

The investigators put the plan into motion around midday in early June. Jensen was listening to the reaction of the GTTF officers over the wire as they checked surveillance cameras and cased the area. These were not things that officers who had been asked to help out other law enforcement officers would do.

"They, particularly Rayam, were very leery and concerned about what they were walking into. Rayam even questioned on the phone if this was an Internal Affairs setup," Jensen recalled later.

Jensen worried that the officers might uncover the sting operation. The officers' arrival was now imminent, and she had to make a choice. If it worked, the sting would provide incontrovertible evidence that the officers were stealing. But it could also backfire and expose their whole investigation.

"We had everything to lose," she said later.

She pulled the plug.

The Harford investigators waved off the city cops, and the FBI was able to remove the motor home from the travel plaza without the officers seeing.

Jensen resolved to continue to listen to the wires, but the officers' paranoia that day served as a warning. A planned attempt to have two undercover agents engage Gondo at a D.C. nightclub was scrapped.

There was also another development that caught the investigators' notice. The day of the sting, Rayam had been the acting supervisor, a title bestowed on an officer when the permanent supervisor isn't available. It was the first hint that changes were coming to the GTTF—changes that would threaten to upend Jensen's entire case.

AS THE GTTF INVESTIGATION proceeded in the shadows, all eyes were on the trials of the officers charged in the death of Freddie Gray—the "Baltimore 6," as some were calling them. Since officers so rarely faced criminal charges, it was viewed across the country as a test case: Could Mosby's office get convictions? But it was also unlike many of the other high-profile cases that had sparked the Black Lives Matter movement: Gray hadn't been shot, and prosecutors weren't alleging that he was beaten. The case was more complicated: The officers were accused of committing an illegal stop and of being so grossly negligent that they caused him to die while he was being taken to jail.

Once Mosby announced the charges against the officers, the next several months consisted mostly of legal posturing by the defense team, a collection of top attorneys from the area. A shadow defense team of lawyers not officially on the case helped draft motions behind the scenes. The attorneys unsuccessfully sought to have the trial moved out of Baltimore and to have the charges dismissed. But they scored a major victory when Judge Barry Williams ruled that the officers would be tried separately. If they were brought to court as a group, the collective weight of the accusations against each officer could be thrown at all six. Tried one by one, however, the officers could shift blame to those not on trial.

Prosecutors continued studying case law and reexamining the evidence, causing a shift in their theory of the case. They still were confident that the knife Gray was carrying was perfectly legal, meaning his arrest was unjustified and thus an assault, but they worried the argument would be too esoteric for a jury. Instead, they would argue that the officers didn't have any reason to stop Gray in the first place. They also had been combing through training documents, seeking to prove that the officers had behaved contrary to official department policies.

The first trial took place in front of a jury and drew national media and small, peaceful protests. Officer William Porter had been charged with involuntary manslaughter and assault, among other things, for failing to secure Gray with a seatbelt or calling for a medic when Gray asked for one. A mistrial was declared after the jury deadlocked—they were one vote away from acquitting Porter on the manslaughter charge, but they tipped in favor of convicting on lesser charges of reckless endangerment and misconduct in office.

In May, the second officer to go to trial, arresting officer Edward Nero, opted for a bench trial—that is, to have the judge determine his fate. Prosecutors argued that Gray had been pursued without justification and that detaining him under such circumstances was tantamount to an assault. Typically, the remedy for a bad arrest was to have charges thrown out or to pursue a civil lawsuit—not to criminally charge the officer. During this same time period, a judge ruled that Jenkins's Special Enforcement Section did not have a valid reason to stop a man they had arrested for allegedly tossing a gun in a housing project. Instead of facing the officers with criminal charges, the judge dismissed the case and praised their work: "They are in a high-crime area, they're checking things out and they're doing what they're supposed to be doing.... Convey my appreciation to the officers for doing their job, notwithstanding my decision." Such outcomes hadn't served as a deterrent, supporters of the charges in the Gray case argued, and it was necessary to take a harder line.

"Police are allowed to make judgment calls. They're allowed to make mistakes," Nero's attorney told Williams, the presiding judge. "And most of the time, the State is arguing that well, yeah, that's a mistake, but it was in good faith, and we still want to have it admissible, and it shouldn't be suppressed—except for Officer Nero. For whatever reason, in this case with Officer Nero, their position is there were mistakes that were made and they're a crime, and he should be prosecuted. And that's just not the law."

Williams acquitted Nero of all counts, saying that his individual culpability was limited by the involvement of other officers and that his own actions were not unreasonable given his training. There were five trials left, but it was clear prosecutors faced an uphill climb.

CHAPTER FOURTEEN

HORNET'S NEST

IN THE MONTHS THAT he'd been leading the Special Enforcement Section, Wayne Jenkins had made sure that top command knew of their good work, regularly emailing summaries of their handgun arrests.

"Not too bad for the first two months," Jenkins wrote to his supervisor on March 1, 2016. "I would like to pick up the pace and break 200 [handgun violations] in 2016."

"Wayne, what you are bringing to the table can not be measured," Captain Kevin Jones, commander of the Operations Intelligence Section overseeing all the plainclothes units, wrote in response to one of the emails. "Each gun, each person extracted reduces violence on a larger scale than we could imagine. Keep up the good work and be safe out there."

In May, a couple of weeks after Jenkins shook the commissioner's hand and received a Bronze Star for his actions during the riot, he argued that his squad could do even more with additional resources. He was emphatic that he must be able to select his new officers.

Tonight, May 4, 2016 my guys made our 50th handgun violation.
I would like you to know that we have won our last 9 jury trials.

Together we haven't lost a GUN case yet in our city. Additionally, this type of pro-active enforcement at this pace usually has complaints from arrestees or civilians. We have one complaint year to date which is in the process of being closed out. Most people think these guns are recovered by me, I want to make it clear that these guns and case are made by my guys. I couldn't do it without them.

I'm asking for three officers of my choosing to train my way, respectful but aggressive in apprehending gun offenders in our city. Based upon what we've accomplished together in over the last year, I believe with two more Impala's and three more officers (of my choice) will lead to the arrest and prosecution of more gun offenders and save more lives.

Three more officers trained by me NOW before summer WILL without a doubt save lives and lead to gun offender arrests. If I have these tools (manpower and vehicles) we will save more lives and lower crime.

After sending it, Jenkins forwarded a copy of the email to Donald Stepp.

A MONTH LATER, LIEUTENANT Colonel Sean Miller sent an email to another commander notifying him of coming personnel changes.

"Monday," he wrote. "Allers to [DEA] Group 52 and Jenkins to GTTF. Three from Jenkins' squad will be absorbed into GTTF. GTTF will have additional responsibilities very shortly."

Wayne Jenkins had been named the new supervisor of the GTTF.

And he was bringing Ward, Hendrix, and Taylor, whom he had been stealing with, to join Gondo, Rayam, and Hersl, who had already been committing their own crimes. It was a monumentally bad decision made by BPD commanders who believed that they were giving one of their hardest workers the resources he needed to clean up the city. Instead they created new opportunities for Jenkins and these officers to turbo-charge their bad behavior.

This was a gift for the federal investigators already looking at

Gondo's squad—if they had wanted to create a supergroup of corrupt officers so they could round them up all at once, they couldn't have done much better than this.

But the feds had no idea what had just happened. Jenkins wasn't yet on the radar. In fact, the federal team now worried that their investigation of the GTTF might have been thwarted—the switch had seemed unusually abrupt, perhaps prompted by leaks. Why in the midst of the wiretap case had the GTTF's supervisor, Thomas Allers, suddenly been shipped to a long-vacant spot on a DEA task force? Just four days before Miller's email announcing the changes, Dean Palmere, the deputy commissioner of the police department, sent a four-word email, inquiring about his former driver: "Has Allers been moved?"

The officers themselves were suspicious that something could be amiss. Gondo called Rayam to say he had been tipped off by another officer that Allers had been moved to the DEA because of an investigation into their unit.

"Listen to what I'm saying," Gondo said. "He just like, 'Yo, I heard y'all getting looked at.' I'm like, 'Who?' He said the gun unit, and the reason why Tommy Boy left was because he was getting looked at. . . . And I said well, anything regarding us . . . I can't foresee that. Ain't nobody doin' nothing. I don't even see that. You know what I mean, anything like that can be happening. I say it could be because of, you know, them [new members assigned to GTTF] coming over."

Gondo seemed worried that the officers joining the squad could be part of a setup.

"He said it's a rumor," Gondo continued. "But I'm just passin' the word."

Perhaps putting on a show for anyone who might be listening, Gondo protested their innocence.

"Ain't doin nothing. You know what I'm saying? We workin'! . . . I don't know. I mean, but I don't know, Rayam."

"So he sayin' that, that that's why [Allers] left?" Rayam replied.

"That's, I had a notion of, I mean I can understand that, and then I can't understand that, because they [DEA] been trying to get him [Allers] for a long time, you feel me?" Gondo said.

"And on top of that, he still a part of it."

"Exactly, I said that as well. You get what I'm saying?"

"Ain't nothing going on anyway," Rayam said.

"All I'm telling you is be mindful. You get what I'm saying. With them," Gondo said, apparently referring to the new members of the squad. "They coming with a lot of heat."

Special Agent Jensen had crossed paths with Jenkins in the fall of 2013 when she worked on the FBI Safe Streets team, a violent crimes task force. Her squad had been running a long-term wiretap investigation when Jenkins and his then-crew crashed in, arresting one of the people they had been tracking. She knew that he was challenging to work with, but she did not know him to be corrupt.

In fact, according to both McDougall and Kilpatrick, Jenkins thought enough of Jenkins at the time to suggest bringing him into the fold and seeing if he could help bring down Gondo and the others. "We've got to tell him—he's walking into a hornet's nest," Kilpatrick recalled Jensen saying.

Kilpatrick and McDougall were wary of pushing their suspicions about Jenkins more explicitly, but they warned Jensen against including Jenkins in anything. Let's give it two weeks and watch what happens, they suggested.

Jenkins, of course, had already been tipped off to the possibility of such an investigation of the GTTF by Guinn six months earlier, after the FBI had reached out to Guinn in December 2015.

"When we first came to GTTF, Wayne said Gondo and Rayam are on federal investigation for selling drugs—this was the second time he told us this," Ward recalled later.

In a wiretapped call shortly after Jenkins took over the unit, Ward told Gondo what to expect from the new boss—namely, that they could come to work late and collect ample overtime.

"This is how this boy be, yo," Ward said. "He don't like to come in on time, yo. He'll come in late every day, yo. So we usually don't come into work until like 10, 11 o'clock, yo. And depend on how he feel, we roll out on regular time, or but he'll try to make you, see if you want to make overtime every day, yo. That's how he is, yo. And then, we just got the green light, we see [another supervisor] last night—said the overtime budget just opened back up, work as much as you want."

Gondo laughed.

"He told us to put slips in for six hours last night," Ward marveled. "Bangin' our overtime shit, yo."

Gondo called Rayam with the good news.

"Just passing the word, brother: Get that check."

"Hell yeah," Rayam said.

The new squad got right to work, and Jenkins continued blasting out email summaries of their arrests. Commanders and other supervisors were enamored with the results.

"Wayne's back!!!!! GTTF tripled their production in one day. LOL," Sergeant John Burns emailed Jenkins.

"I just told your guys I haven't seen a email in a little. They said because u guys were moving. Knew u would be back in the swing. Excellent as usual Wayne," said another.

"Teamwork makes the DREAM work," Jenkins replied.

With the federal investigators unsure of what would happen under Jenkins's guidance, they continued to watch Gondo and Rayam closely.

GONDO AND RAYAM HAD a potentially big score in the works. Officers from the Southwestern District had been looking into a suspected drug dealer named Ronald Hamilton who they believed was moving a large amount of drugs in the area, and they decided to contact the GTTF for help.

"As much as I hate doing this . . . [the] investigation has grown a lot bigger than just our district," a Southwestern District sergeant wrote to a supervisor in an email. "I believe your average patrol officer does not have the necessary resources to complete this investigation."

Hamilton already had multiple federal drug convictions. In 1998, when he was twenty-seven, he had been identified by the Maryland State Police as the person "who controlled most of the drug trafficking in west and southwest Baltimore City and County." Police had intercepted a four-pound package of cocaine sent from Los Angeles to Hamilton's suburban townhome and in a raid had found another 1.5 pounds of cocaine, a loaded .22 caliber handgun, and $496,000 in cash. Hamilton had served nine years in prison after that and had been out only a short time before he was in trouble again. In May 2009, employees at a California shipping company identified a package being sent to West Baltimore that contained a small refrigerator packed with sixteen kilograms of cocaine—about $250,000 worth—and notified Baltimore DEA officials. The cocaine was removed and replaced with sham material; agents flew the drugs cross-country, and an undercover agent posed as a shipping employee at the Baltimore pickup site. Two men picked up the package, then were stopped by federal agents. Hamilton and three others were arrested nearby, and his cellphones would help tie him to the scheme.

Because of Hamilton's prior convictions, the U.S. Attorney's Office filed a notice that the government would ask that he be sentenced to a mandatory minimum of life without parole and slapped with an $8 million fine. Documents show Hamilton helped the government identify the leader and organizer of that shipment, as well as two related shipments of $380,000 cash. Instead of life without parole, Hamilton got six years in prison.

In 2016, two years after his release, Hamilton purchased a 4,100-square-foot home with a pool and two acres of property for $535,000 in the rural exurb of Carroll County. Was it an ex-offender success story, or was Hamilton back to his old ways? An informant—one of Hamilton's own relatives, it would later emerge—told police that Hamilton was dealing drugs again. Gondo and Rayam devised a plan to stick an unauthorized GPS tracker under one of Hamilton's vehicles so they could monitor him remotely.

"The best scenario is that you see a car in the driveway and put that shit on," Gondo had told Rayam in a wiretapped call on June 8.

The operation was successful. The following morning, Rayam excitedly told Gondo what his tracker had revealed.

"You know I save the best for last. That n——out Westminster, yo. He at this big ass mansion with a pool in the back," Rayam said.

"N—— be trippin," Gondo said.

By early afternoon, they were thinking of the possibilities. Gondo urged patience.

"You might wanna wait though, J. I wouldn't get him right just now," he said. "I'm gonna tell you why. . . . You wanna gain a, gain a pattern for him, you feel me. So I would, I would wait. I'm down for it but I would wait especially to see where he takes his profit at. Feel me?"

"Yeah, yeah, yeah," Rayam said.

"You wanna know where the money house is, and where the drug house is before you grab him."

But a few days later, on the night after they had discussed the possibility that they were under investigation, Gondo and Rayam were recorded talking about removing the GPS tracker from Hamilton's car.

They seemed spooked.

The feds worried that the officers' suspicions would cause them to pull back. Maybe the wiretap investigation would be thwarted.

Yet at some point that month and unbeknownst to the federal investigators, the GTTF's new boss and his officers came to an understanding. It would later emerge that Jenkins wasted little time asking Rayam if he'd be willing to sell drugs they confiscated. Shortly afterward—also unknown to the feds—Jenkins, Gondo, and Rayam pulled someone over, then went to his home without a warrant and found a gun and a pound of marijuana, which Jenkins instructed Rayam to sell. Gondo arranged for Glen Wells, his childhood friend and one of Shropshire's associates, to buy the pot from Rayam.

Gondo and Rayam next briefed the new members of the GTTF about Hamilton, and the tracking resumed. This time Jenkins went along, and the three followed Hamilton as he drove around one night. Jenkins relayed to the officers that he had seen Hamilton pull up next to a car with New York license plates and exchange a large bag. "Man, I know there was money or something big in there," Jenkins told Rayam. "I felt like just hitting him and taking the bag."

All the officers of the unit had been put on notice that members of the group could be under federal investigation. Yet the crimes continued.

"We figured Jenkins lied about the federal investigation. I mean how dumb can you be to do illegal shit with someone and you know they are being investigated?" Ward said later. "We kinda thought that Jenkins was trying to keep us separated so while Rayam, Gondo and

Hersl did dirt, he would benefit. He would get a call from, say, Gondo or Rayam, he would tell us we could go home for the day, he was tired. But he wouldn't go home—we would later find out he met up with the other half of the squad."

AT THE JUNE 2016 trial of the third defendant in the Freddie Gray case, Officer Caesar Goodson, who had driven the van in which Gray suffered his fatal injuries, tensions between prosecutors and police became public. Goodson was facing the most serious charges— second-degree "depraved heart" murder—with prosecutors saying he had driven erratically and had failed to secure Gray in the van. City surveillance video showed Goodson rolling through a stop sign and making a wide right turn, crossing the center line in doing so. Less than a block away, Goodson stopped and went to the back of the van to check on Gray without announcing the stop as required over the radio. Prosecutor Michael Schatzow accused Goodson of giving Gray a deliberate "rough ride." Goodson was the only one of the officers who refused to give a statement about what happened that day. His defense team argued that Gray's injury had to have occurred toward the end of the van ride, minimizing the opportunities Goodson had to intervene.

Like the officer before him, Goodson opted for a bench trial instead of a jury trial.

Prosecutors believed the police investigators had soft-pedaled certain aspects of Goodson's case or flat-out refused to examine others. Subsequent leaks to the defense team, and efforts in the police department to compile what prosecutors saw as a "counter investigation," compounded those concerns.

In the leadup to the trial, police files had been turned over to the defense that seemed manufactured to sow doubts or distract from the core issues of the case. One was a document, created the day State's Attorney Marilyn Mosby announced the charges, in which a sergeant claimed Gray had once complained that he "had a bad back." The medical examiner who performed Gray's autopsy said she found no evidence of an underlying condition that would have any bearing on his traumatic injuries—as if a bad back was relevant to a snapped spine, anyway. Another leak seemed aimed to diminish support for Gray, claiming that he had been a police informant.

When the lead detective on the case, Dawnyell Taylor, was called as a defense witness, the prosecutors, Schatzow, went straight at her, telling the judge she had been actively working to undermine the case.

"Detective Taylor, you're aware that you were removed from being the lead detective on this investigation at my request when I accused you of sabotaging the prosecution?" he asked.

To Schatzow's surprise, Taylor said no one had removed her from the case. "I'm aware that you made a request, but you don't have the authority to remove me from the case," she said.

Judge Williams acquitted Goodson of all charges on June 23. He said he felt prosecutors had pushed a case based on inferences about what Officer Goodson must have done to cause Gray's injury but had failed to prove that Goodson had knowingly done so. Moreover, Williams said he believed there were five plausible scenarios that could explain Gray's injury. Pointing to conflicting expert medical testimony, Williams said, "If the doctors are not clear as to what would be happening at this point in time, how would the average person or officer without medical training know?"

The city police union called on Mosby to "reconsider her malicious prosecution" of the officers and said she was wasting taxpayer money. Supporters of the prosecution lamented that it was going down a predictable path. "We have to go back to the drawing board here in Baltimore and Maryland with rules and regulations and laws that affect the police behavior," said the president of the local NAACP, "because it's clear that they can do action that we feel is not correct, but in the courtroom . . . is not a criminal act."

AFTER A FEW DAYS of working with Jenkins, Gondo warned his childhood friend Glen "Kyle" Wells to stay away from where the aggressive sergeant would be patrolling.

"I know they had a pattern of going in the Northeast, and Kyle was my friend," Gondo recalled later. Jenkins "normally targeted people for money in like robberies. So I didn't want him to target my childhood friend and rob him or, you know, I'll be stuck in between 'cause I was working for him. . . . So I just tried to alleviate that by letting Kyle know what was going on."

Though Gondo had worked—and stolen money—with Jenkins before, he was now seeing for himself what Jenkins was like when unleashed on the streets.

Jenkins "was very reckless, you know. I mean, he was just out of control, putting citizens at risk, you know, driving on the side of the street, going in people bumpers. I just never saw anything like this. . . . This dude is out of control. You know, I couldn't believe it," Gondo said later.

"I ain't know it's like that, yo," Gondo told Wells in a recorded phone call.

"That shit real," Wells said.

"That is like some straight, like, off-the-wall-type shit," Gondo said.

"I already know," Wells said. "It's code red."

"Yeah, he code red," Gondo said.

"Like a Rottweiler with the pink thing hanging out," Wells said.

When Wells got a suspicious series of text messages on his phone on July 5, he shared a screenshot with Gondo asking if it could be Jenkins posing as a drug buyer to try to trick Wells into implicating himself. "That sound like [Jenkins], yo?" Wells asked. The message had come to Wells from a number that could receive only texts, not calls, and it made use of Black emojis and slang that seemed forced. To Gondo, it seemed like classic Jenkins trying to pretend to be someone else. He reached out to Rayam, who agreed.

"I'll pull him up, yo," Gondo told Wells, promising to talk to Jenkins.

Meanwhile their daily routine was continuing just as Ward had promised Gondo it would under Jenkins: He was encouraging the officers to "take it easy until around 5 or 6 o'clock, and we'll roll together and get into some street ripping, try to get one."

By early July, the officers were giddy about the amount of overtime money they were making under Jenkins. Rayam said his two-week paycheck was almost $5,000.

"When I looked at it I said, oh my god, who did this? This is a lie," he said, laughing as investigators listened in.

"Damn. Just imagine these n——s been doing this shit yo," Gondo said. "Just imagine yo."

They had been told that one time Jenkins's biweekly paycheck was more than $8,000.

"He got method to his madness," Gondo said. "He, he, he, he off the chain."

"He off the chain," Rayam said.

"Them n——s stay because of that money yo," Gondo said.

"But G like I said, but hey, you know, let's enjoy it now and get it hard now, because all good things come to an end. That ni——s off the chain."

"He's off the fuckin' chain, B."

"He's off the chain, B."

"He is off the chain, yo."

"Yes sir. Yes sir."

"He is off the fucking chain, yo, that n—— yo, he's off the chain, yo."

"Fuck yeah."

CHAPTER FIFTEEN
BUILDING GREATNESS

ON JULY 8, TWO days after city prosecutors began another trial in the Freddie Gray case, Gondo and Rayam followed Ronald Hamilton out of the city and decided to move in.

Hamilton was at a Home Depot with his wife, shopping for blinds, when he noticed a man who seemed to be following them from aisle to aisle. It was Rayam. They left and were headed toward the cleaners when Jenkins, away from the scene, gave the order to move in for arrest.

"Can we pull them over in the county?" Gondo asked, with federal agents listening on the wiretap.

"We can pull them over in the county, and bring them to the academy," Rayam replied. "That's per Sgt. Jenko."

Gondo and Rayam, along with Hersl and Clewell, who were in another car, suddenly boxed in Hamilton's vehicle. Drawing his gun, Rayam dragged Hamilton from the driver's seat and pressed him up against the vehicle.

"Where's your money at," Rayam said. Hamilton was carrying $3,400 in cash, which Rayam tucked inside his bulletproof vest.

The Hamiltons were handcuffed and put into separate vehicles. Gondo got on the phone to update Jenkins.

"We, um, got the package," Gondo said.

"He's in the car with you?" Jenkins said. "Did you tell them anything at all?"

"No," Gondo replied.

"Okay. When I get there, treat me like I'm the fucking U.S. Attorney," the sergeant said. "Introduce me as the U.S. Attorney."

"I got you," Gondo said.

"All right, dawg," Jenkins replied.

The Hamiltons were taken to the Barn, a trailer in the parking lot of a former city public school in Northwest Baltimore, now being used as the police department's training academy. Such satellite offices were designed as discreet places for specialized units to bring informants; they were also isolated from the rest of the agency and command staff. Gondo, Rayam, and Hersl brought Ronald Hamilton inside for nearly an hour, while Clewell stayed outside with Nancy Hamilton. The officers told Hamilton they had been watching him. They had papers in folders that they tossed in front of him. The officers said they knew his history and asked if he had drugs or cash at his home.

"We got you on three controlled buys," Jenkins told him.

"Man, get the fuck out of here," Hamilton later said he told them. "I don't sell no fucking drugs."

The officers didn't believe him. Rayam had already obtained search warrants from a judge for the Carroll County home and also a home in West Baltimore—falsely claiming the GPS tracking as his own observations.

"It was a dud house," Gondo explained later of the West Baltimore place. "It wasn't going to have anything in it. If we believed there was going to be drugs or guns or anything in it, one of us would have split off and went to that house."

Instead, Clewell was sent there, alone.

Gondo said that Clewell was an "analytical guy" who "wasn't going to get his hands dirty."

"To me, he wasn't a street cop," Gondo said. "He never was involved with any money being taken when we were doing search warrants or anything. He was just kept out of that loop in the squad."

"You could basically say he wasn't part of the team," Rayam said later.

The rest of the crew headed to Westminster. Hersl drove Hamilton's truck, while Gondo and Rayam followed in an unmarked car with the couple handcuffed in the back seat.

Hamilton had called the officers' bluff and told them to go ahead and arrest him for the purported drug buys, but instead of heading downtown they were driving north on Interstate 83. Hamilton sensed something bad was about to happen. He leaned over to his wife and said, "Just be quiet. They about to rob me."

The Hamiltons' children were at the home, and the officers had their mother send them away. The cops did a "sneak and peek" inside the house, wanting to get a look at the inside of the house before "officially" serving the warrant. The law allowed officers to enter and "secure" a residence, meaning a cursory look to make sure no one was inside destroying evidence, but a full-blown search was not supposed to happen. Maryland State Police had been notified that a warrant was being served, but it hadn't arrived yet.

Gondo went into the couple's bedroom and in a closet found a block of $50,000 in a heat-sealed bag, plus another $20,000. He counted it out and put it back. Rayam went downstairs and informed Jenkins of the money.

"Hey, what do you want to do?" Rayam asked.

"Go ahead and take it," Jenkins said.

But as the officers continued searching, they found nothing illegal. Hamilton insisted that he made money selling cars at auctions and gambling.

When the state police arrived, troopers collected the $50,000 in the heat-sealed bag in the closet—under asset forfeiture laws, even though no drugs had been found on him or in any of his properties, the officers could take Hamilton's cash and make him account for it later because they said they suspected him of being a drug dealer. The troopers had Hamilton sign a property receipt, and he noticed the $20,000 was not listed. What about the rest? Hamilton asked a trooper, who said he didn't know what Hamilton was talking about.

Gondo would later say he was outside waiting to leave when Rayam emerged with a bag full of the money.

"Go, yo, G, I'm taking it," Rayam told him.

Gondo preferred to skim off the top after arresting someone with drugs or guns. Just taking the money seemed riskier. Too late, Rayam told him.

After the troopers left, Jenkins asked Hamilton again if he would be willing to help set up a bigger target, framing it as he often did by asking Hamilton who he would rob.

"You take care of us, we'll take care of you," Jenkins said, according to Hamilton. "You could wake up one day with ten kilos in your back-yard."

Hamilton said he brushed off the question. Rayam handed him a business card.

"If you change your mind," Rayam told him.

The officers left Hamilton's home and went to a local restaurant, paying for the tab with some of the stolen money. "We can do this three times a year, get three big ones," Jenkins told them. "But don't be greedy."

The officers went back to the city to get their personal cars and then headed to another bar in Southeast Baltimore's Canton neigh-borhood. By now it was 10:30 at night.

On the way, Rayam called Gondo on his wiretapped phone to say he believed the money he had was short.

"I'm counting and counting and counting," Rayam said.

"I would never—come on man," Gondo said. "I would never lie to you."

"Hey all right," Rayam said. "I'ma count it again."

"Come on man, it's me," Gondo said.

"Hey bro, well I'm just letting you know, if it's a mistake . . ."

"I don't make mistakes counting money," Gondo said.

Before Rayam took it, Gondo had counted out $20,000 in the closet—he was sure of it. Rayam had briefly left the money upstairs before consulting with Jenkins about whether to take it. They recalled that Hersl had been upstairs alone at one point. Did he swipe $3,000 without telling anyone? He must have, they thought. They informed Jenkins of their suspicions, but he told them to let it slide.

Special Agent Jensen's head was spinning as she listened to the calls. She didn't expect the officers to talk openly about robbing peo-ple, but this conversation was as close to confirmation as the feds could hope for.

The officers had a few drinks and then split up, with Gondo and Rayam heading to Maryland Live! Casino in Anne Arundel County, and Jenkins and Hersl going to the Horseshoe Casino in downtown Baltimore. Surveillance video showed Rayam clutching $400 cash.

Gondo had used the opportunity at the bar to talk to Jenkins about Glen Wells. There's plenty of other people to target, Gondo said he told Jenkins, who agreed to back off. When Gondo called Wells the next day to tell him—"I got up [Jenkins's] butt for you tonight"—Wells thanked Gondo and invited him on a trip to Miami.

"I appreciate it, sir," Wells told Gondo.

"You ain't have to appreciate shit, yo," Gondo told him. "You my brother."

While the officers partied with Hamilton's money, Hamilton would struggle to get back the portion that had been seized. He petitioned the court in Carroll County, trying to demonstrate his cash business, but had to settle for getting less than half back. After the hearing concluded, Hamilton said, Rayam threatened him. He had earlier texted Rayam, who left his business card, after discovering the missing money. "You robbed me," he wrote. Rayam didn't respond.

"They had more than power. More than power," Hamilton said later in a *New York Times* interview. "They had kryptonite. Them cops did everything they could possibly do to everybody in this city. And everybody that went to jail—there's people that went to jail for something that never ever, ever, ever took place, and all because a guy in a badge got up there and said it."

LATER THAT MONTH, JENKINS sent another mass email touting the unit's work.

"I want to thank the members of the Gun Trace Task Force personally," Jenkins wrote on July 22, 2016. "I push and ask a lot of them on a daily basis and they continue to come to work every day and arrest individuals for firearms. I truly believe without a doubt that the following members have saved lives and prevented violent crime from occurring through their dedication and work ethic."

"Your leadership is what builds greatness. Keep pushing and stay safe," Deputy Commissioner Dean Palmere wrote back. "Wayne, you are truly the engine that drives the train. Thank you for your leadership," said Lieutenant Colonel Sean Miller. "Jesus Christ! You need to be called 'future Commissioner Jenkins,'" said another officer. "Great work, Lt. Wayne!" wrote a supervisor overseeing promotions in the administrative deputy commissioner's office.

Jenkins, of course, was still a sergeant. The sender was alluding to Jenkins's recent efforts to be promoted. He had taken the lieutenants' exam and was number 18 on the list. "You think it's possible?" Jenkins wrote back. "Absolutely. I think the list dies after you!" the supervisor responded.

The commander of the Northeastern District, Richard Worley, asked Jenkins if he could teach his tactics to other officers: "If we could get the rest of the ops teams even close to your production [it] would be a win for the city. Is there something you can teach or train the other units? Can we have other units or officers tag along with your team? Any suggestions would be appreciated."

"Thank you sir, it's all work ethic," Jenkins replied. "One out of ten give their all because it's the right thing to do. People need us and luckily I'm able to hand pick detectives. I want the ones that still work on fixed positions, run without back up, chase the guy in the dark alley. Those few police is what I have and what we need more of."

THE TRIAL OF LIEUTENANT Brian Rice, who oversaw and participated in the arrest of Freddie Gray, also ended in acquittal, on July 18. City prosecutors had no convictions in four tries against the officers charged in Gray's death, including the mistrial. There were three more trials left to go. With each ruling, the judge had made clear that he was rejecting their cases, but the state's attorney's office wanted to press on. The next trial, of arresting officer Garrett Miller, was going to bring a host of additional challenges—the state's attorney's office had to bring on a new team of prosecutors for Miller's case, and the new attorneys objected to going forward with it.

On the first day of Miller's trial—July 27, 2016—the prosecutors who had tried the previous cases walked into court and ended the prosecutions. That included dropping the charges against Officer

William Porter, whom they believed to have lied to investigators and facilitated a cover-up, even if they lacked evidence to prove it.

Reporters rushed to a news conference Mosby held at Gilmor Homes, where Gray had been arrested. Standing behind a lectern, flanked by her prosecution team and Gray's stepfather, Mosby lamented the outcome while blasting the role of forces inside and out of the police department that she said had thwarted their efforts.

"As the world has witnessed over the past 14 months, the prosecution of on-duty police officers in this country is unsurprisingly rare and blatantly fraught with systemic and inherent complications," Mosby said, her frustrations evident. "What we realized very early on in this case was that police investigating police, whether they're friends or merely their colleagues, was problematic. There was a reluctance and an obvious bias that was consistently exemplified, not by the entire Baltimore Police Department but by individuals within the police department at every stage of the investigation, which became blatantly apparent at the subsequent trials."

Mosby said her team remained sure that Gray's death warranted criminal convictions.

"We do not believe Freddie Gray killed himself," she said.

"That's right! That's right!" onlookers shouted. "We know they forced your hand, and the judge was paid off!"

"It has become clear to me," Mosby continued, "that without being able to work with an independent investigatory agency from the very start, without having a say in the election of whether our cases proceed in front of a judge or a jury, without communal oversight of policing in this community, without real substantive reforms to the current criminal justice system, we can try this case 100 times, and cases just like it, and we would still end up with the same result."

Seeking to save face, Mosby claimed the act of charging alone had brought about reform by exposing flaws in the system. When the defense team of more than a dozen attorneys held their own press conference, they elected to have attorney Ivan Bates speak on their collective behalf. The key reason: Bates had already decided to run against Mosby in the 2018 election. Bates, who happened to represent Oreese Stevenson and some others who alleged mistreatment by Jenkins, had taken up the case of Sergeant Alicia White and had come to believe she had been wrongly charged in connection with Gray's death. Bates told the assembled media that the case had been a "nightmare" for the officers charged, brought on by a crusading prosecutor and rebuffed by a fair judge who in a previous life had prosecuted police misconduct. "It is the Baltimore City State's Attorney's Office that has denied justice to the Gray family," Bates said. There were still internal disciplinary cases pending against the officers. Instead of crimes, their conduct would be examined for violations of department rules. Commissioner Kevin Davis asked the suburban departments in Howard and Montgomery counties to take over the investigations and to staff the internal panels that would rule on the cases. Maybe the officers didn't belong in a prison cell for their negligence, but surely someone would lose their job over a man's unnecessary death in their custody. By law, Davis couldn't take any action without guilty findings by the panel.

The two bike cops who had arrested Gray accepted minor punishment. Van driver Caesar Goodson was facing twenty-one administrative counts, and his attorney knew that even if he prevailed his client would be assigned a desk job and not allowed to return to the streets. He sought to work out a deal in which Goodson would get a thirty-day suspension and retire through a clause in the pension rules. City lawyers laughed him off.

Goodson and the other three were cleared of all wrongdoing. All the officers received back pay and returned to work. They remain with the department.

IT WAS ALMOST MIDNIGHT on August 3, 2016, when Baltimore County police officers raided a home in the Rosedale area looking for drugs. The case had originated with Jenkins, who brought it to the county cops and gave a curious version of events. Jenkins said he had been at home when one of his informants called and said a big heroin deal was about to go down. Jenkins said he went to the location—alone— and waited in some bushes, then followed the suspected dealer. When he saw a handoff outside a high-rise apartment building, he said, he moved in and found one hundred grams of heroin and other materials inside a bag. There was surely more at the target's home, Jenkins said.

Baltimore County police sergeant Bruce Vaughn, whose squad was assigned to follow up, questioned Jenkins, saying he needed to know who the informant was. Jenkins demurred, saying the person was not actually a registered informant anymore. Vaughn sent an officer to verify Jenkins's account by watching surveillance footage from where Jenkins said he intercepted the drug deal; it appeared to match. Jenkins was asked to go into the Essex police station and type up information for a search warrant. When they were finished, Jenkins said he was returning home and asked the officers to let him know what they found. The detectives would later realize that the evidence Jenkins had submitted contained only ten grams of heroin, not one hundred as he had reported.

The county officers were carrying out the warrant when a Dodge minivan pulled up in front of the home. County detective Jason Metz shone his flashlight and saw Jenkins and a passenger. Metz did not know Jenkins, but like Kilpatrick he had heard bad things about him.

Jenkins emerged from the van, yelling, "Where's the dope!" Then Metz noticed a completely bald white man, with what appeared to be a police badge around his neck, get out of Jenkins's car. The man looked familiar to Metz, but he couldn't place him.

Unlike the city police force, county police have the functional equivalent of internal affairs officers accompany drug units on search warrants, and the pair of visitors caught that officer's attention, too.

"Can I get your name and badge number?" he asked when he encountered them in the house.

Jenkins gave his information. The second man mumbled a badge number that was similar to Jenkins's, gave his last name, and walked outside.

The county officer turned back to Jenkins, who hesitated. "He doesn't have a badge number," Jenkins said. "He's a member of 'the task force.'" He said the man was his cousin and they had just been playing basketball. It was now past midnight.

The officer pushed again. "What agency did you say your partner is with?"

"The fugitive task force," Jenkins said. He moved into the kitchen of the home, where officers heard him say, "There's more dope and a gun here. Gotta be!" A county officer asked him to pipe down because the subjects of the raid were still in the home. Jenkins and his partner soon left.

At some point, it had clicked for Metz who the strange bald-headed man was.

"What was Donald Stepp doing here?" he asked the others.

Two years earlier, Metz had been assigned to investigate an informant's tip that Stepp was a large-scale cocaine trafficker. Police had received previous tips about Stepp dating back to 2012, but cases never materialized. Metz did surveillance on Stepp's home at least twice in 2015 but said he had never seen any evidence of drug dealing. Still, the last place Metz expected to see Stepp was tooling around with a city police sergeant at the scene of a drug warrant.

The county police officers were all told to write up what they had seen.

In his report, Sergeant Vaughn wrote that Jenkins had misrepresented the status of his tipster by not initially disclosing that he wasn't a registered informant, had been working while supposedly on leave, and hadn't notified the county of his actions or run a deconfliction check on the target.

"Baltimore County would never allow its officers to take actions under these circumstances," Vaughn wrote in his report. "Sgt. Jenkins was in violation of the law and department policy." He said he would await instruction from supervisors and the county prosecutor's office about whether to charge Stepp with impersonating a police officer.

When Metz bumped into Kilpatrick back at the office, he mentioned what he had seen. Kilpatrick, knowing the FBI was looking at Jenkins, made sure the agents knew about the strange encounter. No one told the BPD.

CHAPTER SIXTEEN

HUNTING

AFTER MORE THAN A year of investigating the Baltimore Police Department for civil rights abuses following the death of Freddie Gray, the Justice Department delivered its report on August 10, 2016.

"We found that BPD has engaged in a pattern or practice of serious violations of the U.S. Constitution and federal law that has disproportionately harmed Baltimore's African American community and eroded the public's trust in the police," said Principal Deputy Assistant Attorney General Vanita Gupta, head of the Civil Rights Division. "The agency also fails to provide officers with the guidance, oversight and resources they need to police safely, constitutionally and effectively."

Although it had access to Internal Affairs files restricted from public view by state law, the Justice Department investigation did not note widespread reports of money being stolen by officers. In the 160-plus pages, there were fewer than a handful of such references. The report did find that the BPD had problems with unconstitutional stops and searches, disproportionately targeting Black people with minimal supervision and accountability. BPD made roughly 44 percent of its stops in two small, predominantly African American districts that contain only 11 percent of the city's population. They often stopped people and patted them down or frisked them without reasonable suspicion. One Black man in his midfifties was stopped thirty times in less than four years—with none of the stops resulting in a citation or criminal charge. During a ride-along with Justice Department officials, an unnamed BPD sergeant instructed a patrol officer to stop a group of young Black males on a street corner, question them, and order them to disperse. The officer protested and said he had no valid reason to do so; the sergeant said, "Then make something up."

From the department's outdated technology, to its mishandling of sexual assault cases, to officers' excessive force and First Amendment violations, the report painted a picture of an agency in disarray, one that was regularly trampling on the rights of city residents.

For years, citizens had been complaining about mistreatment while the department's succession of commissioners bemoaned the state of the agency they inherited. Now the problems had been meticulously compiled into a document that paved the way for a consent decree, in which a monitoring team and a judge would enforce reforms—rewriting policies but also generally looking over the shoulder of the department.

That night, the GTTF hit the streets as usual, pulling over several Black men on seatbelt violations and searching them without probable cause, just as the report issued earlier in the day to great fanfare had warned about. "We'd drive around and kinda go hunting and see what we could get into," Hersl once said.

The law allows police officers to stop people for any number of violations and to take further action if warranted by their observations or other circumstances. This is often cited as good police work.

"The biggest cases you'll ever make in your life . . . are the ones off nothing," Jenkins explained to Clewell after stopping a man for being illegally parked.

But, as University of Baltimore law professor David Jaros notes, "What we don't see is all those cases where the subsequent stop does not lead to evidence of a crime—and all of the ways that kind of activity undermines the people being policed, and the police in their community. A lot of the costs of those activities are hidden."

Some of these encounters were now being captured on tape. As part of the reforms already under way, the department had been rolling out body cameras, and one had finally been assigned to Hersl. For years, Jenkins and the other officers had been able to use only their word to detail the arrests they made, or had orchestrated their own videos using camera phones to show they were going above and beyond. But now the department was requiring them to record videos via body cameras that would shed new light on how the unit was racking up such impressive gun seizures. That summer, however, only two of the officers in the unit—Hersl and Gondo—had been outfitted with a camera.

One of the men who was stopped and searched that night in August, hours after the Justice Department report was released, was twenty-five-year-old D'Andre Adams. The security guard and licensed private detective was teaching a young relative to drive. On a busy street downtown, the officers drove at Adams's car to pull him over from the front. Jenkins, wearing a black vest and cargo pants, knelt down next to the passenger side door.

"Sir, I'm Sergeant Wayne Jenkins with the Gun Trace Task Force. The reason you're being stopped today is because you don't have a seatbelt on. How come you don't have a seatbelt on?"

"I didn't wear one," Adams said.

"Are you nervous, sir? We're on camera, you're shaking. Do you usually shake like that?" Jenkins said.

"I'm fine, officer," Adams said, looking calm.

Police had for years cited people acting nervously to justify searches. The body cameras recording from the officers' perspective cast major doubt on how often that was actually true. Adams got out of the car and was told to stand at the rear, facing away, as the officers picked through the car. Hersl's camera recorded Adams, not the others, conducting the search.

"You were advised why we stopped you," Hersl said. "You have to wear a seatbelt."

"That's cool, but why are you searching my car though? I didn't authorize nobody to search my shit."

Hersl waved his hand in front of Adams, unable to muster a response. "We're not arguing with you," Hersl said.

"It's fine. It's fine. Go ahead and do what you gotta do," Adams said, resignation washing over him.

With his daughter in the back seat, Adams asked if he could turn around and at least watch. He offered to let them handcuff him. Hersl told him no.

"It's an illegal search," Adams said, returning to his protest.

"No it's not an illegal search," Hersl said.

"Okay, so you pulled me over for a seatbelt—why am I out of my car right now?" Adams said.

"It's all on camera," Hersl said, as if that answered the question.

"I don't worry about y'all cameras. It's the fact, you gotta know what's right, yo."

According to time stamps from that night, the GTTF officers were stopping someone every ten to twenty minutes, making their way across the city. Immediately after letting Adams go, they saw a car pulling out of a CVS lot. The driver didn't have a seatbelt on and hadn't yet flipped on the headlights. Jenkins and Clewell went to opposite sides of the vehicle, leaning in with their heads touching the tops of the car doors so they could peer inside. Hersl, the only one with a body camera operating, stood back so the conversation would not be picked up on the recording. Suddenly, Jenkins began pulling the passenger out of the car.

"There's a gun in the bag between his feet," Jenkins said to Clewell.

"It's not mine!" the man pleaded.

"I don't care if it's yours. There's a gun between your legs. I don't care if it's yours."

"I just got in the car!"

Jenkins grilled the driver, a paraplegic using a device to drive the car, about his seatbelt. "We just came out of the CVS," he shrugged.

The driver took ownership of the gun, absolving the passenger who might have been charged with it. As the officers processed his information, Hersl chirped to him that he should have his lights on next time.

"Small shit," the man muttered.

"Small shit will get you jammed up all the time, won't it?" Hersl said cheerily.

They were 1-for-3 with finding guns via seatbelt violation stops.

More stops as the night wore on. They chased a man in North Baltimore, searched his car, and found nothing. They stopped another man who had alcohol in his car and who said he was a city worker. "We're out here looking for murderers and guns—we're not interested in the alcohol," Jenkins said. They dumped the alcohol, searched his car, and let him go.

At a gas station in Northwest Baltimore, they stopped a vehicle with four young men inside. The car couldn't have pulled five feet from a gas pump when they were stopped for not having seatbelts on. "You're shaking really bad," Jenkins told the passenger. "Why don't you have a seatbelt on?"

"I just came out the gas station," the man said. "I apologize."

"All right, but when the vehicle is in motion, you have to have a seatbelt on, all right?"

Hersl pointed to a bag on the floor of the car and said they wanted to search it because they had found a gun earlier in the evening inside a similar type of bag—a completely unjustified reason to search this man, and this bag. The man, standing with his hands behind his head, let them search.

They had a small amount of weed, but there was nothing else in the car.

One-for-six.

In the weeks following the Justice Department report, the Gun Trace Task Force committed at least two more robberies, one in which the wiretap picked up Gondo and Jenkins discussing entering a man's home without a search warrant. The officers never activated their body cameras for those encounters. Hersl would later be recorded saying that he was going to put the body camera in his trunk "until someone says something to him" and that "unless a complaint comes out" he doubted anyone in the BPD would be looking for it.

THOUGH THE FBI WAS listening to Gondo's phone, those calls provided only a small window into the GTTF's activities. By the end of August 2016, investigators were ready to take another step in the investigation of the unit: bugging Gondo's car.

For almost two months, Special Agent Jensen and the other investigators had been discussing with prosecutors the idea of hiding a recording device inside Gondo's take-home vehicle, hoping a device embedded in the car might capture more blunt or revealing discussions.

Then there was an incident in mid-August that deepened concern that the officers might change up their behaviors. An agent was conducting surveillance outside Gondo's apartment complex when he was spotted by Gondo. The agent peeled off in his vehicle as Gondo started to approach, but Gondo sped after him. Gondo continued the pursuit for a mile until he caught up to the spy.

"Who are you?" Gondo demanded to know.

"I don't know what you're talking about," the agent replied.

Gondo reached out to Jenkins and told him that they needed to meet.

If there was a time to switch up tactics, this was it. The device would be rigged for both sound and video and positioned at the rear of the car instead of the front, so that the agents could observe phone activity not picked up by the wiretap, like texting or FaceTime.

To get a warrant to record, they'd have to prove to the Justice Department that criminal conversations were taking place in the car. They couldn't. Instead, they decided to lean in on a provision of BPD's take-home car policy that said officers waived any expectation of privacy and could be monitored.

This also meant discontinuing the wiretap on Gondo's phone, as they couldn't have both running at the same time.

After hearing that Gondo was going out of town, they decided to move in. It was daring; the installation was not a quick job, which meant investigators would have to move Gondo's car to another location, then put it back without being detected. Any number of things could go wrong—what if a neighbor saw them in the lot and mentioned it to Gondo? They would park a decoy car in its place until they could return. But what if someone—say, a drunk driver—accidentally hit them as they drove the vehicle? How would they explain themselves?

The agents disabled the car alarm and entered the vehicle. Jensen noticed that the car was very clean inside. Under the front seat, however, they found a cigarette box, and inside was a bag of heroin gelcaps.

Jensen called Derek Hines, one of the federal prosecutors, for advice on what to do. Normally such evidence would be seized, no question. But the investigators didn't want their operation to be discovered—the drugs could have been stolen by Gondo, but they also might be evidence for a case that had not yet been submitted to Evidence Control. They decided to remove one pill, to test and confirm it was heroin, and leave the rest.

The operation was carried out successfully, and Jensen was eager to hear whatever Gondo and the others might be keeping off the phone lines. The next night, August 31, 2016, the hidden device was recording as the officers swept in on a car at a gas station on the west side of downtown. Detective Taylor would later say that the man inside was looking down and appeared to be rolling a joint.

"Might be able to get something dirty," Hersl said.

The car took off, and the officers gave chase.

"No lights, no lights," Rayam said.

The fleeing vehicle plowed through a red light and hit another car, spinning it 180 degrees, before driving up onto a sidewalk, its driver hurt from the collision.

"Shit!" Gondo yelled.

The officers hung back and debated whether to help and whether they could slip away undetected.

"We ain't look too crazy, did we?" Gondo asked. "They got cameras up and down that shit."

"Go back. We're recorded," Rayam said. "I can get on the air and say I just got a report of an accident."

"No," Hersl protested. "Wayne said, I wouldn't say nothing yet. . . . Wayne just wants to stay in the area, close by, see how it comes out."

Rayam wanted to help: "So how about we just go on scene and just act like, 'Oh, is everything okay?' Get what I'm saying?"

"That dude's unconscious. He ain't saying shit," one of the officers said.

"I think we're straight," Gondo said. Of the traffic cameras, he said, "I don't think [the cameras] can zoom in and get tags."

"You only turned your lights on at the very, very beginning at the gas station, right?" Hersl asked.

"Yeah, at that light. I turned it off after that," Gondo said.

"That's the thing with Wayne. He's a little too much with this s—," Hersl said. "These car chases—this is what happens. It's a crap-shoot, you know?"

Hersl proposed that the officers fill out their time sheets to show they had stopped working an hour before the crash.

"'Hey, I was just drivin' home!'" Hersl said, laughing. "I wonder what was in that car . . ."

Jenkins could be heard speaking from a separate vehicle, either by police radio or by phone.

"I don't care," Jenkins said.

"I know. But I'm curious," Hersl said.

"Go back to headquarters."

Jensen said later she was "really horrified" the officers hadn't dealt with the crash. But with the investigation ongoing, the FBI didn't intervene either. The man who was struck that night was a thirty-two-year-old immigrant from Senegal named Serigne Gueye, who was driving home to his pregnant wife when the fleeing vehicle ran the red light. When Gueye was sued months later by the fleeing driver, who falsely claimed that Gueye caused the crash, no one stepped forward to back Gueye's account.

FEDERAL AUTHORITIES LISTENED OVER the wiretap on September 22 as Rayam and Gondo talked about how Jenkins was onto something "big" and wanted to involve only them, cutting out the others. Jenkins had another condition: he didn't want to have his name appear on any paperwork associated with the case. "He's tired of putting his name on shit. I was like, give me the motherfucker, I'll put my name on it," Rayam said. "He was like, yo, this dude's good for at least two hundred. We could get him. I was like 'all right.' [He said] if we do it, it'll be me and you."

Yet being accused of misconduct set Jenkins off. Two days after Gondo and Rayam's recorded conversation, the GTTF chased a man through an alley who had ditched a gun. Body camera video showed Jenkins talking to the man, trying to get him to admit to possessing the gun.

"What I want to know: Is somebody trying to kill you, is someone trying to hurt you. If your life's in danger, you let me know where or who, and I can look into them to try to get more guns off the street. Is your life in danger?"

"Man, everyone's life is in danger. This is Baltimore City," the man replied. "I lost three homeboys in two months last year. I lost two cousins this year."

Just then, the man's cellphone rang. He asked if he could tell the person he was getting locked up. Jenkins obliged, holding the phone open and letting the man talk over speakerphone. "Yo, they found a joint in the alley," the man told the person, using slang for a gun. "[They] put the bitch on me, yo."

Jenkins snapped the phone closed. "Don't do that. We're not cruddy cops. You threw that shit with your right hand. What you just said is very disrespectful. We ain't dirty cops. We don't get down like that. That's dirty case work. If somebody tries to put a gun on somebody, and it wasn't theirs, that cop gets rolled on, and that cop gets charged. We don't police that way. These police right here? We do things by the book."

Albert Peisinger, a longtime city drug prosecutor, remembers similar private conversations with Jenkins. Peisinger, who had worked with Jenkins occasionally for years, said the detective "took constructive criticism, tried to make his cases better. He and other people would listen.

"Toward the end, I think he almost had a dual personality," Peisinger said. "He'd ask, why does everyone think I'm a dirty cop?"

An internal department newsletter went out in October 2016. On the first page, Commissioner Davis wrote to his officers about the looming consent decree. "A consent decree is not a magic pill. It is, however, a court-ordered and enforced mandate that will compel us to make necessary improvements to processes that have been long neglected. At times, it will introduce changes to our organization that may cause anxiety. Police, after all, do not typically adjust well to change. We must not confuse the time-honored traditions of our profession and the growth necessary to improve as an organization. We must honor our traditions, but not cling to them. We must embrace changes that make us better crime-fighters and community ambassadors, and not dismiss them as contrary to the notion of 'real police work.'"

Two pages later, the newsletter highlighted the work of the Gun Trace Task Force as a model for the department, complete with a photo of Jenkins flanked by Hendrix, Taylor, Rayam, and Ward. The blurb was penned by a supervisor, Lieutenant Chris O'Ree.

"It should go without saying that this is an extremely challenging time for law enforcement nationally. Officers are questioning themselves and their role in society, and the changing law enforcement landscape. Against this backdrop, I am extremely proud to showcase the work of Sergeant Wayne Jenkins and the Gun Trace Task Force. This team of dedicated detectives has a work ethic that is beyond reproach."

The squad, up to that point, had seized 132 handguns and made 110 arrests on handgun violations through nine months. "Their relentless pursuit to make our streets safer by removing guns and arresting the right people for the right reasons has made our city safer," O'Ree wrote. "I couldn't be more proud of the strong work of this team."

No one seemed to care much about how the cases were faring in court: From 2012 to 2016, 40 percent of Jenkins's gun cases were dropped by prosecutors, higher than the department average, even as he was winning praise for his skill. Despite police and prosecutors' stated priority of holding people caught carrying guns accountable, officials would later acknowledge that no one was circling back to check or improve the outcomes.

A case in point was the trial of Oreese Stevenson, whose safe was cleaned out of half its contents in March. Stevenson had hired attorney Ivan Bates, who said he had started specifically seeking out defendants whom Jenkins had arrested because the officer's tactics made the cases winnable. At the same time, Bates had never publicly accused Jenkins of stealing. It was too risky for his clients, and a serious accusation for the attorney to make without proof. He recalled one time offering up one such client to a prosecutor—who was more interested in getting the client to talk about his own crimes.

Now in October, Bates and Stevenson were in the courtroom of Judge Barry Williams, three months after he'd tossed out the last of the Freddie Gray cases. Stevenson told Bates that Jenkins had robbed him. Stevenson knew it, Bates knew it, and Jenkins knew it.

Given the GTTF's reported haul—several kilograms of cocaine—and Stevenson's prior record, his case likely would have been taken federal, but the U.S. Attorney's Office knew enough now to steer clear of the GTTF's cases and had quietly dismissed a half dozen that were pending on the federal side.

Bates's game plan was to get the case dropped by scrutinizing the initial car stop. Jenkins was called to the stand and gave his account of the stop. He said they'd approached Stevenson just to chat.

"We always stop and ask if everything's okay," Jenkins said. "We never know who's going to provide us information about current crime that's going on, or past crime. It could be old, young, Black, white, female, male. You never know who's going to speak to the police."

Jenkins said that when he'd approached the car, he'd been careful to follow the rules so that the case would hold up in court. He said he'd learned from past mistakes. That impressed Judge Williams. But Williams noted that in describing their tactics Jenkins also said his squad had surrounded the car, which legally amounted to a detention that was not supported by reasonable suspicion. That made it a bad stop, and Williams threw out the evidence. With no evidence from the traffic stop, the ensuing search at Stevenson's home was also gone, the "fruit of a poisonous tree." Prosecutors had no choice but to ditch the case. Stevenson was off the hook—and so was Jenkins.

When the hearing concluded, Williams called the prosecutor up to the bench.

"Just so you know, I did find your officer relatively credible," Judge Williams said to the prosecutor. "Let him know what the law is. You've got a right to roll up on people, absolutely. But you can't get out of the car and surround the car. He thought the person had drugs. They probably did have drugs. There's no disputing that. There's other ways."

Bates followed Jenkins out of the courtroom.

"I don't know what you're doing, but everybody tells me the same thing. You rob, and you steal, and you're taking everybody's money," Bates said he told Jenkins. "Come on, man."

"I don't know what you're talking about," Jenkins responded.

Having dodged accountability again, Jenkins was about to take some time off. His wife was pregnant again and was about to deliver their third child. Jenkins had informed his officers only a few weeks before that he would soon be taking a leave of absence.

It would last for three months.

CHAPTER SEVENTEEN

READ BETWEEN THE LINES

A FEW WEEKS BEFORE Jenkins went on leave, he pulled Detective James "K-Stop" Kostoplis into the Gun Trace Task Force. This marked a long-awaited reunion for Kostoplis, who had looked up to Jenkins as a rookie officer in the Northeastern District in 2012. Kostoplis had left the department not long after the 2015 unrest and gone to work with a railroad police department back home in New Jersey. When he applied to return to the BPD in early 2016, he was given the runaround by the recruiting section, so he reached out to Jenkins, who sent a message to Deputy Commissioner De Sousa on his behalf.

"I'm sure you remember the name KOSTOPLIS because he was killing the NED with search warrants and gun seizures. In short he is an asset to our department and we should be doing everything we can to hold on to an Officer of this caliber and work ethic. I attempted to speak with recruitment but they basically blew me off," Jenkins wrote. "I'm sure if [the recruitment officer] was contacted by a command member respected like yourself then he would feel the urgency to re-hire this hard charger to help our city through these difficult times."

"10-4 Wayne I know K-Stop well. He was an Allstar like you. I'm sending a separate email to [commander of personnel] Major Handley right now. Didn't know he was trying to come back," De Sousa responded.

Jenkins had said he would add Kostoplis to the gun unit, but it didn't happen right away. He would have to work patrol again, and that was okay—Kostoplis was happy to be back in Baltimore instead of checking train facilities and box cars for freight hoppers.

In late October, the call came: Kostoplis was joining the GTTF. He recalled walking through headquarters with Jenkins, who told Kostoplis that he'd officially "made it" in the department. "You'll never have to go back to patrol after this," Jenkins told him. "You'll be able to work in any specialty unit you want."

Immediately, Kostoplis found the pace of the Gun Trace Task Force frenetic, the hours long. On the streets, body camera footage shows, Kostoplis often stood close to Jenkins attentively, his head going back and forth between Jenkins and the people he interrogated on the street.

"I remember calling my dad on the way home because I couldn't believe it," Kostoplis recalled later. "I think they got seven gun arrests in one day. I've never even heard of something like that before."

When Jenkins went on leave, however, everything ground to a halt. Hersl took a month off to remodel a home he purchased in Harford County. Kostoplis said the other officers stopped working, mostly spending their days sitting around the office. Kostoplis was the new guy in the squad and eager to produce but didn't have any sway. He tried to find other ways to make an impact. He pulled 911 calls for armed persons and proposed going to shooting ranges to check logs for people prohibited from possessing firearms who went to shoot guns. Those were the kinds of things the GTTF had been originally created to do. Kostoplis was told by his new co-workers, "We don't do that."

The possibility that they were under investigation continued to loom for the rest of the squad, even if they weren't particularly rattled by it. Earlier in the month, the recording device in Gondo's car captured him and Rayam once again discussing being tipped off to the federal investigation. Gondo said Jenkins had told him it could be the "feds" and that the investigation could have been ongoing for as long as five years. Gondo scoffed: "It's no Pablo Escobar. It's police." He rattled off the names of other Baltimore cops who'd been taken down by the FBI: "King and Murray, [the length of investigation] was like a year or nine months. That's it. Sylvester, it was months. [Kendall] Richburg, it was months."

AS COUNTY DRUG TASK force cops McDougall and Kilpatrick were finally preparing to bring their yearlong, meticulously compiled case against Shropshire, officers from the city swooped in. It wasn't just any squad, either: it was former Jenkins mentor Sergeant Keith Gladstone and his team, who on their own had obtained a search warrant for Shropshire's home. Gladstone's group should have checked the "deconfliction" databases to make sure no one else was after Shropshire. Kilpatrick later said he suspected Gladstone's unit did check first but didn't care.

As Gladstone and the officers rolled up to Shropshire's home, they encountered Shropshire in the driveway and searched him, finding twenty-five grams of heroin. "Call Wayne!" Shropshire said to the arresting officers, referring to Jenkins. Shropshire said later that Jenkins had once stopped him, given Shropshire his number, and said to call him if he ever ran into trouble with city police. Shropshire said he'd pulled the card once earlier, and after speaking with Jenkins the officer let him go. He claims he did nothing for Jenkins in return.

On its face, the bust was a good one for the city cops: Not only did Gladstone's team report that Shropshire had drugs on him, but the officers found a loaded gun under his mattress and a hydraulic press, which can be used for drug packaging, in the basement. Catching Shropshire with a weapon would automatically increase his possible punishment. In his car, they found a scanner used to detect GPS devices or other trackers. They also collected a phone Shropshire had been using, potentially full of useful evidence. Ideally, this would only add to the case that the feds had built already.

But the feds already had concerns about Gladstone's credibility and weren't taking his cases. Body camera footage could assuage those concerns, but Gladstone's team had turned their cameras on only after an initial sweep of the home, during a secondary search. Instead of contributing evidence to the federal case that was in the works, the involvement of Gladstone's team took key evidence out of the picture—because it was considered tainted. Shropshire was able to post a $100,000 bail and was released.

Six days after the arrest by Gladstone's team, the federal authorities obtained a superseding indictment against Shropshire and another man, using the evidence they had gathered over the past year.

It was a week after Thanksgiving 2016 when Shropshire was taken into custody. Shropshire remembers the detectives climbing out of a white Toyota 4Runner with tinted windows. Not only had Shropshire gone right back to dealing after posting bail, but he was particularly sloppy that day. He had drugs on him—fifteen grams of heroin and 180 grams of cocaine—because a dissatisfied customer had returned them. Kilpatrick approached and identified himself as a Baltimore County police officer. "Baltimore County?" Shropshire thought. "Fuck they want?" Kilpatrick told him they had a federal arrest warrant. His heart dropped. He knew this would be serious.

The case had started with "Brill," the shadowy figure with multiple descriptions. Now they were finally face to face with him, and through more than a year of investigating, the detectives felt as if they had come to know Shropshire. McDougall asked Shropshire if he wanted to call his fiancée and tell her what had happened; he asked Shropshire for her phone number. Shropshire gave the first six digits before McDougall punched in the last four himself—he already knew the number. McDougall also referred to Shropshire's son by his nickname, as if they were family friends.

As McDougall and Kilpatrick drove him to the downtown federal courthouse, Shropshire told the officers they should "get rid" of the drugs they'd seized off him. Use a confidential informant, he said, and then "buy something nice for your wives."

Kilpatrick recalled that Shropshire said: 'Come on, Gladstone took it.'"

ON THE DATE OF his initial court appearance, December 2, 2016, authorities brought Shropshire in for a hastily arranged "reverse proffer" session, in which prosecutors share evidence against a defendant in hopes of getting the defendant to cooperate. Shropshire had no interest in talking about his case. But the investigators might have been even more intrigued about what he had said about Gladstone a few days earlier, and they asked him an open-ended question about what he knew about crooked officers.

The names Shropshire ticked off were exactly the officers already in the crosshairs of federal authorities: Jenkins, Gondo, Hersl, and Gladstone. It was as if the officers' corruption was a huge open secret.

In September, Shropshire said, Gondo had asked to meet him at a Home Depot and had warned Shropshire that he was going to get arrested, according to notes of the meeting.

"You need to chill out," Gondo said, advising him to dump the cellphones he had been using. "Read between the lines."

Shropshire told them of how Gondo had been protecting drug dealers from the neighborhood where they grew up, calling Gondo a "helping hand." He said he partied with Gondo, who had warned him about Jenkins, saying that Jenkins was "no longer on our side" and would lock Shropshire up if given the chance, despite Gondo's attempts to run interference.

Gladstone and Jenkins were "rotten," Shropshire told the authorities. They took money from people regularly and did not report it as seized. In 2008, Shropshire said, Gladstone had arrested Glen Wells and had taken $50,000. Indeed, records show Wells was arrested by Gladstone that year.

All of the Baltimore drug dealers who were "making money" had had similar run-ins with Gladstone, Shropshire said.

Jenkins, meanwhile, made no pretense of doing police work. Word around the city was that he would take not just money but drugs from people he stopped and that he would not file charges or report the incidents. He said he had heard stories where Jenkins had pulled up on people Shropshire knew and had told them that he was looking for guns and was going to search them but that if the dealers gave him drugs without him having to conduct a search, Jenkins wouldn't arrest them. If the dealers complied, Jenkins would drive off as if nothing happened—Shropshire cited two recent examples involving people he knew.

Most of the information was hearsay; the investigators also knew the officers were taking money. But this may have served as one of the investigators' first inklings that Jenkins was taking drugs—for what purposes remained unclear.

ON JANUARY 12, 2017, after months of negotiations, the city of Baltimore and the U.S. Justice Department signed a consent decree binding the police department to judicially enforced reform. Talks had been sped up following the election of President Trump, out of mutual fears that his attorney general nominee Jeff Sessions—who had been critical of consent decrees—would torpedo the agreement. The 227-page pact called for all kinds of new requirements for officers, such as mandating that they "shall stop and detain vehicles only where they have probable cause that the driver has committed a traffic violation, or reasonable suspicion based on specific and articulable facts that the vehicle or occupant of the vehicle has been, is, or is about to be engaged in the commission of a crime." The same went for searches of people and their vehicles. Even if people gave officers consent, officers would have to provide forms to document it, and the subjects could revoke their consent at any time.

While city officials and civil rights groups hailed the move, police officers grumbled about the restraints it would put on their work. Former deputy commissioner Anthony Barksdale told the *Sun* that restricting police interactions on street corners would help drug dealers and people carrying guns illegally.

"They've empowered the criminal element," Barksdale said. "Yeah, it might be great for some people in the community, but what about everybody else?"

AROUND 2 A.M. ONE day in late January 2017, a groggy Wayne Jenkins flipped on the lights inside his home and opened the front door for a Baltimore County patrol officer. Jenkins had summoned the officer, saying that he had returned from work to find that his 2016 Dodge Grand Caravan had been stolen from the driveway.

As the officer took down information about the missing car, Jenkins blurted out that he had seven expensive four-wheelers in his garage and had been worried that they had been taken too. They weren't.

"I was scared as fuck—I've got so much money in four-wheelers, that's the first thing I did was run out back." Jenkins assured him he wouldn't miss the vehicle: "I'll be getting another one in a week," he said.

A week later, a man hiking in a wooded area three miles from Jenkins's home called police to say he'd stumbled upon what would turn out to be the stolen van. Someone had gone to work on it: All of the windows were broken. The front bumper was pulled off. Panels were ripped out from the interior. All of the lights were pulled out. The interior was completely stripped bare. Someone had carved "Fuck you" onto the hood.

County police thought it could have been unruly kids; but the anger, the aggression in the damage, suggested that someone whom Jenkins had wronged wanted to send him a message. No one was ever charged in the case.

Jenkins returned to work. During his leave, the slowdown of the GTTF's productivity that Kostoplis observed had also been noted by commanders, who urged Jenkins's supervisors to get him "back to work and focused." Jenkins, however, was now saying that he wanted a change. Lieutenant Chris O'Ree recalled that Jenkins was "very vocal" about not wanting to return to the same work anymore and wanted to be transferred to the Warrant Apprehension Task Force—where he would serve warrants on wanted individuals instead of building investigations and appearing in court. He told O'Ree he'd decided that his family was more important and that he "didn't want to continue taking the same chances." Lieutenant Marjorie German, another supervisor, also recalled Jenkins asking to be moved to the warrant task force, saying he was upset "about getting all these guns for command and being underappreciated."

Ivan Bates, the defense attorney, remembered a similar conversation after bumping into Jenkins at the courthouse in late February.

"He said, I just want to let you know it's been a good ride battling you, I got respect for you, but I'm never making another arrest," Jenkins told Bates. "Fuck this place. Fuck all them who don't appreciate what I do. I'm going to be a lieutenant. Fuck it."

The warrant squad would certainly be less glamorous work. For years it had been a place where the department hid some of its problem officers so that they could still work but not have to take the stand and be cross-examined. That's because they were carrying out arrests only on cases already compiled by other officers, fanning out across the region to enter homes and try to find people with open warrants. But Jenkins's transfer never came.

One night in February, shortly after Jenkins's return from leave, members of the GTTF were in their office on the sixth floor of police headquarters when Jenkins and Hersl approached Kostoplis. They wanted to go for a ride in Jenkins's van. They didn't tell him what it was about, but sometimes the guys were short like that—sometimes it was just to go get something to eat. Jenkins drove them away from headquarters but not far, pulling over on a relatively quiet block of Water Street, next to a parking garage. Jenkins told Kostoplis to take off his gear and walk to the back of the vehicle.

Jenkins and Hersl stood side by side, two large men facing the slight Kostoplis.

"What do you think about following high-level drug dealers around," Jenkins said, "and finding out where they keep their cash, and just taking it?"

Kostoplis's answer was simple.

"That's a terrible fucking idea," Kostoplis said. "You can't wear a badge and be doing that."

"You're absolutely right," Jenkins replied.

To Kostoplis, the question had been a test of his integrity—to make sure he could be trusted to do the right thing. He remembered how in 2012, when he had first ridden with Jenkins, the sergeant had told him there were two rules for working with him, one of which was that they would never steal.

They headed back to headquarters and didn't discuss it further.

A few days later, however, Jenkins sat Kostoplis down and informed him he was being transferred out of the unit. Jenkins said that he knew Kostoplis liked to be proactive but that because Jenkins was up for promotion to be a lieutenant and had too many open complaints with Internal Affairs, he would be lying low for a while. He told Kostoplis he'd be better off in another squad.

"I know you want to be on the street—I know you hate being in the office," Jenkins told him. "I've got to work from the office now. I've got too many open numbers to get promoted."

Kostoplis protested. He'd been able to work under Jenkins's tutelage for only a couple of weeks, on either side of Jenkins's paternity leave.

"No, I came here to work with you," Kostoplis said. "I want to work with you."

"No, no, no. You're going to this [other] squad. It's the best move for you," Jenkins said.

Kostoplis would later see Jenkins and the GTTF on the street. It didn't seem as if they were lying low. He wondered if he just wasn't up to par.

The truth was that Jenkins couldn't have someone unwilling to play ball in his squad. While he had been telling people he wanted to scale back at work, the officers already in the fold said Jenkins seemed to be looking to step up his crimes. In particular, he wanted another crack at Oreese Stevenson.

Jenkins told Taylor and Ward to meet him in the parking lot near a Northwest Baltimore apartment complex. He was already there with Hersl, and they were drinking Twisted Teas—a malt liquor with tea—said to be one of Jenkins's favorite drinks. He laid out the plan: He knew from researching Stevenson's past that he was part of a crew associated with a restaurant called Downtown Southern Blues, whose members had been taken down on federal drug charges a decade earlier. Some of the names from the case, Jenkins believed, were still big players in town. He had told Taylor that he wanted to hit Stevenson's house again and see what else they could get. Jenkins explained that he wanted to purchase federal agent vests and put GPS trackers on Stevenson's cars and track his movements for a couple of days. If they could identify a routine, they could hit the house when it was expected to be empty, then kick in the door and take drugs and money. Hersl and Taylor were on board, but Ward hesitated. They'd already taken tens of thousands of dollars from the guy—why chance it with a return? When Taylor also changed his mind, Jenkins got upset.

Around this time, Jenkins told the officers that he had a childhood friend who owned a body shop but also dealt drugs and had been shorted by a couple of kilograms on a recent deal. The friend wanted Jenkins to bust the supplier and had provided Jenkins with all the information. Now Jenkins proposed that they track that dealer and rob him too. He mentioned that the supplier could have up to a million dollars—they could split it and "be set," Jenkins said.

"He wanted to dress up as federal agents and wear masks while we went in there," Ward would later say.

Detective Evodio Hendrix, another member of the squad, remembered it the same way: "He stated that he wanted us to actually target him, to basically do investigation to see where he lived, where he possibly had his money and drugs at. And he actually wanted us to rob him."

In the police headquarters garage, Jenkins showed them how he planned to carry out the crime. He opened the doors to his van to reveal a duffel bag packed with a burglar's tool kit: crowbars and machetes, sledgehammers and lock-cutters, binoculars—even a grappling hook. In another bag was a face mask resembling a skull, with mesh covering over the eyes—the kind of thing you might see in a horror movie. There were also balaclava ski masks, binoculars, and gloves and shoes—all black. Jenkins had everything they'd need to carry out the plot, but Hendrix and Ward said they were horrified at seeing the tools and tried to ignore their boss. He seemed to be spiraling out of control.

"Sergeant Jenkins is crazy," Hendrix recalled saying to Ward.

III.

TAKEDOWN

CHAPTER EIGHTEEN
COGNITIVE DISSONANCE

DURING THEIR INVESTIGATION OF the GTTF, federal authorities held off from reaching out to potential victims, worried that word might somehow make it back to the officers through either the streets or the defense bar. Instead, they pieced together accounts of robberies from the wiretap conversations, microphone recordings, and contemporaneous jail calls in which arrestees told friends or loved ones about missing money.

Since Jenkins's paternity leave, there had been no new crimes for investigators to track. Now the GTTF also seemed to be breaking up, with some of the officers moving to other units. Rayam, on light duty following a leg surgery, was working with another unit at the Barn; Gondo and Hersl moved together to the citywide shootings unit, where they were tasked with trying to solve nonfatal shootings.

The federal investigators continued to pick up chatter from the officers discussing the possibility that they were under investigation. On February 15, 2017, Gondo and Hersl were recorded by the bug in Gondo's car as they joked about a possible RICO investigation, the acronym for a racketeering case in the federal system. Gondo again brushed it off, saying that with the current police department regime they would've been suspended already. Hersl told Gondo that Jenkins was supposed to have transferred to the warrant unit but that it hadn't happened. Hersl said Jenkins remained worried about an investigation.

To the FBI, his continued concerns meant he could also be destroying possible evidence.

It was time to start preparing charges against the gun unit.

The first hurdle for Jensen and her team was making contact with victims of the task force and convincing them to talk. Most "did not want anything to do with this," Jensen said later of the victims. Some did not want to expose their criminal dealings, fearful that law enforcement either was tricking them or could later use information they had provided against them. Some considered cooperation, even against dirty cops, to be snitching and wanted no part of that either.

Oreese Stevenson and his wife were among those who did not want to participate. Wise recalls sitting down with Stevenson at a meeting facilitated by his lawyer, Ivan Bates, who urged Stevenson to describe what the officers had done to him. "You hit the lottery," Bates told Stevenson, referring to his charges being thrown out in a case that could have resulted in decades in prison. "You owe everybody else; you've got to step up and tell [the feds] what happened."

Reluctantly, Stevenson told the feds that the officers had robbed him not just of money but also of more kilos of cocaine than the officers had reported seizing. Bates also brought them additional clients from over the years who had reported being wronged by Jenkins and some of the other officers.

Bates told them he "had been beating cases with Jenkins, prevailing on things like suppressing evidence at a rate that was higher than expected," Hines recalled later. "The way he put it was, 'I'm not *that* good.'"

IN ADDITION TO THE illegal searches, extortion, and robberies, federal investigators had uncovered the massive overtime theft committed by the officers. Their open discussion on the wiretap of not going to work or regularly rolling in late had prompted investigators to use Sieracki's access to department databases to pull the officers' timesheets. At one point, Jenkins had received overtime pay while on a family vacation in

Myrtle Beach; Taylor got time and a half while in the Dominican Republic; Hersl was paid extra while working on his house.

One person about whom the investigators found little evidence of wrongdoing was the officer initially under scrutiny: John Clewell. The GPS in his name had sparked the investigation, but they had no evidence that he had taken part in the robberies, and he did not appear to be milking overtime the way the others had been. He had left the squad in the fall, joining a DEA task force.

Despite the months' worth of evidence they'd compiled, the case against the GTTF wasn't a slam dunk. A year earlier, federal prosecutors in Pennsylvania had lost a similar racketeering case against six Philadelphia drug cops. That squad was accused of stealing $400,000, beating suspects—in one case dangling someone from a balcony— and lying in court. Before the case even went to trial, more than 150 convictions based on arrests made by the officers had been overturned. One former member of the squad flipped and testified about the crimes they committed. But the six other officers held their ground and fought the charges, with their defense attorneys urging jurors not to take the word of drug dealers and a dirty cop. In May 2015, a federal jury acquitted all of the Philadelphia officers.

Other than the officers detailed to the FBI, the BPD had been kept in the dark about the GTTF investigation until now. Commissioner Kevin Davis knew only that there had been an anticorruption case in the works but knew none of the specifics. When the details were revealed to him, Davis was startled. It had to have been going on for years, he thought. Davis understood why the FBI hadn't clued him in earlier—he would've felt compelled to take the officers off the street, which would've thwarted the investigation. He tried to focus on the good news: that BPD officers on the FBI task force had been part of putting together the case. "No bullshit, I was proud of the fact that they were arrested while I was police commissioner," Davis recalled later. He hoped the public might give the department some credit.

The moment to act had come.

JENSEN CONSIDERED A NUMBER of options for the takedown operation. The arrest teams could make predawn entry into the officers' homes, the way most arrests are made, but Jensen resisted that approach. The members of the GTTF were armed police whose lives were about to come crashing down, raising the concern that they might harm themselves or others. She thought back to a Cook County sheriff's deputy she had once worked with in the FBI's Chicago field office. For years, he and some other officers had been using their badges to rob drug dealers during traffic stops and home invasions. Within hours of being arrested, the officer hanged himself with a bedsheet in his jail cell.

Jensen and the prosecutors decided they would have to seize the entire squad at the same time. One option authorities considered was to invite the officers to the FBI offices for a bogus awards ceremony—Jenkins certainly craved adulation—and arrest them there. Or they could figure out a way to lure them to the courthouse. Commissioner Davis thought it was important that the arrests happen "on BPD soil, so we didn't leave the impression we are incapable of participating in corruption investigations of our own people," he said later. "I hate to use the word optics . . . but that was a real piece of it."

They settled on summoning the seven officers to the Baltimore Police Department's own Internal Affairs headquarters as part of a ruse. They came up with a solid cover story, related to a failed operation months earlier in late October, when agents had tried to install another recording device in the departmental van used by Jenkins. As Sieracki drove it from the headquarters garage to the offsite location for installation, there was a loud clanging that drew looks from others in the garage. The investigators weren't sure when exactly the damage had occurred, or how—there had been some chatter picked up about a car hitting a pole—but Jenkins had stopped using it. Though the device installation had been a bust, the feds realized they could use the damaged vehicle as a pretext to speak with the officers.

A supervisor in Internal Affairs would call members of the squad and tell them to visit the Internal Affairs office in East Baltimore, on the morning of Wednesday, March 1, 2017. They would tell the officers that they were investigating a hit-and-run case involving an unmarked police car that had struck a child and left the scene and that they wanted to question whether they were involved. "We knew they had this wrecked car in the garage and they hadn't reported it, as far as we could tell. We weren't really sure what [actually] happened,"

Jensen recalled later. They said it was something they needed to clear up in order to process Jenkins's promotion to lieutenant. Because they had no reason to think the GTTF officers had actually struck a child, they believed the officers wouldn't sweat visiting Internal Affairs to be questioned about such an incident. The FBI and BPD worked together to put the arrest plan into motion.

The potential for leaks was now exponentially higher. The night before the takedown, on February 28, the FBI monitored the officers' whereabouts using the GPS on their phones. They wanted to make sure no one started heading toward an airport or out of state. Teams of officers from out of state were on standby in case GPS showed one of the officers making a run for it.

Jensen and other agents arrived around 4 A.M. at the FBI command center just outside the city, where they would monitor the operation. Sieracki, who had gotten about two hours of sleep, was the onsite man at the Internal Affairs office in East Baltimore and trudged in carrying two gallon-sized cartons of coffee and three boxes of donuts. The mood at the command post was quiet. "We knew that [once the case went public] it was going to be a mess," Jensen recalled.

An FBI SWAT team entered to take its place on the second floor, where they would hide in stairwells on either side of an elevator. In dry runs, they learned the elevator would shut quickly, and the Internal Affairs detectives escorting the officers were told to make sure to hold the door open with their arm. Meanwhile, BPD had cleared off the second floor of the Internal Affairs office and had told the detectives who normally worked there that they had to attend a training session. The head of Internal Affairs, Rodney Hill, had ordered a supervisor to quickly mock up a training plan to keep them busy. "Just say the chief is mad about something," Hill recalled telling them.

The officers had been asked to come between 8:45 and 9:00 A.M., and they straggled in. At one point, the GPS on Jenkins's phone showed that he was in Washington, D.C., and Jensen feared they had a runner. But she quickly realized it was only a glitch, as Jenkins was soon observed pulling into the Internal Affairs office. At the command post, Jensen didn't have a live video feed into the IA office. She would have to wait and hear from Sieracki on how the arrests went down.

Jenkins was the first; he arrived on time, around 8:45 A.M. Per standard procedure to enter a secure area, he had to check his gun and phone. Two Internal Affairs officers came down to the lobby and escorted him onto the elevators to the second floor.

As he emerged moments later, Jenkins was swarmed by SWAT members and handcuffed. "I'm one of you! I'm one of you!" he shouted, believing it was a mistake.

Rayam was arrested eight minutes later. Ward and Taylor arrived together a short time after him. Ward recalled being nervous when he arrived—Internal Affairs never called that many people down at one time—but he also didn't think he'd done anything wrong, at least not anything that was on the department's radar. "Being arrested was the last thing on my mind," he said later. Unaware their supervisor was in custody, Taylor called Jenkins several times from the lobby.

They were brought up to the second floor and taken into custody.

Hersl was arrested next, followed by Hendrix. Gondo was last, having shown up nearly forty minutes late.

The officers were taken to separate rooms. Davis, the commissioner, moved from room to room. The FBI didn't want him to say anything, but he at least wanted to look each officer in the eyes. Most of them dropped their heads or looked away.

Jenkins stared back, defiantly.

The feds moved swiftly to carry out searches of the officers' homes and vehicles. Not wanting to ram down the doors to their homes, they had runners take the officers' keys to authorities on site. Almost nothing of value to the investigation was recovered.

Curiously for the investigators, BB guns were found in some of the officers' cars.

Internal Affairs chief Rodney Hill briefed his staff about what had taken place. There were audible gasps. "This is the biggest corruption case in the history of the department," Hill recalled saying. "This is going to be with us for a long time."

AT A NEWS CONFERENCE at the U.S. Attorney's Office downtown a few hours later, Commissioner Davis stood alongside the outgoing U.S. attorney for Maryland, Rod Rosenstein (who was about to join the Trump administration as deputy attorney general), and the head of the local FBI field office, Gordon Johnson. A poster board set up in the briefing room read, "ABUSE OF POWER"; another listed the passage from the Police Code of Conduct about not engaging in corruption or bribery. Rosenstein told reporters that seven officers in an elite plainclothes unit had been arrested on racketeering and other charges and taken into custody by the FBI. The group of officers, he said, had been "involved in a pernicious conspiracy scheme that included abuse of power." Gondo was also charged as a co-defendant in the Shropshire drug conspiracy case.

Davis called the officers "1930s gangsters, as far as I'm concerned."

The phones of defense attorneys and prosecutors around the city started buzzing with word of the arrests. For years they had squared off in court over cases involving the officers; it was one thing for questions to be raised but quite another for them to be validated in such a sweeping fashion. The state's attorney's office hadn't been briefed on the investigation, and some prosecutors at that very moment were proceeding with cases brought by the officers. Assistant State's Attorney Anna Mantegna went back to her office, where some people were in tears.

"They were not tears of sadness," Mantegna recalled later. "They were more tears of anger and betrayal. My biggest nightmare, and that of any prosecutor, I think I can safely say, is the idea that someone may have been convicted and put in jail for something that they did not do. Instantly, all the cases that I had with members of that squad are just kind of flipping through my head."

Another prosecutor at the time said later: "You would hear defense attorneys say in almost every one of your cases, 'My guy said this [officer] is dirty.' Eventually, you're like, 'Unless you have something concrete to show me, I have nothing to go off except your guy doesn't want to be prosecuted.' I think it was a shock to most of the people at our level."

Defense attorneys were struck for the same reason: Clients had often asserted that police took money, but many attorneys had shrugged off the claims. It wasn't necessarily that the attorneys doubted them, though some admit they did. Ultimately, the allegations couldn't be proven and might actually cloud a more viable defense. It was a speed bump to brush past in most client interviews.

Within a few days Davis called plainclothes officers into the same auditorium where he'd rallied them in the summer of 2015, and told them they were being disbanded—put back into uniforms and sent to work out of the districts. The mood in the room was subdued. "This is the absolute, final dismantling of VCID," Davis later said, referring to the tough plainclothes units set up under his predecessors.

The department commissioned an internal investigation of the GTTF's supervisors, focused specifically on the overtime fraud. There was no indication that the supervisors had participated in the unit's robberies. But their exorbitant overtime pay required supervisor approval. How could Jenkins have received time and a half while in Myrtle Beach?

Lieutenant Marjorie German, who had supervised Jenkins on and off since 2015, gave them a broad overview of what it was like to be Jenkins's supervisor: She called him an "administrative nightmare." Many times, she said, she wouldn't even know that Jenkins was working overtime until an email came out from him touting a gun arrest. She'd question why he was on the streets, and he'd respond that a higher-up, like Colonel Sean Miller, had directly called them in for "violence suppression." Miller would apologize and say he had forgotten to mention it. She complained that Jenkins worked from a different office—the plainclothes units including GTTF were supposed to be at the Barn in Northwest Baltimore, but he worked from headquarters instead. "It was common knowledge that Jenkins had a direct line to upper command to get what he wants," German told Internal Affairs investigators. She cited as an example Jenkins getting a rental car—she had denied the request. Two weeks later he had the car. She suspected he had contacted the deputy commissioner, Dean Palmere, which Jenkins's emails confirmed. "What other sergeant in this department has a car personally assigned to him?" German told Internal Affairs investigators.

But German also gushed about Jenkins's ability, calling him "the best gun cop this department has ever seen." She'd seen it personally, she said, when he was on "timeout" while pending discipline in the Walter Price drug-planting case from 2014. Jenkins wanted to make overtime, and Colonel Miller said he could work only if a supervisor rode along with him. She had watched him get two handguns that night, she said.

Another lieutenant interviewed by internal affairs, Chris O'Ree, said Jenkins and his squad were a "tier one asset" and the "top gun-getters" in the city. The decision to move Jenkins to GTTF in June 2016 came from Palmere, and the squad was given the ability to traverse the city.

They were the "only ones producing post–Freddie Gray," he said.

Neither O'Ree nor German had signed the overtime slips for the timesheets when Jenkins was out of town; two other sergeants in a different unit admitted to giving their approval, saying it was a common practice throughout the department for a supervisor to sign the overtime slip of someone who was not in their unit if the supervisors of that member's unit was not available, and particularly so for specialized units.

The Internal Affairs investigator asked German if she had any idea that the GTTF officers were committing crimes or if there were any other warning signs. German said it was a "kick in the gut" and she had been "experiencing a roller coaster of emotions." She didn't know Jenkins's subordinate officers well but "did not expect this from Jenkins."

"He gives 150 percent on the street and is always running and gunning. And that is what they [command] want," German said. While she did not want to absolve the officers of responsibility for their own behavior, she said, "Command created the monster, and allowed it to go unchecked."

THE SEVEN GTTF OFFICERS were charged with racketeering and faced a maximum penalty of twenty years in prison. Gondo was also facing a mandatory five years and up to forty years in prison for conspiracy to distribute at least one hundred grams of heroin in the Shropshire case. At their initial court appearances, the officers were deemed threats to the community by a magistrate judge and ordered held while pending trial. They were initially detained together, in the jail in suburban Howard County.

Jenkins tried to rally the officers to stick together and fight—sometimes speaking to the group as if he was still leading the squad, other times approaching them for one-on-one conversations, according to Ward and Hendrix. He felt the fabricated video of Oreese Stevenson's safe being opened would refute allegations of a robbery and the feds would never be able to prove otherwise. In a separate instance, Jenkins remembered he had sent text messages hounding Rayam to pay him $3,500; he told the others to say that they had been making $500 wagers over Madden football video game matches. When he wasn't urging them to stick together, Jenkins blamed the unit's troubles on Rayam, saying he should accept responsibility for stolen money.

But mostly there was a sense of dread. Jenkins fretted that his phone had been tapped and worried about the kind of evidence authorities might have because of that. "I've been doin' so much stuff outside of work," Hendrix recalled Jenkins saying. "I'm done."

Jenkins reached out to attorneys for representation. Among them: Ivan Bates, the same man who had represented so many of Jenkins's victims. Bates declined because of those conflicts.

Wise and Hines, the prosecutors who would be handling the case, sat back and waited to see if any of the officers would come to them seeking a deal. Ward was the first to reach out through his attorney, followed by Rayam, whom the prosecutors spoke to first. Two others, Hendrix and Gondo, followed. Within weeks, four out of the seven charged were ready to spill.

For a few months, the prosecutors made daily trips to county jails to meet with the officers. Wise and Hines let them set the tone. As the officers outlined crimes the authorities knew about—and ones that they did not—the prosecutors felt a sense of relief as their case was being confirmed and fortified.

Some of the officers said the corruption was widespread, which bothered Sieracki, the Internal Affairs sergeant who had previously worked drugs.

"I didn't do this stuff, and the people I worked with didn't do it," Sieracki said later. "I thought back about whether I'd even suspected anyone was doing anything near what they're doing, and I never had any interaction [like] that."

But these officers were opening a portal into the hidden world. Wise was struck by their lax attitude toward the drugs they had come across—they "threw drugs away all the time. [They] just don't submit them. What we were told is that you drive along Interstate 83 and throw it out the window because it's a pain in the ass to submit the paperwork."

Wise said the officers "still saw themselves as good police officers. There was cognitive dissonance between these roles."

The officers started revealing not just the things that they had done but things others had done or told them about. Gondo told authorities about Rayam's 2014 home invasion of the pigeon store owners, which Rayam himself confirmed. It was a case not previously on the investigators' radar, and Rayam gave the names of his accomplices.

Rayam and Gondo also admitted they had taken part in the home invasion of Aaron Anderson, the incident that had sparked the whole investigation after Clewell's GPS was found on Anderson's car. McDougall's crazy theory was right, after all. The officers said the robbery had been proposed by "Twan"—Antoine Washington—who had heard that Anderson had $100,000 cash on him. Gondo brought the plot to Rayam, knowing Rayam had broken into homes before to carry out robberies. "Gondo had called me and asked me if I wanted to do it. And I told him, 'Yeah, I'll do it,'" Rayam said later. He was the one who stuck a gun in the face of Anderson's girlfriend, while Gondo stayed outside as a lookout. They said Clewell had no clue what his tracker was being used for—the detectives had only told him they were "looking into something."

Hendrix told the agents he had been trying to get away from Jenkins after learning he was likely dealing drugs. Just a few months into his time on the SES squad, Jenkins had asked Hendrix if he had any relatives who could sell drugs. Hendrix told investigators that he later saw Jenkins heat-sealing a bag that contained drugs, and said Ward had told him that he overheard Jenkins on the phone setting up what sounded like a drug transaction.

Meanwhile, Hersl's family was trying to make a public case that he was being unjustly prosecuted. Jerome Hersl visited the Harford County Council and said that if cops like his younger brother were deterred from doing their jobs, crime would spread throughout the region. "The drug dealers control the streets of Baltimore City," he said. "Do drug dealers have political boundaries? How long will it take before they control the streets of Harford County?" He said prosecutors were using flimsy evidence and jail to coerce a plea. "Is this America?" he asked, with no hint of irony.

By late June 2017, the prosecutors had enough new information from the cooperating officers to bring a superseding indictment—more charges—against the officers still fighting the case: Jenkins, Hersl, and Taylor.

And they now had the ammo to indict an eighth officer: Gondo and Rayam both implicated their supervisor prior to Jenkins, Thomas Allers, with taking cash during search warrants. One robbery allegedly involved Allers's adult son, who they said came on a ride-along and got a cut of stolen cash. They also told of another instance that had been missed by the wiretap in April 2016: the officers had waited for a man named Davon Robinson to leave his home, then stopped him for driving on a suspended license. After giving him a citation, they had gone back to Robinson's house and knocked on the door, where, the officers would later claim in court papers, his girlfriend had allowed them to enter and search. In an upstairs bedroom, the officers had found a loaded Ruger 9mm handgun with the serial number removed, Rayam wrote in his report. They had arrested Robinson on gun charges.

The report made no mention of something else they had collected from his house that day: $10,000, which turned out to be money Robinson needed to pay back a drug debt. In the drug world, where ripoffs carry consequences, an offense report documenting that money was seized by police might cut someone a break. In this case, Robinson had had nothing to point to and would very likely have been suspected of lying.

A few months later, Robinson was sitting in his car outside of his grandmother's house. His girlfriend was in a separate car with their three-year-old daughter when a man wearing a hoodie on a blazing hot day approached. They made eye contact as he continued past her car, then pulled out a silver gun and fired into Robinson's car, killing him.

Allers, who had been transferred to a DEA task force as the FBI investigation was getting started, had been suspended as a precaution since the first round of indictments. He rebuffed requests to cooperate and maintained to those close to him that he was innocent; eventually he went on stress medical leave. Allers was indicted by a grand jury on August 24, 2017, on racketeering and robbery charges. Among the charged officers' colleagues in law enforcement, Allers's indictment seemed to be the biggest shock.

The feds were also reaching back further into the past to mine historical allegations of corruption. When the GTTF officers were arrested, authorities had wondered about BB guns found in their vehicles. The cooperating officers later explained how Jenkins had warned them to have something to plant if they ever found themselves in a jam. "He said just in case something happens and you need to get yourself out of a situation, like—'cause basically we have wives and kids that need us—so basically to protect yourself if something was to occur," Hendrix said later.

IT HAD BEEN SEVEN years since Burley's encounter with Jenkins had landed him in federal prison. He was in an Oklahoma facility when he heard the news of the officers' arrests. He soon received a message over the federal prison email system from Brent Matthews, who had served out his own sentence related to the 2010 case in which drugs were reported to have been found in their vehicle following the deadly crash. Matthews told Burley that Jenkins had been among those charged in the new police racketeering case. "It's a possibility you may be coming home from this," he told Burley.

Burley waited to see if authorities would contact him, until a cellmate told him he needed to be proactive. "You've got to move on it now—it's going on right now," the cellmate urged.

Burley, who was moved to another prison in West Virginia that summer, had been sending letters to attorneys, hoping to secure legal representation, when the guards came to him.

"Pack up, you're on the move."

In August 2017, six months after the GTTF indictments, Burley was transported from West Virginia to the Supermax jail in Baltimore. He was there a couple of days before being transported to the federal courthouse, where he met with Wise and Hines.

To his surprise, Burley didn't have to explain his story or plead his innocence. "You don't have to say anything," they said to him. "We already know that they set you up. We already know how they did it."

All of the cooperating officers had told the FBI that Jenkins had relayed to them versions of a similar story—of an incident years earlier when he was working on another squad. It involved a car crash and an elderly man's death, and drugs that had been planted. It did not take federal investigators long to determine it was Burley's case.

Soon Burley was sitting in front of a grand jury, walking the panel through what had happened. He told them about the missed time with his family, and how he had never met his grandchildren. He cried; so did the grand jurors.

Within a few weeks, Burley was summoned to a courtroom for a sealed proceeding, with printer paper taped over the windows on the courtroom doors and his family required to stay outside. The prosecutors laid out the allegations to a judge and asked that Burley be released as they continued to build a case. The judge obliged, and Burley walked out wearing a disposable prison jumpsuit. He embraced his granddaughters for the first time.

"It was amazing," Burley recalled. "They were so accepting of me."

JENKINS, TOO, HAD ENGAGED the feds for a proffer. Most of the officers' proffers were a prelude to a plea. But Jenkins maintained his innocence on certain accusations the authorities considered to be verified. Among them was the Burley case: He conceded that drugs had been planted that day, but he blamed it on another officer involved in the arrest.

The feds began to reach out to other officers who had been there that day. Ryan Guinn and Sean Suiter were the other two officers who'd swooped in on Burley. Investigators had contacted Guinn in the early stages of the GTTF investigation, in late 2015, for information about Gondo. Since then, there'd been eight cops indicted, four who had agreed to plead guilty with a fifth on the way. But Jenkins, who had since emerged as the chief target, wasn't yet one of them. Now, nearly two years later, it was time for Jensen and Sieracki to pay Guinn another visit.

Among their questions for Guinn: Who had planted the drugs at the scene that day?

CHAPTER NINETEEN

HARLEM PARK

SEAN SUITER HAD COME a long way since his days as a drug cop. The forty-three-year-old army vet, who had served in Iraq from 2005 to 2007, had swapped plainclothes for a trenchcoat, moving to the district detective unit, where he investigated nonfatal shootings, robberies, and other serious crimes.

"The writing was on the wall early in his career that [Suiter] was going to ascend the ranks in any path he chose," said Major Martin Bartness. In late 2015, amid the city's surge in killings, Suiter was called up to the homicide unit, where, as usual for him, he was quick to make friends. "He was not only a good cop, he was smart and smiled a lot," recalled retired sergeant Rick Willard. "Everyone that worked with him loved him. Even when you were down he would smile with his mischievous smile and make everyone happy and feel at ease." His partner in the homicide unit, Jonathan Jones, recalled once being on the street with Suiter when someone shouted for him. It was a man Suiter used to chase around the Western District. The man was now employed, and he thanked Suiter for the way he had treated him in the past.

On November 15, 2017, Suiter and Detective David Bomenka ventured out into the Harlem Park neighborhood of the city's west side. Suiter knew the area well from both eras of his career—he'd worked drug cases and shootings here. It was their second visit in as many days; Suiter had tapped Bomenka the day before to accompany him as he followed up on a triple homicide that had occurred in December 2016. In that case, the killer had burst into a home in the 900 block of Bennett Place on the city's west side and had gunned down three people. The home was said to be a "hangout" for the powerful Black Guerrilla Family gang, and leads had been sparse. Bomenka, who had joined the unit just five months earlier, also had a pending case that had taken place in the area and was trying to find one of his witnesses as well.

The 900 block of Bennett Place is just west of downtown, sitting near the mouth of the city's infamous "Highway to Nowhere," an expressway that was started in the 1970s to get suburbanites in and out of the city more quickly but was aborted after about a mile was built. Hundreds of people were displaced as a result of the effort, creating a physical gulf between neighborhoods. To the east of Bennett Place is a community of detached homes with green grassy yards, called Heritage Crossing. It was built on the site of the infamous Murphy Homes: high-rise apartments that were lorded over by the city's biggest players in the drug trade for years until they were torn down in 1999. Just forty feet away, across Fremont Avenue, stand the decrepit, mostly boarded-up row homes of Bennett Place. In the previous four years, eleven people had been shot or killed at that intersection alone. Police set up a floodlight to deter criminal activity and at one point, in an act of desperation, barricaded the block and stationed an officer there around the clock.

Suiter and Bomenka had been out for hours, canvassing various locations around Bennett Place. It was nearing 4 P.M., and Suiter was behind the wheel of an unmarked Nissan Altima, with Bomenka riding shotgun. Suiter's phone rang; he answered and told the person on the other end that he couldn't talk.

As they turned onto Bennett Place, Bomenka said later, both of them noticed what appeared to be a man in a black jacket with a white stripe, crouching in the alley. They didn't know who he was or what he was doing, but they decided to talk to him. By the time they got out of the car and entered the alley, there was no one there. Bomenka came across a pile of trash and wondered if they had somehow mistaken it for the man in the jacket.

Suiter suggested they drive around and come back and see if the person returned. They visited his old post, on Brice Street, and then returned to Bennett Place.

"There's the guy right there," Suiter told Bomenka. Bomenka didn't see anyone, but he said he was willing to follow his more experienced colleague's instincts. Now it was starting to get dark. The detectives got out of the car again and walked down an adjacent alley. Suiter's phone was ringing again, but he ignored the calls. They walked back up the alley, then emerged through a vacant lot back onto Bennett Place.

Their shift ended at 5 P.M.; Bomenka had an evening date and wanted to finish up, but Suiter for some reason was interested in finding out if there was someone in the alley.

This cat-and-mouse stuff wasn't what button-down homicide detectives typically engaged in, but others would later say that it wasn't unusual given Suiter's pedigree working drugs, which more often involved getting one's hands dirty. Still, it didn't make sense to Bomenka that someone was there and they kept missing him.

"I'm just going to wait here to see if he pops back out," Suiter said, according to Bomenka. He directed Bomenka to walk out to the end of the street, taking a position where he would be able to see if anyone emerged from a different opening in the alley. Suiter, meanwhile, stood at the rear of a white van parked next to the vacant lot. Some moments passed. Then, with Bomenka waiting at the corner, Suiter gestured to him. It was a motion that Bomenka interpreted to be Suiter waving him back over, as if to say, "Let's go."

Suddenly, Suiter unholstered his gun and dipped into the lot and out of Bomenka's view.

"Stop! Stop! Police!" Bomenka heard Suiter yell.

Then, gunshots.

Bomenka ran toward the sound and saw Suiter lying face down twenty feet into the lot. Bomenka believed he was still hearing shots, but he said he saw no one. Afraid the shooter was still nearby, Bomenka turned and ran back to the street, fumbled around for his cellphone—he hadn't brought his police radio with him—and dialed 911 to call for help. The alert tone—"wee-wa-wee-wa-wee-wa"—sounded over the police radio, and the dispatcher called out the code for an officer in distress. "Signal 13. Signal 13. Bennett and Fremont, Bennett and Fremont, for the Signal 13 in the Central."

It's not uncommon to hear a "Signal 13" go across the air several times over the course of a day, but the vast majority end up being false alarms. This time the dispatcher commanded "Let's go," reinforcing that this time the signal was alerting to something real. "Bennett and Fremont. Caller reporting that the partner got shot, no description, no further."

Once backup had arrived, Bomenka ventured into the lot with the responding officers. One drew his gun to provide cover as Bomenka rushed to Suiter's motionless body. They rolled Suiter over, revealing his gun on the ground; he had been shot once in the head and was unconscious. His glasses had slipped from his face. In his left hand, he was still clutching his police radio.

Bomenka began performing chest compressions, but officers made the decision to not wait for an ambulance and instead put Suiter into a squad car and rushed him to the University of Maryland Shock Trauma Center, about a mile away. In the frenzy to get to the hospital, the officer driving the car backed into another police car; then, as they crossed Martin Luther King Boulevard near the hospital, he collided with another vehicle. A nearby ambulance collected Suiter and completed the transport.

During the trip, Suiter's cellphone buzzed in his pocket. It was a text message from his attorney.

> You have grand jury by subpoena [tomorrow] at 1 pm
> in federal court. And a meeting at 11 am at USAO
> [the U.S. Attorney's Office].

Then another:

> Dude, what the fuck is going on?

POLICE COMMANDERS POURED INTO the scene at Bennett Place, and a six-block area around it was locked down, with residents prevented from entering or leaving. Bomenka was asked to describe the shooter, but he said he hadn't seen anybody since the man with the striped jacket more than a half hour earlier. When he had turned the corner into the lot, he said, he'd seen Suiter's body hitting the ground and a puff of gunsmoke in the air above him—but no gunman fleeing. "Sean was calling me to come over, he ran over and I came around the corner and shots were fired. I was watching the other side," he said. "I didn't even see where the shots were coming [from]."

The uncertainty led to fear that the shots had been fired out a window or from a rooftop. The dispatcher instructed, "Everybody take cover. Get away from the windows. We don't know where the shots came from." The shooter could be holed up inside of a home, and officers backed off from the block. SWAT units were called and in the hours to come would begin making entry into nearby buildings to search for the suspect. During that time, homicide investigators were kept from the crime scene.

Even with the consent decree in place, officers did not always activate their body cameras as they searched citizens and their homes. A woman who lived across the street from the lot said officers had asked if she lived with anyone and, when they heard a noise upstairs (it was her dog), entered with guns drawn and searched for ten minutes. Others were patted down without reasonable articulable suspicion; later, the consent decree monitor said this showed "a supervisory or training failure to make clear that the circumstances . . . did not automatically justify a pat-down of anyone at or inside the perimeter."

Word traveled quickly within the police department that Suiter was the victim and was gravely wounded. Outside the Shock Trauma Center, Commissioner Kevin Davis could be seen huddling with the heads of the main federal law enforcement agencies—the FBI, DEA, and ATF.

It would be hours before Suiter's wife, Nicole, arrived from southern Pennsylvania, where they'd decided to raise their five children. The first phone call came from a friend, whose husband was also on the force. She told Nicole that Sean had been in an accident—he was okay, she said, but Nicole needed to come to the hospital immediately.

Pennsylvania state troopers picked her up, and they, too, assured her that Sean was fine. But they were driving fast, with their lights and sirens on. She remembers walking into the hospital, where there were scores of city officials gathered. Someone approached her and said, "He was a good man."

As a reporter for *The Baltimore Sun* covering the shooting, I was among a throng of reporters and officials waiting outside Shock Trauma for information on Suiter's condition. A number I did not recognize came up on my cellphone, and I answered. The hushed voice of a woman was on the other end. It was someone whom I had encountered while working on an article, years earlier. We had not kept in touch, but I remembered her. She was telling me that Suiter was due to testify against a dirty cop the next day.

"It was a setup," she said of the shooting. She was whispering, yet sounded frantic, possibly manic. She said Suiter was supposed to testify against dirty cops. "This was not random. It was a deliberate setup against this detective. Nothing here at all random, period!"

After listening to her insist that Suiter's death was an inside job, I hung up and tried to take stock of what she'd said. It was clear that the feds were still pursuing corruption within the ranks: By then, nine current or former city officers had been charged in the growing GTTF case, including a former officer now working for the Philadelphia Police Department whose indictment became public the day before Suiter was shot. The announcement from the U.S. Attorney's Office referred to the investigation as "expanding."

The possibility that Suiter had been killed to prevent him from going to court sent a chill through me, but what court hearing involving corrupt police could she be referring to? There was nothing on the docket for the GTTF case; the pending grand jury proceedings were secret and unknown to the public at the time.

After 9 P.M., a group including the mayor, the police commissioner, the state's attorney, and the hospital's physician in chief gathered to address the media outside. Dr. Thomas Scalea said Suiter was clinging to life.

Davis told reporters the "investigation is very fluid, it's ongoing, it's complex," and said police were looking for a man with a black jacket with a white stripe. "That description could change, but that's all we know now," he said, calling the shooter a "cold, callous killer.

"This is a dangerous profession, this is a dangerous job. Police officers know at any time they could confront someone who wants to do them harm, and that's exactly what happened tonight."

Wise, the federal prosecutor, was in Washington, D.C., when his phone buzzed with the news that the man he was taking in front of a grand jury the next morning had been shot in the head.

Two years later, Wise, who knew things the public did not yet know, recalled his reaction that night: that Suiter had taken his own life.

RYAN GUINN SHOWED UP as scheduled the next day to testify in front of the grand jury.

"I hate to be the bearer of bad news, but Sean just died," Guinn remembers Sieracki telling him.

Guinn kept his composure during his testimony, but when one of the grand jurors asked him a question about Suiter he started bawling.

Suiter's body remained at the hospital for another two days to harvest his organs, delaying a formal autopsy, but emergency room doctors told investigators they believed Suiter had been shot in the left side of his head. Because the gun was found on the ground next to his right side, it was believed the killer had dropped the weapon while fleeing. The area around Bennett Place remained locked down, with residents asked to show ID and officers taking down their information.

At the homicide unit, Bomenka was asked by fellow detectives investigating the case to describe the suspect.

"Physical description: Height, weight. Did you see anything?" asked Detective Joe Brown.

"I didn't see anything, Joe," Bomenka said. "I didn't hear a car speeding off. I didn't hear anybody running."

A reward of $215,000—the largest in memory—was being offered for information leading to an arrest. One person called Metro Crime Stoppers and gave the name of someone they said was a "known hitman"; he was brought in, and lawyered up. A woman called and said her nephew was the suspect—she later said she had made the story up. Another person called 911 and said a group of men had been overheard talking about the shooting, with one saying he did it; all were taken into the homicide section, interviewed, and released. There were other easily dismissable tips: one caller to Metro Crime Stoppers said Commissioner Kevin Davis was the suspect, while other callers said they had a "vision from God" or had psychic powers.

The DEA got wiretaps for every phone connected to drug activity around Bennett Place that they could get, in hopes of picking up any revealing chatter that might aid the investigation, but they only heard dealers lamenting how the police presence was affecting sales. Acting on an uncorroborated tip about a possible suspect, heavily armed SWAT teams raided a nearby home, ordering everyone on the ground and rushing into an upstairs bathroom where a six-year-old boy was showering. The occupants were taken to headquarters for questioning. The BPD had also, without a warrant, raided a vacant home next to the lot where Suiter was shot—and found evidence in a completely unrelated killing that had occurred a year earlier.

Each day, drips of information were released as police pleaded for help: Davis told reporters police had found evidence that suggested the shooter was injured, but he declined to elaborate. He said police were searching emergency rooms and doctors' offices for "anyone with an unexplained injury." Next, he confirmed that Suiter had gotten off at least one shot before he was killed. He said there was also evidence that Suiter had been engaged in a "brief and violent" struggle with his assailant, but he declined to elaborate on what had led him to that conclusion.

A crucial fact changed a few days later, after the formal autopsy: The inspection of his wound showed Suiter had not been shot from the front and left of his head, as ER doctors had believed, but rather from the back-right side, and at close range. Crime scene investigators had found three bullet casings but no bullets to that point and had been searching for slugs on the basis of the direction they believed the bullet had traveled. The lot had been divided into a grid, and nearly every tile of the grid had been dug through—except the one where blood had pooled in the soil. There they located a bullet embedded in the dirt. It would later test positive for Suiter's DNA.

"I'm very encouraged by the recovery of this evidence," Davis told reporters five days after the shooting. "I think it's going to help us identify the killer. I really do."

The official ruling from the state medical examiner's office on Suiter's manner of death was homicide. Yet some police department investigators had already begun to murmur about whether the evidence pointed to something different. They believed it was not only possible but likely that Suiter had shot himself.

If Suiter and the gunman had been engaged in a violent struggle, as the commissioner put it, could the person really have gotten away without Bomenka seeing him? There was no ballistic evidence indicating a second gun had been fired—the three recovered shell casings were from a .40 caliber Glock, the same type of weapon as Suiter's police-issue gun, which had fired three shots. The new angle of the shooting, from the right, was Suiter's gun hand.

On the afternoon before Thanksgiving, seven days after Suiter was shot, Davis confirmed at a news conference that Suiter had been killed the day before he was supposed to appear before a grand jury investigating the Gun Trace Task Force.

"I am now aware of Detective Suiter's pending federal grand jury testimony surrounding an event that occurred several years ago with BPD officers who were federally indicted in March of this year," Davis said, reading from a prepared statement.

Though Davis said he was "now aware," he had known the information about the grand jury testimony since the morning after Suiter's shooting, yet had chosen not to disclose it. Davis said later that he had been assured by the FBI that Suiter was not a target of the investigation, so Davis considered the information inflammatory in the highly charged environment.

"Just because the guy was scheduled to testify before the grand jury next day, that's some chickenshit move of me to say, 'Let me give you this conspiracy theory,'" Davis said later. "I wasn't gonna stomp on this man's grave based on info that did not make me feel uneasy at all about Suiter."

For a week, the city had been on edge over the killing of an on-duty cop, and despite the kind of aggressive all-hands investigation that only cop killings can draw, investigators had seemingly no leads on a suspect. Questions were swirling. Now there was a direct link to the ongoing corruption scandal, which raised new tantalizing questions and provided fertile ground for conspiracy theories. I had to be skeptical of there being a plot behind Suiter's death, but I remained haunted by my caller who had insisted he was "set up." After all, she accurately had told me that he was due to testify in the unfolding case, at a time when no one was supposed to know about that proceeding.

Around town and on social media, some were now openly speculating that Bomenka, Suiter's partner that day, must have been involved. Commissioner Davis dismissed claims of conspiracy, noting that Bomenka's movements had been captured on a street surveillance camera and later on body camera footage and appeared to back his account that he had sought cover after the shots were fired. People who'd spoken with the detective said he was traumatized by the experience.

The reason for Suiter's appearance before the grand jury remained unclear to the public, and Davis said only that there was "no information that has been communicated to me that Det. Suiter was anything other than a stellar detective, great friend, loving husband and dedicated father."

Then came another bombshell, when the department publicly confirmed that they believed Suiter was shot with his own gun. Whoever shot him would have had to have disarmed him.

SUITER HAD A HERO'S funeral on November 29, two weeks after the shooting. Hundreds of officers from across the state descended on a megachurch in Northeast Baltimore for the service. Among the pallbearers was Det. Eric Perez, one of Suiter's best friends, who had been assigned as one of the primary detectives investigating Suiter's death.

Davis, wearing his dress blues, used his own remarks at the funeral to push back on critics of the department: "Suiter gave, and the Baltimore Police Department gives each and every day. It's time for the local and national narrative to start reflecting that reality," he said.

Within the department, however, there were growing concerns that Davis had misled the public by misrepresenting key pieces of evidence in his remarks to the press following Suiter's death. For example, when he said that Suiter had been engaged in a "violent struggle," he was referring to dirt on Suiter's pants leg that to others just as easily could have come from him falling to the ground after being shot. When Davis said that police believed the suspect had been wounded, he was referring to two spots of blood found in the vacant lot that did not belong to Suiter—one of which police said later was determined to belong to an animal, and the other connected to a drug user who had an alibi. The description of a suspect wearing a black jacket with a white stripe was someone Bomenka said they had seen a half hour earlier—and he wasn't even sure of that—making it hardly someone who could be declared the suspect. Some investigators were starting to believe Suiter had taken his own life and staged it to look like a homicide. Davis brushed off the theory.

"There's possibilities, and there's probabilities," he would later say.

The day after the funeral, Wise and Hines obtained a new grand jury indictment against Jenkins, alleging a cover-up in the Umar Burley case. The heroin found in Burley's car—heretofore cited as the reason Burley fled, prompting a fatal crash that had resulted in a manslaughter conviction—had been planted after the fact by Jenkins, the indictment said.

Suiter never made it to the grand jury room, but the indictment painted him as unaware of what had taken place, saying Jenkins had sent Suiter to find the planted drugs because he was "'clueless' or words to that effect." The new indictment charged Jenkins with counts of "destruction, alteration or falsification of records in a federal investigation" and "aiding and abetting deprivation of rights under color of law," alleging that Jenkins had written a statement of probable cause asserting that Burley and his passenger Brent Matthews had heroin, when actually he knew the drugs had been planted.

Though Guinn wasn't identified by name, it was clear from comparing the indictment and Jenkins's original statement that federal prosecutors had relied on Guinn to build their account. Guinn would later say that as far as he knew, the Burley arrest was "legit" and that Suiter appeared to have recovered the drugs straight-up—though Guinn also noted Jenkins's comments at the scene and his strange behavior afterward. Guinn was not implicated in misconduct or the cover-up, but because of his proximity to the case the police department suspended Guinn from his role at the training academy, as a precaution.

On November 29, Baltimore congressman Elijah E. Cummings

pressed the director of the FBI to make the investigation of Suiter's death "a top priority" and called on the federal agency to "do everything" in its power to help. Commissioner Davis had already been told privately that the FBI wouldn't take on the case, but in an effort to apply public pressure Davis sent a formal letter of his own. Mayor Catherine E. Pugh, members of the city council, Governor Larry Hogan, and police union president Lieutenant Gene Ryan all said they supported the FBI taking over. The FBI declined, saying there was no evidence of a connection to an FBI matter. In its announcement, the bureau multiple times used the word *death* instead of *murder* or *killing*.

A FEW WEEKS LATER, Burley and Matthews walked into a federal courtroom in suits, accompanied by their new lawyers. Wise and Hines read from the fresh Jenkins indictment and asked the judge, Richard D. Bennett, who had years earlier sentenced the two men, to vacate their convictions. Bennett stepped down from the bench and strode across the courtroom to shake the hands of Burley and Matthews. "I'm very sorry," he said to them.

Bennett had signed some of the warrants before the GTTF case became public, so he had insight into the wider corruption case. "I'm afraid this is not over yet," Bennett said.

Outside the courthouse, Burley spoke out for the first time. He had new allegations to bring forth, claiming that Jenkins, Guinn, and Suiter hadn't just chased him and planted drugs that day in 2010; his attorney said that Suiter had rammed Burley's car from behind and that the officers had jumped out wearing black face masks with guns drawn.

"For all these years, the scorn has been on Mr. Burley, and living under this dark cloud of taking the life of another, which he truly takes to heart, but which in essence falls on these police officers," said the attorney, Steve Silverman. "*All* of these police officers," he reiterated, referring not just to Jenkins but to Guinn and Suiter as well. "They were a rogue gang of criminals."

CHAPTER TWENTY

GUILTY

ON DECEMBER 13, 2017, a forty-eight-year-old woman drove her SUV toward the power station at the end of Carroll Island Road, in the Bowleys Quarters area of Baltimore County. She then turned right onto Seneca Park Road, passing through grassy lots on either side, the length of two football fields, a quiet street of waterfront residences where nearly every home had its own dock. It was dark when she pulled into Donald Stepp's driveway and sat with her headlights on.

Stepp opened his front door, walked out to the car, and climbed into the passenger seat. A few minutes later he got out and went back into his house.

As the woman driving the SUV pulled away, county police followed close behind.

The cops stayed behind her for five miles as she traveled west, then pulled her over after she rolled through a stop sign. Veteran county drug detective Christopher Toland walked to the passenger side and began talking to her. As he looked inside, he saw pieces of copper-colored wire mesh—commonly used as a filter in glass pipes when smoking crack—scattered throughout the vehicle. The woman said she didn't use drugs and invited the police to search her car. She stepped out and nervously started pulling items out of her purse and handing them to the officer, before suddenly dropping to her knees and trying to shove something from the purse down the back of her pants. It was a yellow envelope containing a half ounce of cocaine.

This was no chance encounter. A month earlier, Toland and another detective had been summoned to the U.S. Attorney's Office in downtown Baltimore. There they met with Hines and Wise, and detectives Sieracki and Jared Stern. Hines told them federal authorities had records showing phone calls between Jenkins and Stepp that had taken place around the same time as, or directly after, robberies Jenkins had committed.

"The cooperators all talked about it—that Jenkins had this shadowy white guy who was a bail bondsman that would show up," Wise said later. "They knew Jenkins had some guy who would get keys cut, to get into cars; that had GPS trackers, to track people; that had access to license plate readers. Stuff to bounty hunt."

Investigators now realized Gondo hadn't been funneling drugs to the Shropshire crew as they had initially believed—instead, the cooperating GTTF officers said Jenkins often was the one who kept drugs, and the prosecutors now theorized that Jenkins was using Stepp to sell them. If the county detectives were able to build a case on Stepp, Hines told them, the U.S. Attorney's Office would take the case federal and see if they could turn Stepp into a cooperator against Jenkins.

The county police had previously investigated the bail bondsman: over the years, informants had reported to police that Stepp was dealing large amounts of cocaine, but the case had been passed from detective to detective, and intermittent attempts at surveillance had produced no results. And there was that odd sighting in August 2016, when county officers reported unexpectedly seeing Jenkins and Stepp together at the scene of a search warrant. The two had scurried away as county officers began questioning Stepp's identity.

Toland had received his own tip about Stepp in the summer of 2017, but the informant had been unable to provide an active phone number for him. Toland did occasional surveillance, but that too hadn't led to anything substantive. Just days before meeting with Wise and Hines, he had conducted a "trash pull" in hopes of finding drug packaging or paraphernalia in the garbage outside Stepp's home. No luck.

After meeting with the U.S. attorney, the county cops stepped up their efforts. A group of nine officers from the county vice and narcotics unit set up surveillance outside Stepp's home. Then, on December 1, the FBI installed a camera focused on his home and gave Toland access to watch it remotely from a tablet.

When Toland arrested the woman leaving Stepp's house with drugs a couple of weeks later, police finally had enough to obtain a search warrant. That same night, just after midnight, the vice unit crept up to Stepp's home, the burbling of the nearby creek the only other noise. They climbed a flight of steps to the main entrance and knocked. "Police, search warrant."

The officers saw Stepp in the kitchen, standing still and contemplating. It had been years since he'd been in prison. He'd built a new life. His five-year-old special-needs daughter was asleep in a crib upstairs. Now officers were breaking open his front door with a battering ram.

As the cops made their way through the home, they found tens of thousands of dollars in drugs—cocaine, crack, heroin, and Ecstasy—in an electrical box that was screwed shut and stashed under a bed.

Stepp had to know his time might come—in a desk drawer, investigators found a printout of the superseding indictment against Jenkins, Hersl, and Taylor. Yet he kept dealing, even keeping the drugs in his own home.

Stepp's bail was set at $100,000, and he was able to post it and walk out of jail the next morning.

By 8:31 A.M. that same morning, Hines already had an indictment typed up and emailed it to the detectives asking them whether they would be available to go in front of a grand jury after lunch. Before the end of the day, they had obtained a federal indictment against Stepp on drug charges that carried a mandatory minimum of ten years in prison and a maximum of life behind bars. He was reapprehended the next day.

Stepp flipped immediately and completely. The feds had theorized he was selling drugs for Jenkins, but they had no evidence. Now, just weeks before Jenkins was set to go to trial, Stepp was outlining years of drug dealing and other crimes with Jenkins in hopes of reducing his sentence. He had saved pictures of himself committing some of those crimes, along with pictures of him and Jenkins at Delaware Park Casino, at the Super Bowl, and goofing around inside police headquarters. Stepp even told the cops they had missed another three kilograms of cocaine when they searched his home and told them where to find it. He told them about an expensive watch Jenkins had given Stepp after stealing it from a drug suspect: Stepp had thrown it into the creek behind his house. An FBI dive team plunged into the waters and recovered it—just where Stepp said it would be.

Stepp estimated that he had sold $1 million worth of drugs with Jenkins, at pure profit.

And Jenkins's car that was reported stolen from his driveway and found stripped down in the woods with "Fuck you" written on the hood? Stepp said Jenkins told him he had had it destroyed because he didn't want to make payments on it anymore—some casual insurance fraud dropped in with the robberies and drug dealing.

The prosecutors thought they already had evidence of a startling array of crimes committed by Jenkins. Stepp's confession opened a whole new dimension.

FOUR OFFICERS HAD PLEADED GUILTY, and the three others—Jenkins, Daniel Hersl, and Marcus Taylor—were nearing trial scheduled to start in late January 2018.

But on January 3, three weeks after Stepp was charged, and after considerable negotiations between prosecutors and his defense attorney about the statement of facts, Jenkins agreed to plead guilty.

At a rearraignment hearing two days later, Jenkins stood and raised his right hand, like so many people he had arrested over the years, and spelled his name for the clerk.

"How do you wish to plead to counts one through six of the superseding indictment?" asked Judge Catherine C. Blake.

"Guilty, ma'am," Jenkins said.

Judge Blake read through the long list of crimes Jenkins was pleading guilty to, from racketeering to robbery to illegal searches and seizures to drug dealing. His plea agreement cited many crimes that had not been previously disclosed—he admitted he had stolen dirt bikes from people riding them illegally on city streets and then sold them through an associate, and that he had swiped twelve pounds of high-grade marijuana intercepted by law enforcement from the mail. Then there were the crimes he'd committed with Stepp. It took several minutes for Blake to wind through the depths of the plea.

"Do you agree, sir, that the statement of facts is correct and you did what it says in there you did?" Blake asked.

There was only one thing Jenkins wanted to correct: Blake had said that Jenkins was "responsible for having heroin planted in that vehicle," referring to Umar Burley in 2010. Of all the terrible things Jenkins was admitting, he objected to the characterization of his role in the Burley case.

"He's not acknowledging that he planted the drugs," Jenkins's attorney, Steve Levin, told Blake, "although he's acknowledging that he authored a false report with respect to another officer planting those drugs." Was Jenkins accusing Suiter? Or someone else? The claim went unacknowledged by prosecutors, and Blake wound down the hearing. His sentencing would take place at a later date.

"Any questions at all, sir, for me or your lawyer about your guilty pleas or the terms of your plea agreement?" Blake asked.

"No ma'am," he said. "I'm ashamed of myself."

CHAPTER TWENTY-ONE
COPS AND ROBBERS

"THIS IS A DYSFUNCTIONAL police department," Police Commissioner Davis acknowledged in an interview days after Jenkins's plea. "I'm telling you that as a person who has seen what a healthy organization looks like. This is not one of them, but we're making huge strides in getting there."

Davis was fighting for his job. He'd taken over a few months after the death of Freddie Gray, an outsider trying to build enough bridges in the community to suppress more civil unrest as the court cases against the officers crumbled, while trying not to alienate an easily alienated police force whom he needed to combat the increased violence. The GTTF scandal had happened on his watch, but he had moved to end plainclothes policing and had come up with a plan for tracking the quality of gun cases and how they fared in court instead of just tallying arrests.

"We inherited a culture that looks at accountability as a four-letter word," he added. "And that's years and years of neglect—years and years of chasing the two H's, homicide and heroin.

"Should someone have known [about the GTTF officers]? Absolutely they should have known."

Two weeks later, on January 19, the Friday before the start of the trial of Marcus Taylor and Daniel Hersl, the two Gun Trace Task Force officers who had not pleaded guilty, Mayor Catherine Pugh fired Davis. She didn't cite the GTTF scandal or the handling of the Suiter case but instead referred to the continuing high rate of crime in the city. For the second time in three years, there had been 342 homicides, a per capita record. "Crime is now spilling out all over the city, and we've got to focus," Pugh told the media.

She named Darryl De Sousa, an agency veteran, as the next commissioner. It was a name the federal prosecutors had heard during their investigation.

But first, they had two Gun Trace Task Force detectives to put on trial.

Many details of the GTTF case had remained under wraps, with the officers' crimes tightly summarized in the indictments and plea agreements. Had Daniel Hersl and Marcus Taylor pleaded guilty like the others, it would have likely stayed that way. A trial required laying the evidence bare.

On the first day of trial, Wise stood up, buttoned his suit jacket, and walked to face the jurors. "In the course of this trial, you will go inside the Baltimore Police Department, inside the operations division, and into special elite units, including one called the Gun Trace Task Force where detectives and other senior officers operate, including these men, Defendant Daniel Hersl and Defendant Marcus Taylor," Wise said. "And the evidence will show that these men engaged in racketeering, specifically that they committed robberies and extortions and overtime fraud. . . . What these defendants did at its base was to abuse the trust placed in them as police officers, as senior officers assigned to elite units, to enrich themselves.

"The Gun Trace Task Force wasn't a unit that went rogue," Wise said. "It was a unit of detectives who had already gone rogue. . . . They were, simply put, both cops and robbers at the same time."

Hersl's attorney, William Purpura, was trying a novel defense strategy: He admitted that Hersl stole money, but he argued that an officer taking cash during an arrest was theft, not robbery, and therefore not a federal racketeering offense. As a law enforcement officer, he said, Hersl was authorized to seize money if he believed he had probable cause, and any money later pocketed was theft from the police department. Wise and Hines, "the Twin Towers of justice," over-charged the case as a conspiracy, he said.

The subsequent testimony of the cooperating officers revealed publicly, and for the first time, the depth of the misconduct carried out by the unit. Beyond robberies, they talked about racial profiling and warrantless stops as a normal part of their work. They talked about overtime fraud being widespread, with Ward naming a high-ranking Internal Affairs commander, who, prior to that assignment and while working in the plainclothes division, was the first official he'd heard employing the concept of "slash days." That was the term used when an officer received an unofficial paid day off as a reward for getting a gun.

At one point, two duffel bags were dragged to the middle of the courtroom floor and Hines started pulling items out. One contained black clothing and gloves and a mask. The other was full of tools. They'd been found during the search of Jenkins's van. Detective Evo-dio Hendrix, who had earlier pleaded guilty to racketeering, testified that Jenkins told his officers that "he had all that stuff just in case he ran into a monster or a big hit."

"And what is a monster?" Hines said. "What did you understand that to mean?"

"Someone with a lot of money or drugs," Hendrix said.

When Stepp took the stand, Hines displayed screenshots of his Amazon order history, showing he was the one who had purchased the tools and other gear contained in the duffel bags.

Stepp testified that he had committed several break-ins at Jen-kins's direction, including one in which another, unidentified Balti-more County police officer was a participant. He said he had once met a Dominican drug supplier at the Scores strip club and that Jen-kins had officers provide security. Stepp said he and Jenkins had once tracked Kenneth "Kenny Bird" Jackson, a strip club owner notorious for his past alleged ties to the drug world, and had broken into his silver Acura in a Sam's Club parking lot and stolen between $12,000 and $19,000.

"You—you!—broke into Kenny Bird Jackson's car?" Purpura asked, incredulously.

"No offense to Kenny Bird Jackson or any of the other people, but I didn't know who they were," Stepp said.

Prosecutors also brought in victims of the GTTF's crimes—drug dealers who normally would have been on the receiving end of trial testimony by cops. Protected by immunity, they admitted to dealing drugs and then walked jurors through their encounters with the task force. Oreese Stevenson, saying candidly that he didn't want to be there, told jurors that he had far more drugs than the GTTF officers had submitted as evidence.

Hines asked a man named Shawn Whiting, who said he was robbed of cash and drugs by Ward and Taylor in 2014, why he didn't make a complaint about being charged with a lesser amount of drugs than he knew he had.

"Mr. Whiting, why didn't you complain about the missing drugs?" Hines said.

"Who gonna complain about more extra drugs?" Whiting responded.

Whiting had, however, complained to internal affairs and the Department of Justice about stolen money, to no avail.

Ronald Hamilton, who had been grabbed while leaving a Home Depot with his wife, was shown the Rolex watch recovered by the FBI dive team in the creek behind Stepp's home.

"Is this the first time you've seen it since March twenty-second of 2016?" Wise asked.

"Yes."

The defense peppered Hamilton with questions about whether he was an active drug dealer. He insisted that he made his money gambling and selling cars, but a casino ledger showed minimal winnings or losses, and his own record of auto sales simply didn't add up. As Taylor's attorney pressed him about how he could afford such a nice house, Hamilton snapped.

"This right here destroyed my whole fuckin' family," Hamilton said. He apologized to the judge, but continued: "This destroyed my whole family. I am in a divorce process right now because of this bullshit. This destroyed my whole fuckin' family, man. You sit here asking me questions about a fuckin' house. My fuckin' wife stays in the fuckin' Walmart every fuckin' night until I come home. If you want to know that, worry about that. That's what the fuck's the matter in here, man. Everybody's life is destroyed, man. My house don't have nothing to do with this."

Rayam also broke down on the stand as jurors listened to a wiretapped phone conversation, in which Rayam's children's voices could be heard in the background of the call. He again got emotional when prosecutors played audio from the night in August when he and the other officers chased a suspect who then crashed his car into an oncoming vehicle.

"It was bad. It was real bad. It was—it was bad," Rayam said of the crash scene. "I wanted to go back just to check on 'em, and I wanted to go back because we can get in trouble. I mean, although I was doing so much wrong, it was just to a certain point where like too much is too much."

Hines asked why none of the officers stopped to help.

"Cause we were foolish. I don't know. We just didn't. . . . It was pretty bad. And—and it could have been any of us," he continued, turning to the jury. "It could have been any of you guys or my mother or father. And—but we just—we just didn't stop."

Gondo was the last of the cooperating officers to testify. On crossexamination, the defense attorneys drew out things from Gondo's proffer sessions. Gondo testified that his longtime partner Rayam had told him that his third shooting in 2009, which killed thirty-year-old Shawn Cannady, was unjustified and covered up. Cannady's vehicle hadn't bumped the leg of Rayam's partner as they said at the time, Gondo said he had been told.

"Fuck it, I just didn't want to chase him," Rayam said, according to Gondo.

He said the current deputy commissioner, Dean Palmere, had coached Rayam on what to tell investigators. Palmere denied the accusation as he announced his retirement midtrial.

One of Taylor's defense attorneys asked Gondo about comments he had made to the FBI about stealing money well before he was on the GTTF.

"You started talking about how you started taking money about ten years ago when you were on VCID?"

"That's correct."

"Okay. And it was you, Detective Suiter, Ward, Ivery, and Tariq Edwards—"

Suiter.

"That's correct," Gondo said.

"And so the five or six of you, you'd take money and split it out amongst yourselves, right?"

"That's correct."

Questions had swirled over Suiter's role in the Umar Burley drug-planting incident, and now one of the government's star witnesses was directly accusing Suiter of stealing money. Some believed the evidence suggested Suiter might have taken his own life, but with the feds saying he wasn't a target of the Burley investigation, it was unclear what he might have been afraid of. Gondo's accusations now raised the possibility that Suiter had more to hide: Could he have feared that prosecutors might eventually start looking at him for stealing money?

The trial wasn't about Sean Suiter, however, and the accusation wasn't explored further.

Suiter's family pushed back, with an uncle saying: "Sean has never done anything wrong in his life. People will say anything, so I don't pay no attention to what they say."

PROSECUTORS CALLED DETECTIVE JAMES Kostoplis as their final witness. He told of the night when Jenkins and Hersl took him for a ride and asked what he thought of stealing money from drug dealers. Every trial is a morality play, Wise explained later, and Kostoplis illustrated the path not taken by the corrupt officers.

"At some point during the career of these two men . . . they were given that exact same opportunity to make that choice," Hines told the jury in his closing argument. "And if 26-year-old James Kostoplis could stand up to Wayne Jenkins and 17-year veteran Daniel Hersl, then these two men certainly could have made that same choice. But they did not."

The trial had laid waste to what remained of the Baltimore Police Department's credibility. This wasn't a one-off, disputed incident or a case of one "bad apple"—the public had heard from officers themselves, who had come together into an elite and well-regarded unit, admitting to an array of pervasive misbehavior unobstructed for years by any systems designed to stop them.

The jury deliberated for about twelve hours over two days. When word came down that a verdict had been reached, spectators filed in and Hersl and Taylor were brought from lockup. Taylor leaned back in his chair, while Hersl, his hands clasped in front of his face, looked back at his family and exhaled deeply. Wise and Hines stood together. "Take this all in," Wise whispered to Hines. He told him to be proud of their effort regardless of the outcome.

The jurors were mostly white and mostly women. But they had selected as their foreperson the only young Black man among them. It seemed to be a symbolic gesture, given who had been the targets of the police squad.

As the foreperson announced the verdicts—guilty of racketeering, conspiracy, and robbery—Hersl's head dropped. There was little reaction among the spectators. Special Agent Jensen, sitting at a table behind the prosecutors, wasn't sure how to feel. It was the desired outcome, but she wasn't in a celebratory mood. "The whole thing was such a mess that it didn't really feel great at all," she said. "It was just kind of sad."

Not for those terrorized by the officers. Alex Hilton, thirty-eight, had attended the trial and said Hersl had arrested him multiple times years earlier. He was relieved: "Every time I see a police car or knocker car, I'm looking to see if he's in there. I can't get his face out of my mind."

Outside the courthouse, Wise and Hines stood with the acting U.S. attorney, who told reporters that the corruption probe of the Baltimore Police Department was ongoing.

FOLLOWING THE SENSATIONAL REVELATIONS at the trial, the new police commissioner, Darryl De Sousa, said he was creating an anticorruption unit to probe all of the claims arising out of the GTTF scandal. "Let me make it clear: I have ZERO TOLERANCE for corruption," De Sousa said in a statement. At the same time, in response to crime, he was moving to reinstate plainclothes units, for years the source of so many corruption scandals and complaints. De Sousa was a thirty-year veteran, and the agency had always relied on these units.

In mid-February, De Sousa said he was also appointing an outside panel of experts to review Suiter's death. While it was still officially classified as a homicide by the state medical examiner's office, the number of voices arguing Suiter had likely taken his own life was growing.

"Go where the evidence leads," De Sousa told the panel at its first meeting at police headquarters.

He would not see the work through.

Ward had told the federal investigators that Jenkins had once pulled over a female acquaintance of De Sousa and caught her with drugs and that Jenkins had let her go after a phone call with De Sousa. And it was De Sousa who had signed off on making Jenkins's discipline case go away in 2015.

Federal investigators had been looking into De Sousa and found that he had been cheating on his taxes for years. Wise and Hines brought federal income tax charges in May. City leaders at first tried to rally behind him, but he was pressured to resign and would eventually land in prison after pleading guilty to tax fraud. For the second time in four months, a police department on the ropes was looking for a new leader.

CHAPTER TWENTY-TWO

POSSIBILITIES AND PROBABILITIES

AS HE WOUND DOWN a forty-six-year career in law enforcement, Detective Gary T. Childs had planned on taking a seven-week trip to the Grand Canyon with his wife and then spending more time on his turkey farm. He'd started the farm years earlier with an eye on this occasion: he named it "Dunlawin Farms," for when he would be "done law-ing."

For twenty-two years he had chased drugs and killers as a detective with the Baltimore Police Department, and he'd spent the last twenty-one years with the Baltimore County force. All told, he had been involved in the investigations of well over six hundred homicides.

One case stood out above all. Child's partner and friend, Marcellus "Marty" Ward, was working undercover on December 3, 1984, posing as a drug dealer from Philadelphia and taking part in a heroin deal. He was wired to record the interactions and sat in a third-floor apartment above a store called the Kandy Kitchen in Southwest Baltimore. He had made two smaller purchases in previous meetings, and this time authorities were planning to move in for an arrest. As the arrest team made entry on the first floor, the target, twenty-six-year-old Lascell Simmons, got spooked and shot Ward. The body wire recorded the entire ordeal—the loud bangs of Simmons's .357 Magnum, Ward groaning, and Childs rushing in to aid his partner. "Marty, Marty, Marty! Marty, where you at?" Childs yelled. From a hallway outside the room where Ward lay dying, Childs urged Simmons to give up. "Here's my badge!" Childs said, tossing his wallet into the room. "Now throw the gun down and walk down and if that man dies, I'll kill you!"

The case changed the way police in Baltimore handled undercover drug buys; they started being more selective in such operations, and they hoped that their discretion would in turn carry more weight with judges. Things stayed that way until the mid-2000s, when the New York policing model of cracking down on drug areas was brought to Baltimore. As a result, thousands more minor cases flooded the courts and in turn carried less weight.

For Childs, the lasting effects were personal. Ward and Childs had first met in the mid-1970s, when Ward worked as a plainclothes officer and helped Childs in a battle with a man trying to wrestle away his gun. They would later work in a narcotics squad and then on a DEA task force; they became close friends off the clock and their children played together. Childs anguished over the loss. "I was there and I heard it and I couldn't do anything. It came so fast, it came so sudden in what we thought was a routine investigation. There was really nothing that we hadn't done a hundred times before," he said in a 1985 interview. To this day, discussing Ward's death causes Childs to lose his composure. "There are times," Childs says, welling up, "that it just comes and gets me. That's what drives me to solve cases."

Now Childs was part of the team pulled together to review the investigation of Sean Suiter's death.

There was precedence in Baltimore for outside panels to review controversial police cases: They'd been used for a 2011 "friendly fire" shooting outside a downtown club that killed Officer William H. Torbit Jr., and for the 2013 death of Tyrone West, a man who died in a confrontation with police after a traffic stop. But those reviews had been initiated after prosecutors had already declined to bring criminal charges—this group would be asked to review what was technically an open and pending homicide investigation, the details of which are typically held very close to the vest.

The Independent Review Board (IRB) would be chaired by a consultant based in Virginia, James "Chips" Stewart, a former director for the National Institute of Justice, the research arm of the U.S. Department of Justice. He had led boards in the cases of Tyrone West and Torbit. Also on the panel were a retired New Jersey State Police superintendent and a retired chief of detectives from the Rockland County, New York, district attorney's office. In addition to Childs, another retired city homicide detective, Marvin Sydnor, was tapped for the panel.

There were ground rules. The panel was told not to reinvestigate the case but to look over the work performed by the homicide unit. Childs nevertheless was hopeful that their involvement might generate new leads; maybe someone who had been reluctant to call the city police department would be more willing to help an outside team. Though attitudes had shifted and many in leadership viewed Suiter's death as a likely suicide, Childs was more than open to the possibility that Suiter had been murdered—it was listed as a murder case, and Childs wanted to solve it.

"To me, that would be like winning the Super Bowl, if we could get enough evidence that city homicide could arrest a guy for this murder," Childs says.

Childs, sixty-nine, was given the investigative file on a hard drive. He started reviewing while on his postretirement road trip to the Grand Canyon and later pored over it from his home office in a rural community north of Baltimore.

He was first interested in the unsolved triple homicide case from Bennett Place that Suiter had been investigating. Maybe Suiter was getting close to locking up a suspect, Childs thought, or his investigation had angered someone who wanted him dead.

As Childs read further into the file, he was struck with questions. The triple murder had happened in December 2016. Detectives are supposed to enter "progress notes" in a computer to detail their efforts on a case. Childs was surprised to find that Suiter's last notable progress report for the case had been filed at the end of the same month as the murder. There was a canvass for undisclosed witnesses in September, and then another the day before Suiter was shot. Suiter reportedly told people he was looking for a prostitute named "Mary" who potentially had information on the case, but there was no mention of such a person in the notes. At the same time, there was a promising lead that Childs says Suiter had overlooked: the crime lab informed Childs that someone had been arrested carrying the gun used in the triple murder, but Suiter hadn't made any note of the information or followed up on it.

Childs focused on the physical evidence. The apparent lack of any other person's DNA found on Suiter's body and the fact that Suiter appeared to have been shot with his own gun were troubling. He thought back to Marty Ward's case. "You can't have a life-or-death struggle, like I heard for the 10 seconds that Marty went through, and not leave some definite DNA on something," Childs said. "Suiter had no other injuries—no injuries to his hands, no defense wounds, no injury from falling on his face."

Suiter's movements just before the shooting were captured on surveillance camera at the far end of the block, and, while the footage was difficult to discern, it appeared to show him standing behind a van parked at the mouth of the vacant lot. If Suiter was hiding from a suspect in the lot, Childs surmised, he should have been on the opposite side of the van, using it as a shield. But instead he was at the back of the vehicle, potentially exposing himself to the person.

Childs conducted tests to challenge some claims and assumptions. He fired a gun at a range to see if gunsmoke would linger over Suiter's body the way Bomenka had said he observed (it did). Had someone rushed past after the shots were fired, as the test suggested, the cloud would likely have dissipated. The chief of the crime lab helped explore what might have caused Suiter's DNA to get inside the barrel of his gun, and whether the explosion of a fired bullet would eliminate it (it would not). The medical examiner worked through trajectory theories using probes put through a mannequin's head. The extra gunshots Bomenka said he had heard could be attributed to a "canyon effect" of echoes due to the surrounding buildings, the panel would say.

Suiter's last known words, "Stop, police!" also didn't add up for Childs. "You're not going to be hollering 'Stop, stop, police.' You're gonna be hollering get the f off me, or hollering 'Dave, Dave' [at Bomenka]. Or nothing," he said. "That's something you yell when you're chasing somebody, not when you're in a confrontation."

Then there was what the panel said was an overlooked piece of evidence: blood spatter from Suiter found inside the cuff of his right shirtsleeve, consistent with blowback from Suiter's gun hand being up near his head and the sleeve facing open when the shot was fired.

There could be no shooter, Childs and the panel concluded on the basis of the physical evidence.

Childs surmised that when Suiter had used his hand to motion to Bomenka, he was trying to direct him to go away from the lot and get Bomenka completely out of view. But Bomenka instead interpreted it as a gesture to come toward him, and that meant Suiter's window of opportunity was closing. Childs thinks Suiter darted into the lot, went down to the ground, and fired two shots into the air, hoping it might cause Bomenka to seek cover or at least pause. "Suiter catches him out of the corner of his eye—he knows he has seconds," Childs explained. "He fires two shots to slow him down. As a police officer, when shots are fired, your instinct is you head for cover. You're not going to hear shots and stick your head around right away. He fires two shots, makes Bomenka hesitate a few seconds, and then in the same motion shoots himself" while in a prone position.

Why involve Bomenka at all?

"He knew he needed a witness," Childs said.

To Childs and the rest of the IRB, Suiter's impending interview with the U.S. Attorney's Office was no small matter, and it provided a reasonable motive to support the physical evidence. Childs remembered being a nervous wreck after being brought in for questioning once by Internal Affairs early in his career. Why had Suiter picked that day to re-engage the triple-homicide case, after letting it lie dormant for months? "If I knew I had to go to the U.S. Attorney, on an allegation that's something I could go to prison for, I wouldn't be out looking for no 'Mary' on a case I ain't done nothing with in a year," Childs says.

The IRB learned through its interviews that Suiter had met only once with the FBI, on October 24—he had given no statements, had requested an attorney, and had asked agents if he was going to lose his job. Though the board didn't interview Suiter's attorney, Jeremy Eldridge—who was maintaining attorney-client privilege—they were able to read text messages between the two from Suiter's phone that shed some light on their interactions.

They'd exchanged messages the day before the shooting to set up a time to get together. Then, on the day of the shooting, at 4:01 P.M., a half hour before he was shot, Suiter received a call from Eldridge. Bomenka said he remembered Suiter taking a call and telling the person that he was unable to talk. He then rejected two subsequent calls from Eldridge.

Gondo had testified at the GTTF trial that he'd stolen money as far back as nine years earlier when he was working with a group of officers that included Suiter. There were other indicators of a relationship—and perhaps an attempt to cover it up: an analysis of Suiter's phone showed that Gondo and Ward had been deleted from Suiter's phone contacts. Seventy-five messages and 313 call log entries were also deleted. It's unknown how many, if any, were conversations with Gondo or Ward. But his phone still showed contacts with Gondo in March 2016. The board was also given a letter, summarized quickly in their report, that the incarcerated Hersl had sent discussing an encounter he'd had with Suiter and Gondo just before the officers were arrested. Hersl recounted that Gondo "would disappear a lot and go down to the homicide unit and hang out with Det. Suiter, and Suiter on occasions came down on the 5th floor to come get Gondo before the 2 of them would leave the office too [sic] go talk in private, sometimes disappearing for up to 20 to 30 minutes."

In August 2018, the review board issued its findings.

"The Board concludes that, based upon the totality of the evidence, Detective Suiter intentionally took his own life with his service weapon," the report said.

"Suiter had every incentive to make his death not appear to be a suicide if, in fact, he had decided to take his life," the panel added. They noted that the BPD benefits package available to the family of a police officer who is killed in the line of duty is far more lucrative than that for an officer who has taken his life, and that the Department of Justice provides funds to families of fallen law enforcement officers.

"We do not know what Detective Suiter's state of mind was on

November 15, 2017," the panel concluded. "We do know that he loved and was loved by his family and that he left many friends behind. We also know that Detective Suiter was under more stress than most of us endure. Being a BPD officer is highly stressful under the best of circumstances. These were far from the best of circumstances. He was due to testify the very next day before a federal grand jury investigating perhaps the worst scandal in BPD history. He did have an offer of limited immunity, at least as to the Umar Burley evidence planting allegations. But if Gondo and others were providing truthful information to federal law enforcement, Detective Suiter faced a difficult choice. He could testify truthfully and be protected by federal immunity. In acknowledging personal illegal conduct while with the agency, however, he would likely end his career. His admissions would be a firing offense, and the specter of state criminal prosecution might also exist. Indeed, when the FBI agents approached Suiter about a month prior, he asked if he would lose his job. Alternatively, Suiter could have denied wrongful conduct before the grand jury. That might subject him to federal charges, however, if the grand jury and prosecutors concluded that Suiter was not truthful. Detective Sean Suiter spent the last hour of his life ignoring his attorney's calls and texts. Instead, he drove around Bennett Place repeatedly, ostensibly looking for a mysterious 'Mary' and perhaps another mystery suspect, but, as Detective Bomenka suggested, 'maybe [they were] just seeing things.' He had a meeting at 5 p.m. to prepare to face his difficult choice before the grand jury.

"Time was running out. Suiter's futile searches may have signaled a quiet desperation before a final, tragic decision."

A DAY AFTER THE release of the IRB report, Nicole Suiter traveled to the downtown law office of Eldridge, her husband's friend and attorney.

Nicole had not made any public comments following her husband's death. She thought a suspect would be apprehended by the time she got out of the hospital that first night, on the basis of how shootings of police officers were typically handled. And she kept quiet as information started to emerge about his grand jury testimony, and as the investigation started to turn away from looking for a killer. Every time a story was published about his case, she scanned the comments section, where she said the majority of posters asserted his death was part of a conspiracy. Still, she hoped fresh eyes might discard the BPD's emerging theories and find something new in the case file.

Now she decided to break her silence. She read a prepared statement to the press.

"I understand that the public has been patiently waiting for Det. Sean Suiter's wife to speak out, and before now, I did not have the strength in me to do so," she began. "I will not go on allowing anyone to shame my husband's name and ruin his legacy with these false allegations of suicide. . . . I have the same views and thoughts as the majority of the community, and that is, my husband did not commit suicide.

"I don't make this statement as a heartbroken widow; I make this statement as an aware individual who has evaluated every piece of evidence that has been shown to me, with the knowledge that much evidence has not been presented. . . . Based on the fact that no one knew my husband better than I did, I will not accept the untimely death of Sean as nothing other than a murder, which is being covered up for reasons unbeknownst to me or our family.

"What the community does not know," she continued, "is that I spoke to my husband less than one hour prior to his murder. Sean was in a great mood [and] happy spirit, and we briefly joked about a video of him dancing that I captured. Who knew that would be the last time I spoke with my husband."

"My husband is a stand-up guy," Nicole said later in an interview. "If he committed a crime or did something wrong, he's gonna take it like a man and deal with it. . . . My husband was no coward at all."

What had Suiter discussed with her about his impending testimony?

"I found out about it when everybody else found out about it," Nicole Suiter said.

She rationalized that seemingly significant omission by saying that Suiter often had to appear in court as part of his job and that—

because he had nothing to worry about—the case wasn't remarkable enough to merit a mention.

WHILE SUITER HADN'T TOLD his co-workers, or even his wife, about his impending testimony, he and his attorney Jeremy Eldridge had talked about it extensively. Eldridge remains convinced that Suiter did not take his own life.

"I was never, ever fucking worried about him," Eldridge said. "This was never a situation where he was going to be charged—it was never a situation where I was worried about him being one of these people implicated in some of these robberies."

But his account raises additional questions.

The two had met years earlier when Eldridge was a young prosecutor and Suiter was a drug cop. Eldridge became a defense attorney and Suiter rose to homicide; they were Facebook friends and competed in a fantasy football league together but didn't see each other much.

In late October 2017, Suiter reached out after meeting briefly with the FBI. As Suiter relayed it, Sieracki told him investigators had an allegation on an evidence-planting incident that they wanted to talk to him about. Suiter was uncomfortable and asked if he should get a lawyer. "Do you think you need a lawyer?" Sieracki responded. It was in that meeting that Suiter asked if he was going to lose his job.

Eldridge agreed to represent Suiter free of charge and began speaking with Wise, the federal prosecutor, to assess the situation. Eldridge said Wise had told him that Suiter was not a suspect in the evidence-planting case they were investigating and that other witnesses had cleared him. But Wise declined to tell Eldridge the specific case that they wanted to talk to Suiter about. Eldridge was put off by the evasiveness. "It was like kids who don't want to share toys," he said. After Eldridge figured out that it was the Burley case, he asked for documents related to the case, but Wise declined.

"I want a clean crack at Sean," Wise said, according to Eldridge. "I want to make sure he doesn't have an invented memory, because we know Wayne wrote the statement of probable cause, and we believe Wayne lied about it."

Eldridge sought to pull the documents anyway, asking Suiter repeatedly if he could track them down. "I felt like I had to do my job, which is, let me figure out what's going on, let me make sure my client is prepared to answer questions," he explained. "The feds knew everything, they wouldn't share anything—I asked innumerable times. I cannot tell you how uncomfortable that made me."

Suiter seemed to brush off Eldridge's frequent requests for the statement of probable cause from the Burley case. "I was obsessed with getting this report. I was like, 'Can you get it, can you get it.' He was like, 'Uh, I can try,' then he'd forget. I wouldn't say he wasn't taking it seriously, but he wasn't losing sleep over this shit."

Eldridge tried to think a few paces out. So Suiter didn't know about drug planting, but what else might the feds ask about? Eldridge had been in proffer sessions where things went sideways after clients were asked questions that they didn't see coming. He remembered telling Suiter, "'Let's not be naive. If you heard Wayne stole money, you're gonna have to tell them.' He was like, 'Well I heard some stuff.' I was like, 'You better be able to tell them what you heard.'" Suiter also told Eldridge that other officers including supervisors had recommended that he get away from Jenkins, and Eldridge told him to be prepared to explain why.

In their conversations, Suiter asked lots of questions. He'd testified in court many times, but this was different. The GTTF case was the first instance, at least in some time, that police corruption was being taken seriously, and it was still evolving. "So many of our conversations had nothing to do with him doing anything wrong. It was, 'What's it going to be like if I have to testify? What's my life going to be like, is everyone going to hate me? Am I still going to be working? Jeremy, they didn't catch all these guys . . .'"

Eldridge said he'd "drilled" Suiter about whether he knew about drugs being planted, even after the fact. Suiter was adamant that he had no knowledge. Wise was giving Suiter proffer immunity for his testimony, and Eldridge said he had no concerns when it came to Suiter's potential criminal culpability.

After finding out about Suiter's shooting, Eldridge stayed at his downtown office overnight and didn't sleep. The next morning, he went to visit Wise and Hines and urged them to get involved in the investigation of his client's death. "I want to know, why are local PD on this? It's your fucking witness," Eldridge recalled saying.

"They were shell-shocked. That's just the honesty of it," he said of Wise and Hines. "And politically, what I saw after that, within a week, they're saying, 'He wasn't our witness, he didn't even make it in here.' So it's like, because he got fucking killed, we're not responsible for him, which to me always felt like a copout."

They sparred over Eldridge asking Suiter to pull reports on the Burley crash, with Wise saying to Eldridge at one point: "Well Jeremy, if you told him to go hunting for something, did you get him killed?"

Wise and Hines later explained why federal authorities did not take over the case, saying they saw no possible nexus between the shooting and his testimony. The members of the GTTF "were all locked up," Wise said. "It wasn't like there was another list of officers we were on the verge of charging and Suiter had the key piece of evidence. There was nothing like that. This was a historical evidence-planting episode, and the primary target is Jenkins, who's already locked up. . . . Gondo gave us a whole list of names [of officers involved in misconduct], so had Rayam, so had Ward. What would be the motive to kill the guy? At that point, four of the seven had flipped. Those four aren't killing him. The guys who implicated [Suiter] aren't going to kill him. They're already cooked."

Moreover, they had always believed that Suiter had likely taken his own life, and the prosecutors said that later briefings regarding the investigation didn't give reason to believe otherwise.

"Given that he [Suiter] was a federal witness, we certainly asked if there was any evidence of a shooter, but we were told repeatedly that there was no evidence of a second shooter," Hines said.

Eldridge was successful in convincing the federal officials to have Suiter's car searched before the BPD could get to it. He believed Suiter should have had materials for their meeting in his personal car, and in those early moments he wanted to know if the papers were still there or could have possibly been swiped. The FBI impounded and searched the car—without telling city police—and did not find anything. Eldridge thought nothing of it, though it would seem to at least raise the question of whether Suiter hadn't prepared for the meeting because he wasn't planning on attending.

Eldridge lambasted the IRB's claims about Suiter's anxious state of mind before the shooting. Anyone who interacted with Suiter in his last days and moments, Eldridge insists, would have found the IRB's description to be totally off. He remembers their last phone call, a short time before the shooting, when Suiter told him, "Hey J, I'm finishing up on some shit, I'll be there when I'm done."

"I've never forgotten that sentence," Eldridge said.

Eldridge said the IRB also got one potentially key detail wrong: The panel asserted that Suiter had picked Bomenka to accompany him to Bennett Place that evening because he was a junior detective who could serve as a patsy. But it was Bomenka who tapped Suiter to accompany him, as Bomenka followed up one of his own cases. A homicide prosecutor had asked police to locate a witness in a pending case who was wavering on her testimony. It was decided that Bomenka might be able to convince her to follow through. "The only person willing to go with Dave was Sean," said a law enforcement official. "If [the squad that helps locate people] had been able to pull her in, they wouldn't have been there at all." And if it was Bomenka's errand, Eldridge offers, then it was less likely that Suiter had plotted that moment to carry out his plan.

Despite his concerns, Eldridge does not believe that Suiter was killed as part of a conspiracy to silence him. The four officers pleading guilty and cooperating against Jenkins had already given the feds plenty of ammo. "He wasn't 'doing' anybody outside of the dude that was already in jail, who everybody else was doing," Eldridge said, referring to Jenkins. "So that doesn't make any fucking sense."

What if there were more buried secrets, secrets that only the officers engaged in corruption knew about?

"Then that begs the question, who knew, who was scared, and did Sean know something about somebody and he should've been scared, and that person had a motive to kill him? But that's all supposition."

IN CROSS-EXAMINATION AT THE GTTF trial, Gondo testified that he'd taken money with Suiter—an explosive claim that hung in the air after the trial ended. But he—and other officers from the squad—had

had more to say in the closed-door proffer sessions with prosecutors, months before the shooting, that never became public.

One of the very first things out of Gondo's mouth in late March 2017 had been that the first time he could recall stealing money had involved Suiter. The incident stood out for him: It was Gondo's first search warrant, a dope house on Druid Park Drive, and they had found $700 and some gelcaps of drugs. After the search, he said, they went to the parking lot of the Western District with Suiter and Ivery, where they split up the money. Gondo wasn't lobbing accusations at everyone he'd ever worked with: he explicitly excluded two other officers from being involved, saying that one was a stand-up guy who never took money and that he hadn't trusted the other.

But he maintained that Suiter, whom he referred to as a "mentor figure," was involved.

Gondo went on to say Suiter had told him that in 2010, when he was with the major crimes squad with Jenkins, they "took money on every stop" and Suiter requested a transfer because of it. Regarding the Burley case, Gondo said Suiter knew about drugs being planted and was "scared" that it had happened.

Rayam too, in a proffer session in April 2017, implicated Suiter with stealing, telling investigators that Jenkins had told Rayam that he and Suiter "took money all the time."

Jenkins, meanwhile, insisted he wasn't the one who planted the drugs in Burley's car, even as he pleaded guilty to helping cover it up. He never publicly identified the person he claimed was instead responsible. Jenkins told the feds, however, that it was Suiter.

These were claims made well before Suiter was shot, and the feds had been carrying the information around in their back pocket. When the federal prosecutors told Eldridge and Commissioner Davis that Suiter wasn't a "target" of their investigation, it very well could have been because they were laser-focused at the time on bringing Jenkins down.

Maurice Ward, one of the GTTF detectives who pleaded guilty and cooperated with the racketeering investigation, vouches for Suiter and questions Gondo's testimony that they all stole money together. "I still don't understand when Gondo said we all used to take things together, which is not true, I never did anything with Suiter or [their supervisor Kenneth] Ivery," Ward said. But Ward also said he never openly stole with Gondo either, highlighting that the officers' corruption wasn't as blatant as it sounds. "I heard of things he was involved in; he probably heard the same about me, but we never did anything like that together."

Notably, no one else from the squad that Gondo said he had taken money with in the late 2000s was ever charged by the feds as a result of Gondo's accusations. If the accusations were true, and Suiter did kill himself over fears of going to prison, those fears might never have been realized if he had stuck it out.

THE THEORY THAT SUITER took his own life gradually took hold as a consensus within the department, but Eldridge continued to push back against an investigation that he increasingly felt everyone involved wanted to abandon. He came across what he considered to be a tantalizing lead that had been discarded by police and never touched by the IRB: In December 2017, one month after Suiter was shot, a former Black Guerrilla Family gang member turned informant named Donte Pauling sat down for an interview with detectives and gave information on a range of crimes. Among them, Pauling told police that on the night that Suiter was shot, Pauling was outside a bar a few blocks from Bennett Place when his cousin arrived, upset. He said that someone he knew had just shot someone who had suddenly come up on him "in his [drug] stash."

"When he told the story, we didn't know it was an officer 'til shit hit the news," Pauling told the detectives.

Pauling, whose information on other cases had been used by federal prosecutors at a high-profile gang trial, told the detectives the name of his cousin but said he did not know the name of the supposed shooter.

When footage of Pauling's interview with police surfaced in the news, the police department was forced to respond and said they had deemed Pauling's information to not be credible. But they declined to explain why.

The story caught the attention of Assistant State's Attorney Patrick Seidel, who believed police had failed to follow up on the lead.

Detectives were sent to locate the man in Pauling's story. He was now in the Midwest, and detectives interviewed him and collected a DNA sample. The case suddenly seemed as if it could have new legs.

The department was on its fourth commissioner since Suiter's death two years earlier, with New Orleans veteran Michael Harrison taking the helm in early 2019. Harrison had no stake in the case, though he did have an interest in turning the page. He had Maryland State Police do a second outside review; after it came back without raising significant issues, he announced in late 2019 that Suiter's case was being closed. State's Attorney Marilyn Mosby, however, told reporters that her office considered Suiter's case "open and active" while questions related to Pauling's tip were being run down, forcing Harrison to reverse course. But in the months that followed, police and prosecutors refused to discuss the case. Sources said the leads had hit a wall.

The state's chief medical examiner was presented the information about the shooting being a likely suicide and decided not to revise the ruling. Dr. David Fowler said that Suiter had been trained on the significance of contact wounds. "If you wanted to fake a homicide, he was too smart to put the gun to his head, in my opinion," Fowler said after his retirement in late 2019. At the same time, he acknowledged that the relationships with Suiter among the investigators were a problem. "It's probably not appropriate for a police agency to be investigating the loss of one of their own, especially if it's a homicide detective," Fowler said.

Others believe there's still room for someone to have had a brief struggle with Suiter and either to have shot him or to have caused Suiter to accidentally shoot himself—with none of it captured by the physical evidence.

Among those who staunchly believe Suiter was killed is his partner, veteran homicide detective Jonathan Jones. Though Suiter never mentioned the GTTF grand jury to him, either, Jones vividly recalls his partner being in great spirits the day of his death. He believes that if Suiter wanted to take his life and ensure his family received line-of-duty benefits, he could've simply run his car off the road on the way home. "Why would he put a scenario into effect where everything had to work out perfectly?" he said. Jones strongly defends Bomenka from the conspiracy theories of his involvement, but also questions whether Bomenka got tunnel vision after seeing Suiter was shot, and could've missed other observations. "This isn't television. In real life, it takes a split second [to shoot someone]," said Jones, who has investigated homicides for thirteen years. "If you have tunnel vision and you're only focused on your partner on the ground, somebody could be standing right next to you and everything else goes blur."

On the second anniversary of the shooting, Suiter's surviving relatives and Eldridge staged a protest outside of City Hall. "Sean Suiter was murdered. Solve it!" read one sign. Another said: "How many times are you going to kill my father?"

Eldridge continues to press investigators to do more. "Our joke at home is that I'm a 'finder.' I find shit. I find my wife's keys; I find everything everyone loses. It's why I'm good at my fucking job. It's why I was good as a prosecutor, it's why I'm good as a defense attorney. My kid sees Sean's picture on TV. She says that's your friend who died—who killed him? 'I don't know.' She says, 'You can't find him? Dad, you're the finder.' . . . I don't understand why I am one of the few people that still gives a fuck."

Childs, meanwhile, said some in the department have tried to make him feel bad for his conclusions. "Look, I've handled over 125 suicides in my career. Many family members do not want to believe that their son or their daughter killed themselves and didn't come to them for help. . . . I get it, I understand it. That's a tough pill to swallow," Childs said. "They asked me to look at [the Suiter case], and they wanted the truth. It is what it is. The evidence is overwhelming."

Sean Suiter's death officially remains classified as an unsolved homicide.

CHAPTER TWENTY-THREE

THE ABYSS STARES BACK

ON JUNE 8, 2018, Wayne Jenkins stood before U.S. District Court Judge Catherine C. Blake waiting for his sentence on the racketeering and other charges to which he had pleaded guilty. He'd been held without bail since his arrest fifteen months before, moving around between at least four facilities in Maryland and Virginia. Wearing a maroon, V-neck prison jumpsuit, he looked down as he was led into the courtroom. He sat at the defense table and stared forward. He had a couple of rows of family in the stadium-style seating of the ceremonial courtroom but looked back at them only briefly, a flash of emotion crossing his face. His attorney, Steve Levin, handed him some tissues.

Ahead of the hearing, Jenkins's family and friends had sent the judge a number of letters asking for leniency, saying he had been a good cop and a good father who had made mistakes. His mother, using the same term her son used for his biggest robbery targets, wrote: "I promise you, he is not a 'monster.'"

The court allowed two family members of Elbert Davis, the man killed in the Umar Burley crash, to give victim impact statements.

"We have no father to share our lives with. We miss our dad. We no longer have the special occasions, birthdays, holidays that we spent with my dad," said Shirley Johnson, one of Davis's daughters. "And then to find out seven years later that Officer Jenkins was involved in the accident that took my father's life, that he is no more than a common criminal and his task force, 'cause my dad would be alive today had it not been for his actions on that day. Our family's hearts are broken. We'll never be the same again."

Assistant U.S. Attorney Wise said Jenkins's criminal misconduct was "breathtaking." "People that should have been charged with drug crimes were let go because Jenkins took their drugs," Wise told Blake. "People that were charged had false descriptions of the circumstances of their arrests provided to judges in our city and in our state courts and even in our federal courts."

As a sergeant, Wise said, Jenkins was supposed to play a key role in looking out for misconduct, not facilitating it. "If a sergeant is corrupt, is compromised, there is almost no way to design a system to prevent it," he said. "There's simply no way to imagine, going forward, how we won't face this problem again if deterrence—if a strong deterrent message isn't sent from this sentencing and from the sentencings of these other defendants."

The terms of Jenkins's plea called for a sentence of between twenty and thirty years. The sentencing guidelines called for twenty-four years. Wise and Hines asked that Blake impose the maximum.

Levin hoped to convince Blake to give his client twenty years.

"Your Honor, in Gene Fowler's book, 'Good Night, Sweet Prince' John Barrymore said the following words: 'A man is not old until regrets take the place of dreams.' Although he is not quite 40 years of age, Wayne Jenkins, filled with regret, is old," Levin said. "Wayne Jenkins knows he's let his community down; he's let his loved ones down; he's let himself down. And for all of that, Your Honor, he is racked with remorse.

"Growing up in Maryland, Wayne Jenkins had a host of dreams. He dreamed of being, like his father, a good and decent man, a man Wayne Jenkins has described to me and others as his best friend. He dreamed of defending bullies—defending others against bullies, things made clear in the letters to Your Honor that he did as a young man. He dreamed of serving in the United States Marine Corps, like his father. And he did serve, and he served honorably, as reflected by the records, his awards, and his certificate of discharge, some of which was shared with Your Honor.

"He also had personal dreams, some of which were realized. Mr. Jenkins married his high school girlfriend, to whom he remains married to this day. He dreamed of having a big and loving family, of being a big presence in their lives. As you know—as you've heard, Your Honor, he certainly was.

"But those dreams have died. Those dreams are no more.

"They have been replaced by pain, by hurt, welling up in his heart. And I don't mean the physical pain he has suffered while detained. I will address that a little bit later, Your Honor. I mean the pain caused by regret that keeps Wayne Jenkins up at night, wishing he had acted differently. It's what causes tears to well up in his eyes, knowing that he acted in a manner in which he should not have acted. It's what causes his heart to break when he considers his conduct."

Jenkins had been held in the same northern Virginia jail as the soon-to-be-convicted leader of a Baltimore Bloods gang who had accused Jenkins years earlier of planting a gun on him. Levin said Jenkins had been attacked and badly injured by a fellow inmate who learned Jenkins was a former police officer; Jenkins had warned corrections officers that the attack was coming, to no avail, Levin said. He did not mention that Jenkins, while held in the Allegany County Detention Center in late 2017, had instigated two fights himself. Records show that Jenkins tried to head-butt another inmate in a dispute over what to watch on TV and that he had prompted a lockdown of the facility two months later when he started punching an inmate in the head during a card game.

"In short," Levin continued, "Mr. Jenkins will serve much harder time than other inmates. His prison sentence will likely include substantial isolation, enhanced levels of fear and anxiety, and almost complete separation from his family. So his dream now is that he will still have some shred of a life after a sentence of 20 years. . . .

"It is, as dreams go, not much and certainly very different than what he had in mind at one time early in his life. But it is something to hold onto."

Blake then asked Jenkins if he wanted to address the court. He stood and turned around, first speaking to Davis's family members.

"To the Davises, who lost their loved ones, from the bottom of my heart, I wish I could take that day back and not stop that vehicle. I sat at the University of Maryland and held the woman's hand for over an hour in the bed. I held her hand for over an hour with her, the passenger in that vehicle."

Davis's family would later say they didn't recall him there; Guinn says he himself was the one at the hospital bedside holding Phosa Cain's hand.

Referring to Burley, who was not in the room, Jenkins continued to maintain that he had not planted the drugs that day but that he had known of it and had failed to speak up: "I didn't come forward after I found out about that. I should have came forward, and I didn't.

"I've tarnished the badge.... I made so many mistakes, Your Honor. In my whole life I said 'I'm sorry' when I make a mistake, but that don't—'I'm sorry' don't cut it. Nothing ever hurt so bad as to see my sons through glass and not be able to touch them when they cry. I have a 1-and-a-half-year-old son I don't even know. And when he comes into the room to see me, he won't even get close to me."

Jenkins was now sobbing, his voice occasionally raising into a higher pitch as he tried to push through.

"Ms. Davis, about your father, I'm so sorry for what you're going through, 'cause my father is my best friend. I love my father more than life itself—mom, you, too. I wish I never would have stopped that vehicle. I can't take it back. And I put my heart and soul into my job for so many years.

"And, Your Honor, I've been alone mostly for this year and a half 'cause I can't be around people in jail, obviously. . . . But, again, it's my fault. I know it's my fault, 'cause I did it. And I deserve to be punished. I deserve to go to jail."

He said he had turned to the Bible while in jail, reading it thirty-one times, seeking forgiveness. He turned to his wife. "Kristy," he said, "I'm so sorry. You deserve better than me.

"I'm so sorry, Your Honor. I'm so sorry to the citizens of Baltimore. Mr. Umar Burley—God forgive me. I wish I would have came clean when I found out that drugs were planted. I should have came clean, and I didn't. I'm so sorry, Your Honor."

Blake said she believed Jenkins was remorseful. But "the message must be clear that officers who break their oaths by robbery and fraud will be prosecuted; they will be justly punished for that conduct," she said.

She handed him a sentence of twenty-five years.

Jenkins winced as the U.S. marshals placed handcuffs on his wrists, and he did not turn back as he was led out through the back of the courtroom. In a few weeks, he was shipped out west to a high-security prison in the Arizona desert, while back home city prosecutors continued to throw out convictions in many of the arrests he had made.

CHAPTER TWENTY-FOUR
THE PLACE TO BE

THE CRIMES OF THE GUN TRACE TASK FORCE members were so significant, so sustained over an extended period of time, that it seemed impossible that supervisors and commanders didn't know about them. But the federal investigators uncovered no evidence of such top-down collusion with regard to the officers' crimes. Poor supervision, definitely. Tacit encouragement of bending the rules, likely. But robberies, drug dealing, and evidence planting? None of the cooperating officers indicated that any supervisors had specific knowledge. As Leo Wise said about keeping the feds' investigation of the officers close to the vest: "The best way to keep a secret is to keep a secret."

Institutionally, having worked the streets, at least some commanders had to have known what went on in a general sense, though. Bad behavior seemed to be passed down through the generations. "You've got to realize," said retired attorney Richard C. B. Woods, who had gone after Jenkins twice around 2010, "that these cops put on trial are just the present tip of an iceberg that's existed in Baltimore police for decades. These cops didn't learn how to trick it by themselves. They were taught."

With the GTTF behind bars, the federal investigators continued to work toward Jenkins's onetime mentor, Keith Gladstone, who also had a swirl of misconduct allegations around him dating back years.

Gladstone had retired just a few weeks after the arrest of the GTTF members. For most of his career, dating back to the 1990s, he had worked in some of the agency's elite drug units and federal drug task forces. And he'd faced years of misconduct allegations. But it was his relationship with Jenkins—helping him out in the 2014 case of Demetric Simon—that ultimately led to criminal charges.

In 2014, Simon had fled from Jenkins, who ran Simon down with his car. Simon wasn't armed, but a BB gun was recovered from the scene. After the GTTF arrests, federal authorities found BB guns in some of their cars, and the cooperating officers said Jenkins had told them to carry such weapons to plant on the scene in case they got in trouble. The Simon case had all the hallmarks of a case of planted evidence.

Around the same time that Jenkins pleaded guilty, investigators would later learn, Gladstone arranged to meet with one of the officers who worked under him, Carmine Vignola. Using their wives' cellphones in an effort to avoid detection, they arranged to meet in the swimming pool of a YMCA near Gladstone's Pennsylvania home to ensure neither was recording the other.

"Do you have anything to worry about now, you know, since Wayne was arrested? Do you have any concerns?" Vignola asked Gladstone, according to prosecutors.

Gladstone said no—except for the Demetric Simon incident. Vignola knew of the case too: he had been the officer eating with Gladstone when Jenkins called, and Vignola had gone to the scene with Gladstone. Standing there in the pool, Gladstone told Vignola that if Vignola was questioned by the feds he should tell them that he had gone to the site of the arrest only for "scene assessment" and to protect a third officer who was involved.

Their small conspiracy didn't matter. Gladstone was indicted on February 27, 2019, on charges of depriving Simon of his civil rights and witness tampering. Gladstone agreed to cooperate and pleaded guilty.

While awaiting sentencing, Gladstone sat for a deposition in a civil suit in June 2019 and said he was never all that close with Jen-kins. Why, then, did he risk his career to plant the BB gun in 2014?

"I think it has to do with self-worth," Gladstone said. "You know, I didn't come from the greatest home. When I was living in my house, I had some brothers, and we were very close, and that's how we got through was my brothers. I got out and went into the military, cama-raderie again. I got into the police department, camaraderie. And just, you know, you go into these situations, and this person is always there behind you and, you know, who takes care of them? Nobody. So he called me and asked me for help. I did it, and I threw away everything to do that because I thought he would do it for me."

"You considered him like a brother?" the attorney asked.

"I considered pretty much most police I work with as a brother. And I would have done that probably for one hundred people," Glad-stone replied. "I had two families, and I think I put one of them far ahead of the other one. And now my other one is paying."

Vignola was indicted on charges of lying to the federal grand jury about the BB gun incident. Even though he had been given immunity by Wise and Hines, Vignola told the grand jurors that he hadn't seen what Gladstone retrieved from the trunk of his car that night and that they had headed straight to meet Jenkins at the scene. But that wasn't true—the officers had first traveled to the home of a third officer in their squad, Robert Hankard, to pick up the BB gun, Vignola would later admit. Hankard was charged with lying to the grand jury about the incident too.

Wise would later remark that—despite all he'd seen through four years of digging into the misdeeds of Baltimore police officers—he couldn't believe that two officers offered immunity had gone into the grand jury room and lied. That caused Gladstone's indictment to con-tain false information—the first time Wise said he was aware of that happening in his fifteen years as a prosecutor. Wise said the episode for him pierced the "mythology" that the federal grand jury room was a sacred space where law enforcement officers came in to tell the truth. Vignola had delivered a carefully crafted story—"He knew how to game the system," Wise said.

The feds, reaching deeper into the past, learned new information about the forty-one-kilogram cocaine bust that Jenkins had made in 2009 while part of a squad with Gladstone. It was billed at the time as a record seizure for the department.

It was actually larger than they knew.

Gladstone had transported the drugs back to headquarters in a van, with a SWAT team supposedly assisting and standing guard through then–police commissioner Frederick Bealefeld's news conference. But three more kilograms of cocaine were left behind in the van—whether accidentally or on purpose is unclear. Gladstone and two other officers from that squad hatched a plan to have one of their confidential informants sell it and kick back the proceeds. The officer whose informant sold the drugs took a $20,000 cut; another, who continued working big cases with the ATF throughout the GTTF saga, received $10,000. The statute of limitations to be charged for the crime itself had passed—but prosecutors were able to hit them with charges of lying to federal investigators.

In all, eight members of the Gun Trace Task Force had been sentenced to federal prison—Jenkins for twenty-five years, Hersl and Taylor for eighteen, Allers for fifteen, Rayam for twelve, Gondo for ten, and Hendrix and Ward for seven—and seven other current or former officers, including the onetime commissioner, had been charged with federal crimes.

By comparison, Antonio Shropshire, whose drug operation sparked the investigation that brought the officers down, received twenty-five years.

Officers on the periphery of the scandal began leaving the department. Michael Fries, who had handpicked Jenkins for the plainclothes units early in his career, and William Knoerlein, who had been his supervisor as his stock rose in the late 2000s, retired. Jenkins's partner in 2013 and 2014, Ben Frieman, resigned in early 2019. So did Clewell, who—though he had never been implicated in any of the GTTF crimes—had been suspended and eventually left the department. Thomas Wilson, a twenty-four-year veteran who had been accused by Stepp at the GTTF trial of providing security for a meeting of drug dealers at a strip club, also retired in July 2018. Two former city officers working in Baltimore County who had been implicated left that agency as well.

Most of the cooperating officers had testified not just that they had lied and stolen but that they had done so for years, without real fear of detection. They described it as "part of the culture" of the BPD. Now anyone who had worked with the convicted officers also had a cloud over them—Had they known what was going on? How couldn't they know? Just how many more dirty cops had been out there, operating with impunity for years? Matthew Ryckman, a former officer who worked with Jenkins in 2013 and 2014 and became a federal agent in California, told the FBI of crimes he had committed with Jenkins. Ryckman was never charged, raising the question of how many others avoided accountability by cooperating.

Then there was the wider impact: How many unjust convictions existed? How many guilty people would be let out because the officers tainted their cases?

All of this happened during a time when the consent decree was supposed to be restoring confidence in the city's police.

Marilyn Mosby went into her reelection campaign having forged an image as a fighter for the community, but also carrying the baggage of the failed prosecutions in Freddie Gray's death, record homicide rates, and accusations that her office had failed to do its part to detect the GTTF detectives' misconduct. She prevailed, earning 49 percent of the vote, with Ivan Bates and a third challenger splitting the other 51 percent. Her office spent two years reviewing cases involving the GTTF officers and others tainted by the scandal, and announced that the review would result in more than eight hundred criminal cases being dismissed or overturned. That number was expected to grow as more officers were implicated. "Some of these individuals who have been convicted are really dangerous individuals," Mosby said of the cases being overturned in the scandal's wake. "It's drained a great deal of resources. It's extremely time consuming."

Remarkably, despite the revelations of systemic and ongoing corruption exposed by the case, more than eighteen months after the GTTF trial the Baltimore Police Department had still not launched an internal review of the circumstances. There were many current and former officials whose actions or lack of action raised questions that might have fallen short of federal crimes for the prosecutors to go after but still called for some type of accounting if there was any hope of preventing this from happening again. After all, the federal investigation itself was initiated only after suburban drug investigators stumbled onto the crimes while pursuing a heroin crew. Almost all of the direct supervisors and commanders who had failed to spot or curb the misconduct, from bad searches to overtime theft, remain with the department.

New commissioner Michael Harrison, the New Orleans veteran, who had been hired in January 2019 after a months-long search to replace De Sousa, told a state commission that—despite pledges from past commissioners to investigate—his agency had done no far-reaching review into how the corruption was allowed to fester for so long. Pressed on why, he deferred to the city solicitor, who cited one reason: the potential to encourage more civil lawsuits against city police—which were expected to exceed millions in liability. Finally, toward the end of 2019, the city appointed former Justice Department inspector general Michael Bromwich to conduct an independent review.

The city sought to be excused from having to pay lawsuit judgments resulting from the officers' conduct, calling them "criminals who just happened to be officers of the Baltimore Police Department" whose actions were so far "outside the scope of their employment" that taxpayers should not foot the bill for their crimes. The judges on Maryland's highest court were not swayed.

"Given the egregiousness of the conspiracy, the length of time of the conspiracy, the number of former members of the department's Gun Trace Task Force who participated in the conspiracy, and the department's acknowledgment that examples of members of the Gun Trace Task Force planting evidence were plentiful, it is reasonable to conclude that the Department should have known of the misconduct by former members of the Gun Trace Task Force," Judge Shirley M. Watts wrote for the court. "The ultimate responsibility for the officers' misconduct rests with the governmental entities that employed and supervised them—namely, the city and the [police] department."

EARLY IN THE SUMMER OF 2019, shortly after Gladstone pleaded guilty, Ryan Guinn sat in his living room just beyond the county line in Northeast Baltimore. He was wearing sweatpants, sneakers, and a hooded sweatshirt. *Mad Men* was queued up on Netflix; a docile old pit bull was asleep on the couch.

In the dining room were boxes of his things from work.

"Fuck them," Guinn said of the Baltimore Police Department. "I'm done."

Guinn had been asked by the FBI to testify in front of a federal grand jury about the Gladstone BB gun–planting case—as in the Burley incident, Guinn was on the scene when it happened. Also as in the Burley incident, Guinn said he had not been aware of the crimes committed but was able to help provide a framework of who was there and their movements.

Yet after Gladstone was indicted, Guinn found himself among a group of officers suspended by Commissioner Harrison. The cloud over those who had worked with the corrupt officers was hovering again. Guinn had been initially suspended after the Burley case too, but that suspension had been short-lived—then-commissioner Davis had been assured by federal authorities that Guinn didn't do anything wrong, and he was reinstated. And it had since been revealed in the press that Guinn had played a role in reporting Gondo and Rayam and providing assistance to the FBI in the early stages of the GTTF case. One of his former supervisors nominated him to receive the department's Medal of Honor, its highest award.

Then not only did the police department's new regime move to suspend Guinn again, but he was told he was being transferred from the police academy to the juvenile detention center—an undesirable assignment, and a place where problem officers were typically shipped. A couple of months after his suspension, more than two years after the initial arrests and more than a year since the GTTF trial, Guinn was hit with Internal Affairs charges related to "tipping off" Jenkins to the Gondo investigation.

"You've got to be fucking kidding me," Guinn said when informed of the charges.

Guinn had spoken to Jenkins about Gondo, but at the time Jenkins was not under criminal investigation or working with Gondo. Guinn said Jenkins had always talked about Gondo being dirty, and he had believed Jenkins might be able to help provide information about him to the FBI.

He had never liked Gondo and Rayam. He didn't particularly like Jenkins, either, but mostly he felt let down by him.

"I trusted him," Guinn said. "A lot of people did. A lot of people held Wayne in very high regard, including me. I could pick apart all day things he did wrong, tactics-wise, but at the end of the day, we all thought of him as just a very aggressive 'super cop.' That's the way he portrayed himself to be. Everyone loved Wayne.

"People can say they knew he was dirty—bullshit. Nobody thought Wayne was dirty. And everybody who says that is a fucking liar. He cut corners—yeah, what cop doesn't cut corners? Show me a cop who goes A-to-Z and hits every letter in their investigation. With the pressure we're put under to produce?"

Guinn had at different times worked side by side not just with Jenkins and Gondo and Rayam but also with a host of other cops accused over the years of misconduct. Could you really operate in that world and see and hear no evil?

"They didn't steal around me," he insisted. "They knew better than that. They didn't trust me."

"I know I didn't do anything wrong," he continued. "I put my life on the line, testifying, giving information on these guys. I didn't have to do it. I could've kept my mouth shut like every other fucking cop that knew Gondo and Rayam were dirty. I came forward. I did what I was supposed to do."

Guinn never took the new assignment to juvenile detention. He went out on medical leave with often crippling anxiety and depression, trying to strike the right balance of medications. Guinn started keeping a log of his dreams in a notebook, a suggestion from his therapist. He recounted a recent one where he was in his parents' home in New Jersey, but he and his family were living there. He heard children crying and screaming, and he ran toward the sound, which took him to the basement, where he encountered a large pine door that his father built. He opened it and saw two men wearing hoodies. His children were on the ground, and the hooded men turned around to reveal Gondo and Rayam. Guinn reached for his gun, but it wasn't there.

He woke up in a panic and checked on his boys that night. He no longer lets his kids sit on the couch by the front windows of his home, and he does not let them go outside without being there with them.

Guinn was biding his time until he could separate from the force. Soon he expected to be in New York State, working on insurance claims for his father-in-law's business. He took the test and aced it. He wanted to be as far from Baltimore as possible, but three hundred miles would have to suffice.

AT DUSK ON A FALL Saturday in 2019, Umar Burley was driving along a tree-lined West Baltimore street when a marked Baltimore police cruiser pulled behind him, its emergency lights flashing. Burley felt the rush of panic—but he knew not to flee. He immediately pulled over and looked around to see if there were witnesses. He wondered if the officer might have been friends with Jenkins, and he waved his license out of the window as the officer approached.

"You okay, sir?" asked the officer, whose body camera captured the encounter.

"No, I have a problem with police," Burley said. "My name is Umar Burley, the one [Wayne] Jenkins planted dope on. So I got issues with officers. So I would like this to hurry up."

The officer said Burley had a brake light out. He had been pulled over for the brake light before, and the state police had issued a tow order. The officer said the car was being impounded and asked for his keys. Burley fumbled for his phone to call one of his attorneys.

"I don't trust you," Burley told the cop. "I don't trust you."

Since he had gotten a car, city police had pulled him over six times.

"I'm a sitting duck," Burley said later. "It's like they're cutting me off on all ends, so that way I end up going back to the streets."

As his lawsuit against the Baltimore Police Department wound through the courts, Burley was told that he could not work because of post-traumatic stress disorder, and even if he did, the money he earned would go toward the million-dollar civil judgment against him from 2014. Finally, in November 2020, the attorneys representing Burley and Brent Matthews, who was in the car with Burley when Jenkins pulled him over, reached a historic settlement with the city for

$8 million—more than what the family of Freddie Gray received. But Burley was in no celebratory mood the day the settlement became official: "The only good thing about this I see is that I'm still living," he said.

JAMES KOSTOPLIS REMAINED ON the force. In late 2019, he was assigned to one of the revived plainclothes units, the Pennsylvania Avenue task force, and worked the streets in sneakers, dark-blue BDU pants, and a hooded sweatshirt. Kostoplis had been conducting one drug investigation for more than six months, using a GPS tracker—lawfully—and other surveillance methods.

"I'm hoping once we hit that, it'll be done. It'll shut this block down," he said. "At least for a while. That'll create a void and someone else will try to come in, but hopefully we can squash it so it doesn't happen."

It was a rainy Tuesday as he and his partner, Joshua Rutzen, crisscrossed the area looking for targets with open warrants. There had been no roll call with a commanding officer to start their shift, or to reiterate the rules and regulations, or to generally let them know there would be accountability for their actions; they know what to do, their superiors said. Rutzen, whom others called "Rain Man" because of his uncanny ability to remember names and faces, stuck his head out of their Ford SUV, eyeing a busy area around Lexington Market for one of the targets, and spotted him standing outside a corner store. He climbed out and approached the man, who offered no resistance and was loaded into an arrest van outfitted with a rear-facing video camera—technology adopted after Freddie Gray's death.

Both officers repeatedly checked their phones throughout the shift. They had applied to be sergeants, and word was going around that the promotional list would be disseminated that day.

"I don't see anything," Kostoplis said.

"I think that's a good thing," Rutzen said. "I think you only get an email if you didn't make the list."

Kostoplis had left the department in 2015 and returned in 2016, but he considered leaving again after his experience testifying at the

Gun Trace Task Force trial. "This is what I came back for? This mess?" he remembered thinking as he waited two anxious days at the federal courthouse before taking the stand.

But he had since strengthened his resolve. They now tell his story during the ethics course for trainees at the police academy.

"I left; the grass is not greener. There's a lot of opportunity to do a lot of good things here. A lot of people that need help," Kostoplis said.

"This is the place to be."

SPECIAL AGENT ERIKA JENSEN left the Baltimore field office, moving on to a new assignment at FBI headquarters. She lamented that she had never been able to get a wiretap on Jenkins's phone. During their investigation it was clear Jenkins was participating in robberies and false reports, but she said that alone hadn't satisfied the criteria to tap his phone. The scope and depth of his behavior didn't become apparent to them until after the charges were filed and people started flipping. The FBI also had found nothing during their search of his home after his arrest. To investigators it seemed as if Jenkins, whether through leaks or his own conscience, had anticipated the end even as he continued to plot additional crimes.

"Sometimes I look back and wonder if he knew [his arrest] was coming, the freight train was coming off the tracks, and he couldn't help himself," Jensen said.

What about all the money? In addition to the robberies and drug sales, Jenkins was raking in $170,000 in city pay between his salary, overtime pay, and the fraudulent overtime work. Though he did have work done on his home and acquired a few cheap houses as rental properties, Jenkins never moved from the small ranch-style home he had bought with his high school sweetheart in 2005. One officer told the FBI that Jenkins had once said he had $200,000 buried somewhere and was building toward $500,000. No such stash has been located. "We have done investigations to try and find [the money]," Jensen said. "Not to be an armchair psychologist, but he had impulse control issues. Did it slip through his fingers as fast as he got it?"

WAYNE JENKINS REMAINED PUBLICLY silent for three years after his sentencing, despite a crush of overtures from reporters and filmmakers. Initially held at an Arizona prison, he was transferred in late 2018 to the medium-security Edgefield Correctional Institution in South Carolina.

In January 2020, a manila envelope landed on my desk. It contained a stack of papers and a CD. The note on the papers' first page, typed on a prison typewriter, was labeled "Special Mail" and addressed to "American citizens and public media abroad."

"It is of interest that somehow you afford me a moment to express myself, please," it began.

Using stilted and often difficult-to-decipher language designed to sound like legalese, Jenkins sought to highlight a civil lawsuit that had been recently brought against him and dismissed. The plaintiff, Andre Crowder, had taken part in 2018 in a news conference held by Ivan Bates involving people who said they had been victims of the Gun Trace Task Force. Crowder told reporters that he'd been pulled over by Jenkins for a seatbelt violation, and the officers had searched his car and found a gun. He said they later went to his home and stole $10,000. While he was locked up, his three-year-old son had died. His story had been a particularly wrenching example of the damage inflicted by the officers. In his lawsuit, Crowder claimed the gun had been planted, but in the course of litigating the lawsuit Jenkins's city-appointed attorney located body camera footage of the stop that clearly showed, from start to finish, officers finding the gun ditched under the vehicle. Crowder was on tape taking ownership and explaining to the officers how he'd obtained it.

Crowder's arrest was not one of the incidents charged in the federal racketeering case. His fraudulent claim of a gun being planted had been made after the fact, amid the piling-on against the officers. You could hardly blame some of the arrestees for trying to even the score after years of police lies.

But Jenkins seized on Crowder's disproven allegation as an opportunity to win his reputation back: The body camera clip showed that people making claims were lying, Jenkins was saying, and he had done good, honest police work all along.

Hersl, Taylor, and Allers have also continued to maintain the cases against them were fabrications; Hersl went so far as to say in letters sent from a Missouri prison that he had found himself "in a 'Serpico' position of being a good cop working with bad cops."

"As an officer in the line of duty, Wayne Earl Jenkins never planted drugs, firearms or stole money from individuals in custody, nor elsewhere," Jenkins wrote in his letter. Donald Stepp's testimony, he said, had sunk any hope he had of taking his case to trial, while Wise and Hines had "badgered" him and "scared and intimidated co-defendants and witnesses to fabricate, lie, and articulate what they need to secure conviction [sic] or make their case. This is why myself, Detective Hersl and Detective Taylor ended up with no cooperation deal at sentencing and excessive terms of imprisonment. Because we refused to lie on others!" Jenkins's wife, who forwarded the letter and body camera video, said Jenkins would grant an interview if I published the materials, which I was planning to do anyway. But attempts to follow through were unsuccessful.

Through the inmate email system, I relayed to Maurice Ward what Jenkins was saying. "Oh Wayne still up to his old tricks, lol," he replied.

Wayne Jenkins is officially scheduled to be released in January 2039.

EPILOGUE

AS THE UNREST OVER Freddie Gray's death reached its crescendo in the spring of 2015, I found myself wading into the epicenter of the riots at Pennsylvania and North avenues. My reporter's instincts were drawing me there, but I wasn't sure whether it was, well, safe. These concerns were affirmed multiple times: when I first tried to make my way south on the avenue, a police officer told me he could not let me through for my own safety. Give me a break, I said. I need to be there; that's where the story is. "Well you're not getting through this way," he said. I headed west down a side street, where a van carrying a family had stopped and a woman inside warned me not to go any farther. "They'll kill you in there!" she said. I kept going, and as I turned the corner on North Avenue, it was pandemonium. People were everywhere, a vehicle was on fire, and a police car was being destroyed. I pushed closer to the intersection where a CVS was being looted. I pressed up against a row home, hoping to go unnoticed as much as possible.

It was then that a six-foot-six man walked up to me and, without any introduction, slung his arm around my shoulder. In this atmosphere, it did not feel friendly. My first reaction was that he had me in a vulnerable position and that at any moment he was going to move his forearm from my shoulder to under my neck and put me into a headlock to rob me. If that was going to happen, it was going to happen, so I tried to stay calm.

I told him I was a reporter, and he said that he was going to protect me. They won't do nothing to you if I say you're with me, he said; we need you to be okay so you can tell the story of what really happened here today. He brought me over to the front of a row home on West North Avenue with a full view of everything transpiring. The door was open; several people stood out front. Some had blue bandannas; he said they were members of the Crips. I stood with them, taking in the chaotic scene, including watching young men crack the trunk of an abandoned police cruiser and ransack its contents.

I felt the pull to go deeper into chaos. Though the Crips members had said I would be safe with them, I thanked them and left. I didn't get far when I heard someone run up behind me and say, "Kick it out." He had a hoodie pulled tight over his face and wanted my cellphone. He pulled out a can of pepper spray, and I turned away just in time. It hit the back of my head.

I retreated back to the strip of row homes where I'd been safe and continued watching, at one point behind the shark tank–like gate of a business whose owner locked us inside. I'd watched the scene unfolding beginning at Mondawmin Mall for hours, and, with a story to file, I told the tall man that I was leaving and thanked him for looking over me. He insisted on walking me out, and we went to the same route I had come in—a cut-through aptly named Retreat Street. For a second time, I was wary that there was still a chance to rob me if he were so inclined. But he simply said goodbye.

"Wait," I said. "What's your name? How can I get in touch with you?"

I scrawled in my notebook: "Charles Shelly," followed by a phone number.

THE ENSUING MONTHS CONTINUED to be a chaotic period for Baltimore: continuing unrest, then the charges against the officers, then exploding violence. My wife was eight months pregnant during the events of April 2015, and she had our first child one month later. While learning to be a dad, I continued to document the officers' trials and the street violence.

While I thought about reaching out to Charles often, it was probably a couple of years before I fished out the notebook from that day and decided to try to find him. When I dialed the number I'd written down for him, it had been disconnected. As I searched for a way to reach him, I was reminded of a story from the unrest that had generated national media coverage, about a truce worked out between the city's gangs. Charles figured prominently into the story—he was shown in one picture wearing a Chicago Bulls jersey and a yellow bandanna around his neck, with his arm around a man who was identified as a Bloods member. He refuted a report from police, made hours before Gray's funeral on the day of the riot, that gangs were teaming up to attack police.

"It's false, absolutely false," Charles had said. "If that was the case, why wouldn't we do it today? We were on their side today."

Who was this guy, I wondered?

A month after the riot, the police and DEA had raided the same home where I had been offered refuge. The gang set leader had been charged with possession of a gun and drugs, and the case was taken federal. The DEA proclaimed that the gang had played a part in fueling the pharmacy looting, but they never made the allegation in court.

By the time I found Charles and tried to meet face-to-face, he had left the city and moved to Georgia. Our attempts to connect via phone always fell through.

With the five-year anniversary approaching in the spring of 2020, I tried again. Now Charles was back in town, and we met at a home in Northeast Baltimore where he was staying.

HE WELCOMED ME INSIDE to the cluttered home he was sharing with a few other people. The lights were off. We had barely begun catching up when Charles told me that we were going down the street to a corner carryout store to pick up food for the others in the home. It was one month into the coronavirus pandemic. He seemed to know everyone both outside and inside of the store. When I later asked him a question about the membership of the Crips in Baltimore, he said,

"I had you around quite a few just a second ago. You would never know."

Charles explained that, though he hadn't been quite aware of it then, he had been approaching a crossroads in his life at the time of the riots. He was, and remains, a Crips member. "I can't just wake up in the morning and be like, I'm not a Crip no more. That's not how that works," he said. But he had also been enrolled in community college at the time and working toward his GED when the unrest began to play out. He lived a few blocks north of Pennsylvania and North avenues, the epicenter of the riot, and he said he had no choice but to enter the fray. He said the gang truce was real, at least as far as those who were involved in urging it were concerned.

Charles said that during that time period he walked the streets with other gang members, promoting peace and unity to the people they encountered.

If this seems like gang propaganda, Charles also dismissed the narrative that police alone provoked the riot. He said he personally heard youth discussing the "Purge"—a planned riot that was said to have appeared on social media before the event took place—on the subway before it happened. "It was going in one ear and out the other—it's kids, they bluffing, they not going to put their hands on police. Lo and behold, the shit happened," he said.

The gang truce was organic, he insisted, and more simple than it appeared: people who had connections and prior contacts but had become members of rival organizations decided to put those ties to the side. "We looked at like, I wear blue, you wear red—the majority of us out here are Black. If you ain't never ever had any sense of Black unity, now would be the time to start," Charles explained. "Y'all got a powerful enemy right now—you can't look at the enemy in front of you if you looking for the enemy behind you."

Charles said in the wake of the unrest he met influential leaders who came to the city—Al Sharpton and Jesse Jackson, as well as rappers and other celebrities who visited—and he appeared on national television in addition to local media. He didn't seek to capitalize on the attention, he said, nor did it translate into any new opportunities beyond the moment. But the experience did affect his mindset.

"It showed me, I can do great things . . . I can get a job and do positive things on a smaller scale, as far as my own life. Since then, I haven't sold no drugs, I haven't been a part of any gang violence," he told me. "I've been trying to work, pay my bills, work on my credit, take care of my kids. Just be as positive as I can."

I still wanted to know: Why did he look out for me that day? I was an outsider in a moment when he was looking out for his own.

"It was everybody doing whatever the fuck they want," he said. "The chances of [something happening to you] was like 100 out of 100."

But I pushed him: So what?

"I care about people. I'm a nice guy. No matter what type of evil shit I've been into—I'm kind of like a paradox," he said. "I will hurt you. I will hurt you bad. But I've got to have a reason. At the same time, I'm not gonna let something happen to you. After it's done, it's like, I could've saved that man. That was a transitional period in my life. I believe in karma. It wasn't necessarily for you. It was for me."

Charles had held legitimate jobs in his life but often found himself confined by office work or any situation where he felt disrespected. On the streets, he knew he could make easy money slinging drugs, but it came with risks. "It finally came to a head. I can't keep making excuses. I can't keep—every time shit gets too hard—just go back there [to the streets], because if I keep going back there, one day I'll wake up and be forty and I'ma still be on somebody's corner selling drugs and go to jail. I just have to make something different happen."

His move to Georgia was not planned. His father had moved down there and asked him to stay with him for a month. Charles had lost a job through a temp agency and decided to take his dad up on the offer. He liked the change of pace. The air smelled better there. He got a job and decided to stay. He even applied for and received a concealed carry permit, which he showed me with pride.

"That was one of the happiest moments of my life," he said. "All the shit I've done—I'm changing. It's like society is slowly accepting me back."

CHARLES SAID THE RIOT was a result of people being repeatedly forced into a corner and pushing back. I asked him about police treatment of people in his community. Charles had been arrested many times in his life, including once by eventual Gun Trace Task Force officer Danny Hersl, in 2011. He said Hersl was a jerk but didn't plant drugs on him or rough him up. Still, he had bad interactions with others, including being strip searched in public—a practice documented in the Justice Department civil rights report—and detained without justification in an attempt to pump him for information.

"They wonder why, when police—good cops—try and do their investigations and do their job the right way, and they get so much kickback and flak from the community," he said, lighting a cigarette. "Because we don't fucking trust them. What have y'all done to make us trust you?

"Let's be honest," he continued. "Nobody wants to live next door to a killer. Nobody wants to see people selling drugs all day on their street, especially an area like this—although it's fucked up around here, these are people who actually own these homes and they don't want to see that shit. But they can't call [the police]. They can't assist you."

For years, the officers who eventually came together on the Gun Trace Task Force had searched people without justification, lied about entering their homes without warrants, stolen money, and recirculated drugs in the community. There are documented examples of evidence being planted or misappropriated to serve the officers' goals. People often didn't even bother to complain; those who did were mostly ignored. That is a major reason, of course, why those cops were able to get away with their crimes for as long as they did and to become ever more brazen about them. While the police department leadership begged citizens to cooperate, and many officers were working to improve community relations, some of its most elite officers were running roughshod on Black men in poor neighborhoods, creating a free-fire zone for anyone seeking to exploit them. Between those who had experienced the abuse and the relatives, friends, and coworkers who heard their stories, people who had never trusted the cops in the first place became only more contemptuous of them. Baltimore's Black communities have been both overpoliced and underpoliced.

———

A COUPLE OF WEEKS after the anniversary of Gray's death, video of the killing of a Georgia man named Ahmaud Arbery went viral. The two white residents who accosted Arbery as he was jogging through their neighborhood said that they believed he had committed a crime, so they tracked him down and shot him in the street—a modern-day lynching. Then, a national outrage was prompted by the videotaped killing of George Floyd by a Minneapolis police officer who kneeled on Floyd's neck for more than eight minutes as he said, "I can't breathe." The dormant Black Lives Matter protests roared back, this time in even larger numbers and with a renewed urgency. Massive protests occurred in nearly every American city; Minneapolis burned, and looting prompted curfews in several cities including New York, D.C., Atlanta, and San Francisco.

Baltimore was not among them.

The mood during the first three nights of local protest was tense; Baltimore had been through this once before, and many felt that five years later little had changed. For those who believed "No justice, no peace" should mean just that, another uprising would be understandable, if not outright merited. But on the streets this time, people spoke about how the last round had stained the city's reputation and how other individuals had paid a personal price.

At youth-led protests at City Hall, organizers demanded that the assembled protesters not do anything that might provoke an aggressive police response that might get members of the crowd hurt. One activist chased away a man who knocked over a trash can during a march. The next night, whenever a bottle flew in the direction of police clad in riot gear, young community leaders sliced through the crowd and shut them down. Fireworks were later thrown at officers, and other protesters pulled to the ground the people they suspected to be responsible. Police held the line and watched the crowd handle itself. The message had been sent, and for weeks to come, thousands took part in passionate, peaceful protests and organized for future lobbying efforts. They vowed this time to create lasting change.

In his 2018 testimony, Donald Stepp, Sergeant Wayne Jenkins's drug-dealing partner, remarked that the police officers of Baltimore "owned the city." And he's right in the sense that for years they were able to enrich themselves and assert their authority on the streets. But the task of building trust and keeping people safe, the job they took an oath to provide, was not something all the officers' power was able to achieve.

Watching the community once again take to the streets, this time also reining in those who sought to escalate, I thought back to what Charles had told me earlier that spring.

"We still run this shit," he had said. "As a police officer, you can literally only do what we allow you to do. We—as far as the community itself, even the drug dealers—we run this city."

ACKNOWLEDGMENTS

I could only tell this story through conversations with those who lived it. I am particularly thankful to Umar Burley, Gary Childs, Jeremy Eldridge, Ryan Guinn, James Kostoplis, Antonio Shropshire, and Maurice Ward for sharing their stories, as well as the U.S. Attorney's Office, the FBI's Baltimore field office, and the Baltimore Police for granting access to interviews with investigators including assistant U.S. attorneys Derek Hines and Leo Wise, FBI agents Erika Jensen and Gregg Domroe, and BPD sergeant John Sieracki, who I thank for their time and perspective. Thank you also to Harford sheriff corporal David McDougall and Baltimore County sergeant Scott Kilpatrick.

D'Andre Adams, Gary Brown, Serigne Gueye, Malik McCaffity, and Demetric Simon deserve additional thanks for being among those who provided crucial insight into their interactions with officers and the impact on their lives. Attorneys Ivan Bates, Joshua Insley, Deborah K. Levi, Erin Murphy, and Steve Silverman lead the many attorneys in town who helped me report this story, while Kevin Davis and Anthony Barksdale are among the former top police officials who were particularly accessible. I also want to thank Robert F. Cherry for his insights over the years.

And finally, thank you to Charles Shelly, for looking out for me—and others—in April 2015 and for sitting down to talk about it five years later.

As discussed in the notes section, there are scores of other people who were interviewed over the years and for this project who do not appear credited in any way, either because their information did not make the cut or because it generally contributed to an understanding of certain topics or events. Others still stuck their neck out and spoke on the condition of anonymity—they cannot be thanked by name, but please know that I valued your time and insight.

I am indebted to David Simon, who raised the idea of a book to me during the Gun Trace Task Force trial and connected me with his literary agent, Rafe Sagalyn, who guided the process along with his assistant Brandon Coward. David's nonfiction writing set an un-achievable bar for police reporters across the country and especially those at *The Sun,* and I have been privileged to be able to reach out to him over the years. Rafe and Brandon were patient with me as I took on this new type of writing challenge, and found a home for the project.

I am so grateful to Andy Ward at Random House, who decided to take on the project, and who along with Marie Pantojan provided editing and guidance. Andy took the time to meet with me when the project was being pitched, and stayed involved even as he ascended to a new role with the company. He and Marie were attentive and careful editors who improved my words while working around the demands of my daily newspaper reporting.

What would I have done without Peter Griffin? Peter was enormously helpful working with me closely as an editor-before-the-editors during the most intense six months of writing and beyond.

Wil Hylton and Tom French provided crucial guidance and support during the proposal process. Wil was a supportive ear and mentor, while Tom agreed to a marathon editing session on the proposal when I felt lost. Alec MacGillis and D. Watkins provided further counsel for which I am also appreciative.

I want to thank my family—past and present—at *The Baltimore Sun,* where I was hired in 2005 and eventually placed onto the police beat in 2008, allowing me to report on events that occurred during much of the period covered by this book. Thank you to my partners in covering crime for those years, particularly Peter Hermann, Gus Sentementes, Melissa Harris, Justin George, Ian Duncan, Kevin Rector, Jessica Anderson, and Tim Prudente. The tumultuous events of

2015 in particular were truly a group effort, and the reporting in this book draws from all of their work. Those not already named include but certainly are not limited to Luke Broadwater, Colin Campbell, Meredith Cohn, Scott Dance, Doug Donovan, Erica Green, Jean Marbella, Mark Puente, Catherine Rentz, Dan Rodricks, and Yvonne Wenger, as well as editorial leadership including Trif Alatzas, Eileen Canzian, Sam Davis, Kalani Gordon, Richard Martin, Laura Smitherman, and Sean Welsh. There are so many others, the great photo staff, copy editors, and designers, who are integral to bringing our readers the news. Also thank you to the many other journalists who covered these events side by side with us, in particular Juliet Linderman and the staff of the late *Baltimore City Paper*, who were silenced at a pivotal point in our city's history.

A special mention to Diana Sugg, who helped guide many of my important projects in recent years and generally provided support to me and so many others.

Thank you also to Tribune Publishing attorney Mike Burke for working with me to lift barriers to this project.

I appreciate the readers who have supported local journalism, those who provide productive critiques that keep us on our toes and thinking critically, and anyone who has let me into their world to tell stories over the years.

Thank you to Jennifer and Charlotte for your patience and support during the nights and weekends as I toiled away on this project, and generally tolerating the demands I placed on myself over the years as I attempted to do this job as well as I could. Thanks also to my parents—who subscribed to two newspapers, helped me with my paper route when I overslept on the weekends, and later supported my career goals—as well as my brothers and other extended family.

Rest in Peace Shawn and Kevin Cannady, Kendal Fenwick, Freddie Gray, Gregory Harding, Walter Price, and Sean Suiter.

This is a book that takes on years of cover-ups and lies, so I have endeavored whenever possible to cite sources within the text. In this notes section, I attempt to pin down specific pieces of information that can be traced to a particular conversation, document, or event. Reporting for this book included interviews with more than two hundred people, not including incidental interviews as part of my reporting for *The Baltimore Sun*. Whenever possible, interviews were conducted on the record, but some subjects requested anonymity either because they were not authorized to speak or because they wanted to speak candidly about sensitive topics. Some sources were consulted multiple times and for hours; others were engaged about a particular fact or aspect.

The number of court records and internal records involving the officers that I reviewed is in the thousands and incalculable. The trials of Daniel Hersl and Marcus Taylor, and of Antonio Shropshire and others charged in his narcotics conspiracy case, are central to the story, but there were dozens of other trials involving the officers or their targets for which I watched courtroom tapes or read transcripts that are not specifically cited. Those included people arrested by the officers and also cases of other officers accused of misconduct prior and unrelated to the Gun Trace Task Force case.

Significant insight was gained through public records requests of body camera footage of GTTF officers who had been issued cameras, as well as emails of Wayne Jenkins and, to a lesser extent, Thomas

Allers. Baltimore County Police produced hundreds of pages related to their investigations of Donald Stepp, with the Maryland Insurance Administration providing additional hundreds also on Stepp.

In Maryland, despite the revelations from this case and others, police misconduct records remain secret by law despite repeated pushes to provide greater transparency. Revelatory information reported from Internal Affairs and personnel was obtained through sources who took a risk in providing it, and whose efforts are appreciated.

While the Justice Department report on the Baltimore Police Department released in 2017 is cited, another study of the department that I used as a reference was the No Boundaries Coalition's March 2016 report "The People's Findings Regarding Police Misconduct in West Baltimore."

I. KNOCKERS

3   **Months earlier, Burley:** Umar Burley, interview, October 7, 2019.

4   **Members of a plainclothes police squad:** Ryan Guinn, interview, June 24, 2018.

4   **"Let's go":** Ibid.

5   **the "Vikings":** Kevin Davis, interview, August 14, 2018.

5   **They would often be given names:** Ryan Guinn, interview, June 24, 2019.

6   **"Hey Sean":** Police radio recording.

6   **The chase lasted less than a minute:** The vehicles traveled about eight-tenths of a mile before the crash.

6   **"Why did you pull off?":** Burley, interview, October 7, 2019.

7   **Guinn caught the passenger:** Guinn, interview, June 24, 2018.

7   **"The shit's in the car":** USA v. Jenkins indictment, 2017.

7   **The couple was taken downtown:** Guinn, interview, June 24, 2018.

7   **He had spent years in the game:** Burley, interview, October 7, 2019.

8   **In 2007:** Court records, USA v. Burley.

8   **But Burley swore:** James Johnston, interview, April 29, 2019;
     Johnston was Burley's attorney for the state charges. These as-
     sertions are also reflected in the notes of Thomas Crowe, his
     later federal attorney, whose pleading is quoted next.

8   **Guinn later said:** Guinn, interview, February 18, 2020.

9   **"If this case goes to trial":** USA v. Jenkins indictment.

2. WHATEVER IT TAKES

10   **"There was no question":** Donald Kimelman, "Baltimore Mayor
     Charms City with Unusual Style," Knight-Ridder, August 22,
     1979.

11   **It burst into public view:** Peter Jensen, "Killer of Two Men,
     Their Pregnant Wives Gets Life, No Parole," *Baltimore Sun*,
     December 16, 1989.

11   **His father, Lloyd "Lee" Jenkins:** Matthew Jenkins, letter to
     Judge Catherine C. Blake, submitted May 24, 2018.

11   **Not only was Wayne the youngest:** Ibid.

11   **"Wayne didn't take shit from no one":** Andy Janowich, inter-
     view, 2019.

12   **Jenkins attended Eastern Technical High School:** Eastern
     Tech yearbook, 1998.

12   **"Rudy":** Lloyd Lee Jenkins II, letter to Judge Blake.

12   **The football coach, Nick Arminio:** Nick Arminio, interview,
     2019.

12   **A few months later:** Enlistment information from U.S. Marine
     Corps.

12   **He connected with a fellow Baltimore-area native:** Patrick
     Armetta, interview, February 15, 2020.

13   **In 2000, Jenkins reached the rank:** U.S. Marine Corps.

13   **"the utmost flawless character":** First Sergeant Todd A. Brown,
     letter to Judge Blake.

13   **Jenkins was perhaps most focused:** Armetta, interview, Febru-
     ary 15, 2020.

13   **"This is my community":** Eric Baumgart, former chief of Bow-
     leys Quarters Volunteer Fire Department, letter to Judge Blake.

He went on to say, "That night, I assigned Wayne dozens of rescues saving countless lives. Without him, I am not certain of the outcome of the families he rescued."

13   **Jenkins was rejected:** Jenkins's personnel file information.

14   **His military pedigree and toughness:** Interviews with class members Jason Rathell, Dan Horgan, and Gillian Whitfield, spring 2019.

14   **"With drugs the way they are":** David Simon, "In Police Front Lines, Sense of Duty Falters," *Baltimore Sun*, February 8, 1994.

14   **"broken windows theory":** James Q. Wilson and George L. Kelling, "Broken Windows: The Police and Neighborhood Safety," *Atlantic Monthly*, March 1982, 29–36, 38.

14   **Baltimore's commissioner in the late 1990s:** Peter Hermann, "Police to Begin Ticketing in Oct.," *Baltimore Sun*, September 18, 1996.

15   **"We're the police":** Peter Hermann, "Wanted: Less Social Work, More Law Enforcement; 'I'd Like for Us to Be the Police Again,' Says Commissioner," *Baltimore Sun*, April 20, 2000.

15   **Black political leaders had concerns:** Ivan Penn, "Black Officials Raise Zero-Tolerance Fears," *Baltimore Sun*, December 21, 1999.

15   **Their eventual 152-page report:** Van Smith, "Believe It . . . Or Not," *Baltimore City Paper*, August 27, 2003.

15   **Davis angrily described the police affidavit:** Gail Gibson, "U.S. Judge Rebukes City Police After Rejecting Evidence," *Baltimore Sun*, March 10, 2003.

16   **Horgan, the recruit class commander:** Dan Horgan, interview, 2019.

17   **"Write the violation!":** Del Quentin Wilber, "Police Commissioner Begins Plan to Drive Drug Gangs off Streets," *Baltimore Sun*, May 12, 2003.

18   **The makers' stated message:** Ethan Brown, *Snitch: Informants, Cooperators and the Corruption of Justice* (New York: Public Affairs, 2007), 172.

18   **At their trial, King testified:** Matthew Dolan, "City Detective Speaks Out at Corruption Trial," *Baltimore Sun*, March 28, 2006.

19   **City officials treated the case:** Another bellwether case at the time was that of the Southeast District "Special Enforcement Team"; in a series of lawsuits its members were accused of some of the very same types of misconduct the Gun Trace Task Force would be charged with ten years later: making bad stops, entering people's homes without a warrant, and taking money. Attorneys for the plaintiffs wrote in one filing that Assistant State's Attorney Tony Gioia told them that one of the SET team members agreed to cooperate and in exchange was allowed to remain an officer in good standing. Gioia told the attorneys that the cooperating officer gave detailed testimony admitting to "falsifying charging documents, lying and stealing" on the part of the squad. No one was ever criminally charged. The sergeant, William Harris, was placed on then–state's attorney Patricia C. Jessamy's "do not call" list, but the list was abolished in 2010 by her successor, Gregg Bernstein, and was never restored by Marilyn Mosby. Harris in recent years worked on the SWAT team and through overtime was annually one of the highest-paid employees in the city.

19   **One man that year:** Gus G. Sentementes, "O'Malley, Hamm Hear Criticism of Arrest Policies," *Baltimore Sun,* January 5, 2006.

19   **Former officer Eric Kowalczyk:** Eric Kowalczyk, *The Politics of Crisis: An Insider's Prescription to Prevent Public Policy Disasters* (Oceanside, CA: Indie Books International, 2019), 24–25.

20   **One Saturday night:** Testimony from O'Connor v. Fries et al., 2008.

21   **"All this happened over nothing":** Charles Lee, interview, 2019.

22   **"They're just treating these people like animals":** Michael Pulver, interview, 2018.

22   **Cirello, who has since left:** Robert Cirello, interview, December 2018.

23   **When Fries was promoted:** Mike Fries, testimony, George Sneed v. Michael Fries et al. trial, 2010.

23   **In late 2005:** State property records.

3. BAD GUYS WITH GUNS

25   **The department eventually settled a lawsuit:** Though Bealefeld immediately began disavowing zero tolerance tactics, the 2006 lawsuit by the ACLU and NAACP (Maryland State Conference of NAACP Branches et al. v. Baltimore City Police Department et al.) was not formalized until June 2010.

25   **Barksdale believed that tough policing was necessary:** Anthony Barksdale, interview, April 23, 2018.

26   **"There was so much pressure":** John Skinner, interview, May 20, 2019.

27   **"I don't want 2,900 scarecrows":** Annie Linskey, "From the Sidewalk Up," *Baltimore Sun,* May 18, 2008.

27   **Though such lists exist now in other cities:** Patricia Jessamy, emailed statement, June 6, 2020.

27   **Another signature program:** The unit was initially called the Gun Tracing Task Force and over the years would eventually be called the Gun Trace Task Force.

27   **One of the inaugural members:** Ryan Guinn, interview, March 18, 2019.

28   **The task force's mission:** In the Baltimore Police Department's 2007 annual report, the unit's mission was described as follows: "Task Force investigations can be in-depth and time-consuming, and may involve extensive database analyses and street surveillance to prepare a case for indictment and prosecution. Among a variety of investigative avenues to pursue, task force members inquire into the identity of the original buyers of firearms that are seized from criminal suspects; determine the amount of time between the original purchase of the firearm and law enforcement's seizure of it; investigate the relationship between the original purchaser of the firearm and the criminal suspect; and review ammunition records at retail outlets to learn if convicted felons have attempted to purchase firearms ammunition."

28   **In its first full year:** Baltimore Police, "Annual Report, 2008," 41.

28   **After they took down a gun dealer:** Stephen Janis, "Mayors Vow Action on Illegal Firearms," *Baltimore Examiner,* February 14, 2008.

28   **Asked on the stand:** Wayne Jenkins, testimony, Troy Smith et al. v. Knoerlein et al. trial, March 24, 2011.

29   **"To get a 41-kilo seizure":** Ben Nuckols, "Baltimore Police Make Largest-Ever Drug Seizure," Associated Press, February 21, 2009.

29   **One officer recalled:** Interview with an officer who spoke on condition of anonymity, 2018.

29   **Another recalled him this way:** Interview with another officer who spoke on condition of anonymity, 2018.

29   **Others, however, were skeptical:** Interview with a third officer who spoke on condition of anonymity, 2020.

30   **In Jenkins's spare time:** From the Official M.A.S.T.E.R. System Website—the discontinued site of Jenkins's MMA trainer, James Guy.

30   **One drizzly afternoon:** Rodney Bailey, testimony, USA v. Mickey Oakley, 2010.

32   **the bar case went before a civil jury:** Antonio Lee was shot dead on January 23, 2011, when a van pulled up alongside his car in East Baltimore and opened fire. The civil trial commenced on March 22, 2011.

32   **The attorney representing Jenkins:** The defense attorney for the officers was Michael Marshall.

33   **Woods delivered an impassioned rebuttal:** Video of proceedings in Eric Smith et al. v. Baltimore City Police Department et al., March 30, 2011.

33   **"They have free rein":** Brendan Kearney, "Baltimore Jury Awards $1 to Bystander in Bar Bust," *Daily Record*, March 30, 2011. Plaintiff Troy Smith gave this quote. Jury foreman James Morrison added: "We just felt like there was not really enough evidence to convict any of the defendants. Basically, these guys were located at a site where there was . . . a drug bust going on."

33   **Guinn said Jenkins refused:** Ryan Guinn, interview, June 24, 2018.

34   **One detective who worked with Jenkins:** Interview with a fourth officer who spoke on the condition of anonymity, 2019.

35   **A peculiar incident:** This alleged incident is documented in an internal report by Detective Sergeant Robert Velte dated April 2011.

4. EYES AND EARS

36   **Wayne Jenkins was promoted:** Wayne Jenkins's personnel file.

37   **James Kostoplis had joined:** James Kostoplis, interview, May 8, 2019.

37   **"would try to freestyle battle":** Maurice Ward interview, [September or October 2018?].

38   **he had a front-row seat:** James Kostoplis, interview, April 28, 2020. Three people—two men fleeing from police and an innocent bystander—were killed in the fiery crash that occurred September 24, 2013. Rumors have circulated since his indictment that Jenkins, known for getting into high-speed chases, played a role in the chase and it was covered up. With the caveat that many cases have been shown over the years to have a different sequence of events than was reported at the time, my reporting could not substantiate that Jenkins was involved other than getting onto the police radio to inquire about the chase after another sergeant had instructed the officers to discontinue the pursuit. Dispatch records show that a sergeant named Tashania Brown ordered those officers to cut off the chase. Jenkins then jumped onto the radio, asking where the vehicle had been last seen. One of the officers then moved to another radio channel and called out locations of the chase until the crash. As reported in this chapter, Kostoplis says he was riding with Jenkins at the time and they were in a different area of the city. They were headed that direction to assist and then heard there'd been a crash. The chase "was not a very long thing," Kostoplis told me.

38   **In less intense scenarios:** Kostoplis, interview, May 8, 2019.

38   **Two weeks after his promotion:** Donald Stepp, testimony, USA v. Hersl et al., February 1, 2018.

39   **Former Baltimore County police commissioner:** James Johnston, interview, 2019.

39   **"Seven years ago"**: Sentence modification hearing transcript, State v. Stepp, February 2, 2004.

40   **He became the top loan officer**: Dennis Danielczyk, letter of reference to Maryland Insurance Administration, 2013.

40   **With a mortgage to pay**: Stepp, testimony, USA v. Hersl et al., February 1, 2018.

40   **a crowdsourced online design site**: I tracked down the man who responded to Stepp's solicitation pitch for a logo, and he forwarded me Stepp's message.

41   **"I guess there are some feminists here"**: Tyler Waldman, "Racy Bail Bonds Sign Draws Ire," *Towson Patch*, November 15, 2011.

41   **In a two-page typed letter**: Wayne Jenkins, letter to Maryland Insurance Administration, January 21, 2003.

42   **Since their Delaware Park Casino trip**: Stepp, testimony, USA v. Hersl et al., February 1, 2018.

43   **But Jenkins was again playing with fire**: Baltimore County Police Department records.

5. DON'T FREEZE UP

44   **In January 2014**: Video of court hearing, Shirley Johnson et al. v. Umar Burley, January 14, 2014.

44   **He was emotionally destroyed**: Umar Burley, interview, October 7, 2019.

47   **With homicides and shootings**: Despite cutting hundreds of positions, the Baltimore Police Department remained at one of the highest staffing levels in the country. The department budget also jumped considerably under Rawlings-Blake's tenure, from $352 million in 2011 to $476 milion in 2016. But the numbers are misleading: the police budget rose $70 million—16 percent— in a single year (fiscal 2013) on the strength of a simple accounting change, with pension costs shifted from central budgeting to the agency level that year. "Other personnel costs" within the police budget rose from $46 million in fiscal year 2012 to $111 million in fiscal 2013 as a result of the pension shift, even as salary spending dropped that year. Actual spending did not increase by $70 million, and the long-term increase is misleading as a result.

48   **Batts had fled Oakland:** Tasion Kwamilele, "Anthony Batts, the Exit Interview: In Oakland, the Police Department Is Seen as the Necessary Evil," *Oakland North,* November 7, 2011.

48   **Demetric Simon had been driving:** Demetric Simon, interview, 2018.

49   **Jenkins got onto the dispatch radio:** Dispatch audio of Wayne Jenkins.

49   **"What the fuck did you do?":** Ryan Guinn, interview, March 18, 2019.

50   **Gladstone was eating:** Keith Gladstone, plea agreement.

50   **"I didn't see it":** Ben Frieman, Internal Affairs interview transcript, 2014.

50   **"I tell my clients":** Paul Polansky, interview, 2018.

50   **But in their subsequent investigation:** Investigative file for Force Investigation Team review of Demetric Simon case.

50   **The Internal Affairs investigator:** Wayne Jenkins's personnel file documents.

51   **When she followed up with him:** Internal Affairs investigation summary report, dated March 17, 2015.

51   **And Price's attorney said:** Bryan Mobley, interview, 2017.

52   **"When I saw the video":** Molly Webb, interview, 2017.

53   **"I think he's given us all he's going to":** This is from an account of the conversation that I obtained through a source in late 2017.

53   **The two officers sat for separate interviews:** Internal Affairs file, Walter Price investigation, 2015.

6. GROUND SHIFT

55   **During one radio appearance:** Marilyn Mosby, interview on *The Marc Steiner Show,* WEAA, June 5, 2014.

56   **"In point of fact":** Gregg Bernstein, news conference, January 24, 2013.

56   **Mosby expressly praised police:** Marilyn Mosby, campaign kickoff speech, accessed from YouTube, June 24, 2013, https://www.youtube.com/watch?v=iXu4-zZeXGM.

57   **In her 1998 high school yearbook:** Mark Puente, "Mosby Says

She Learned from Mistakes of Family Members in Law Enforcement," *Baltimore Sun,* July 15, 2015.

58   **Jenkins himself had been involved:** Investigative file, Internal Affairs investigation of September 4, 2013, shooting.

58   **Witnesses disputed:** Justin George and Justin Fenton, "Man Killed in Police-Involved Shooting Is Identified," *Baltimore Sun,* September 5, 2013.

59   **Meanwhile, *The Baltimore Sun*:** Mark Puente, "Undue Force," *Baltimore Sun,* September 28, 2014. Puente's deep-dive report showed that since 2011 taxpayers had paid $7.5 million on such settlements, and he illustrated it with stories from alleged victims. It should be noted that the *Maryland Daily Record*'s Brendan Kearney had documented the financial impact as of that time in a series of articles in 2011, reporting that the city had paid "at least"—one official said it was likely "a significant undercount"—$16.8 million from July 2004 through early 2011. A 2006 *Sun* article said the city had paid out $3.5 million in 2005 alone, and $5 million in 2004.

59   **It wasn't uncommon:** Interview with former city official who requested anonymity.

59   **"People kept telling me":** Anthony Batts, remarks to President's Task Force on 21st Century Policing, February 13, 2015.

7. LET'S STAND TOGETHER

61   **a study found:** Amanda Petteruti, Aleks Kajstura, Marc Schindler, Peter Wagner, and Jason Ziedenberg, "The Right Investment? Corrections Spending in Baltimore City," Justice Policy Institute and the Prison Policy Initiative, February 25, 2015, www.justicepolicy.org/uploads/justicepolicy/documents/rightinvestment_design_2.23.15_final.pdf.

61   **The development's history:** Lawrence Lanahan, *The Lines Between Us: Two Families and a Quest to Cross Baltimore's Racial Divide* (New York: New Press, 2019), 11–12.

63   **Another resident, Kevin Moore:** Catherine Rentz, "Videographer: Freddie Gray Was Folded Like Origami," *Baltimore Sun,* April 23, 2015.

63   **Jacqueline Jackson, fifty-three:** Kevin Rector, "The Forty-Five Minute Mystery of Freddie Gray's Death," *Baltimore Sun*, April 25, 2015.

65   **Around this time:** Terrence McCoy, "How Companies Make Millions off Lead-Poisoned, Poor Blacks," *Washington Post*, August 25, 2015.

66   **Jenkins, who just a month earlier:** "The Baltimore Uprising— Part 1," uploaded to YouTube by Baltimore BLOC. Uploaded May 26, 2015, https://www.youtube.com/watch?v=Vz5urb dwjCg. Other videos, posted by user "The AList" on Vine and YouTube, show a uniformed Jenkins responding to a disturbance. "Protesters put in back of the police wagon in front of shake and bake": https://vine.co/v/ea0636lIeuA; "Protesters Surround a police car Pennsylvania Avenue #FreddieGray #JusticeForFreddie #BlackLivesMater": https://vine.co/v/ea06 MDIZrUF; "Police arrest Freddie Gray protesters on Pennsylvania Ave": https://www.youtube.com/watch?v=UoW7PLlQtjs &feature=youtu.be.

67   **Inside police headquarters that night:** Published and unpublished material from *Baltimore Sun* reporter Justin George. Published material ran in the *Sun* series "Looking for Answers," October 9, 2015. Unpublished material was provided by George.

70   **A decade earlier, Baltimore juries:** Jeffrey Alston won a $39 million verdict from a jury after he was paralyzed from the neck down after a 1997 police van ride. Dondi Johnson Sr., who told a doctor in 2005 that he had not been buckled in and had gone face first into the van after the van made a sharp turn, suffered a fractured neck and died two weeks later from pneumonia. His relatives won a $7.4 million verdict. The city settled the former for $6 million; the state's cap on damages resulted in the latter being reduced to $219,000.

70   **The next day:** Reporting from Justin George.

70   **Batts's eyes were bloodshot and blurry:** Ibid.

71   **Kowalczyk later said authorities had an informant:** Eric Kowalczyk, *The Politics of Crisis: An Insider's Prescription to Prevent Public Policy Disasters* (Oceanside, CA: Indie Books International, 2019), 97.

71   **the FBI would later say:** Jason Leopold, "Fearing a 'Catastrophic Incident,' 400 Federal Officers Descended on the Baltimore Protests," *Vice News*, June 24, 2015.

71   **The first rock was reported thrown:** Kevin Rector, "What Happened at Mondawmin? Newly Obtained Documents Shed Light on Start of Baltimore Riot," *Baltimore Sun*, April 20, 2019.

72   **Wayne Jenkins stood in the dim light:** This account is compiled from sources including Jenkins's own write-up of the event and the version superiors submitted for a commendation, as well as an account from the Division of Correction driver Corporal Andre Jones, other internal reports, video footage from news outlets and citizens, and interviews with people on scene. I obtained a disc of aired footage from CNN while footage archived online includes from a Fox affiliate (https://www.youtube.com /watch?v=sCtKKU64e1M, around the 14:40 mark); CBS news (https://www.youtube.com/watch?v=UBNRj1eRWLs, the 5:45 mark); and RT (https://www.youtube.com/watch?v=_5kHRQ GMyC0, at the 21:10 mark). Notably, none of the seven other officers awarded for helping Jenkins that day was willing to speak about the incident, and reports from the corrections officer indicate Jenkins may have identified himself as another officer when he commandeered the vehicle. All of the DOC reports identified the officer who took the van as Sergeant John Berry, who was not involved.

73   **Jenkins would later write up his own account:** Wayne Jenkins, email, May 18, 2015.

73   **A supervisor on the ground later recalled:** Interview with an officer who spoke on the condition of anonymity because of not being authorized to speak.

73   **Other officers remember:** Multiple officers who were not authorized to speak recalled this in interviews.

73   **clashes were pushing into residential side streets:** These next two paragraphs are drawn from my own observations from being at the center of the unrest that day.

73   **"Looting expected":** Baltimore City Fraternal Order of Police, Lodge #3, "After Action Review: A Review of the Management

of the 2015 Baltimore Riots," July 8, 2015, https://fop3.org/wp
-content/uploads/2019/08/AAR-Final.pdf, 30.

74   **Asked after his arrest:** Court documents from USA v. Donta
Betts.

74   **Nearly 315,000 doses of drugs:** Meredith Cohn, "DEA: 80 Percent More Drugs Taken During Pharmacy Looting Than Previously Reported," *Baltimore Sun,* August 17, 2016.

74   **Later that night:** Donald Stepp, testimony, USA v. Hersl et al.,
February 1, 2018.

75   **They said the public had lost confidence:** Sam Cogen, interview, April 18, 2020.

75   **Meanwhile, Mosby felt:** Wil Hylton, "Baltimore vs. Marilyn
Mosby," *New York Times,* October 2, 2016.

76   **About five minutes before the news conference started:** Ibid.

77   **Back at police headquarters:** Justin George, "Tension Mounts
Between Police, Prosecutors as Charges Announced in Freddie
Gray Case," *Baltimore Sun,* October 9, 2015.

78   **"Well, we are all fucked":** Text messages included in Freddie
Gray case investigative file released by police.

78   **Within a half hour:** Wayne Jenkins, email, May 1, 2015.

78   **Jenkins next organized a fundraiser:** Wayne Jenkins, email,
May 14, 2015. Liquor board records show Danielczyk's ownership tie.

79   **One prosecutor:** Interview with a source who spoke on the
condition of anonymity.

79   **"All we heard":** Interview with a source who spoke on the condition of anonymity.

80   **Andre Hunt:** Hunt was arrested in October 2013 by Jenkins
and Frieman. The DEA's Group 52 joined the case and recovered two kilograms of heroin during a search warrant. Hunt
flipped and pleaded guilty, and was set to turn himself in on
May 18, 2015. He was shot dead in broad daylight on April 29,
2015. Biographical details come from Peter Hermann's May 17,
2015, article in the *Washington Post,* "After Rioters Burned Baltimore, Killings Pile Up Under the Radar."

80   **A thirty-one-year-old woman and her seven-year-old boy:**

This refers to the killing of Jennifer Jeffrey-Browne and her son Kester "Tony" Browne on May 28, 2015.

80   **The twenty-two-year-old son:** Ronnie Thomas III was fatally shot on May 31, 2015. He was first shot in 2013 after knocking somebody out in a fight outside a Southeast Baltimore seafood restaurant. The next year, Thomas was charged with shooting someone. Three days after Carlos Wheeler, the man charged with shooting Thomas, was convicted, Thomas was killed. The violence continued: prosecutors say Wheeler's brother was later killed as retaliation for Wheeler shooting Thomas in 2013.

80   **He met with officers:** Recording of Anthony Batts's address to officers at union meeting, May 26, 2015.

80   **Mayor Rawlings-Blake felt Batts couldn't lead:** Stephanie Rawlings-Blake interview, July 1, 2019.

81   **"We are pushing for an all-hands-on-deck approach":** Stephanie Rawlings-Blake, news conference, July 12, 2015.

81   **Community members and officers alike:** Kevin Davis, interview, August 14, 2018.

82   **"Any hope I had of continuing":** Kowalczyk, *Politics of Crisis,* 131–33.

8. CLEARED

83   **Ward considered it "an honor":** Maurice Ward, interviews.

84   **Sometimes, when they came across groups:** Maurice Ward, testimony, USA v. Hersl et al., January 23, 2018.

85   **They'd often take people's keys:** Ward, interviews.

85   **The oldest of three children:** Maurice Ward, sentencing memorandum, May 29, 2018.

86   **"I was excited":** Ward, interviews.

87   **In late 2015:** Wayne Jenkins, email to Dean Palmere, December 24, 2015.

87   **"Sir I hate to call you":** Wayne Jenkins, email to Darryl De Sousa, January 4, 2016.

87   **Ward had been working with Jenkins:** Ward, interviews.

88   **Later, Jenkins did more than talk:** Maurice Ward, testimony, USA v. Hersl et al., and interviews.

89   **In November, Jenkins and his wife:** Various family and friends referred to the lost child in their letters submitted as part of Jenkins's sentencing memorandum.

90   **But nothing happened:** Rodney Hill, Summer 2018 interview with *Al Jazeera,* and Jenkins's personnel files. Jenkins's personnel records show that De Sousa and later another deputy commissioner, Jason Johnson, approved the punishment. De Sousa, for his part, said in May 2019 that he did not recall the case: "All disciplinary decisions were put through the proper consideration by command staff and BPD legal department. No single person was in a position to make unilateral discipline decisions." *Al Jazeera* provided a full transcript of the interview, including extensive unaired portions.

90   **A few months prior, Jenkins had text-messaged:** Jessica Lussenhop, "When Cops Become Robbers," BBC News, April 3, 2018.

90   **He chose to rip into Internal Affairs:** Wayne Jenkins, statement to Captain Kevin Jones, personnel file, January 15, 2016.

91   **Jenkins set up a meeting:** Arrangements for the meeting are documented in emails from September 30 and October 6, 2015.

91   **Meanwhile, Jenkins was also lobbying commanders:** Wayne Jenkins, email, December 3, 2015.

91   **Jenkins, who showed up trying to coach Laronde:** This account is drawn from interviews with three sources, as well as documented by Baynard Woods in the article "Internal Affairs," *Real News Network,* May 23, 2018.

92   **"He knew where that line was":** Hill, *Al Jazeera* interview.

9. TRACKERS

95   **As a drug cop working:** Scott Kilpatrick, interview, August 30, 2019.

96   **Sometimes they would refuse to assist:** In addition to Kilpatrick's observations, Baltimore County prosecutors confirmed

that in February 2015 they dropped a case brought in their jurisdiction by Jenkins and Frieman, after the defense attorney Ivan Bates said the officers had credibility concerns. The prosecutor, Fran Pilarski, said he called a county officer he knew, who agreed that Jenkins had integrity concerns.

96 **In 2012, Baltimore County:** Maryland Department of Health reports.

96 **As he and other county detectives:** Kilpatrick, interview, August 30, 2019.

97 **"Your man Jenkins":** Pen register application, March 14, 2016.

97 **Antonio Shropshire had grown up:** Antonio Shropshire, interviews.

98 **Among the officers who arrested him:** Court records.

98 **He said he took the nickname:** Shropshire, interviews.

100 **McDougall, working:** David McDougall, interview, June 25, 2019.

100 **A nineteen-year-old from a beach town:** Tim Prudente, "How Heroin Overdoses in the Suburbs Exposed Baltimore's Corrupt Police Squad, the Gun Trace Task Force," *Baltimore Sun,* March 16, 2018.

100 **"Got any boy?":** Testimony, USA v. Shropshire et al.

100 **"The supply of OxyContin dried up":** Kenneth Diggins, testimony, USA v. Shropshire.

101 **McDougall checked "deconfliction" databases:** McDougall, interview, June 25, 2019.

102 **"These guys would be dealing all day":** Kilpatrick, interview, August 30, 2019.

102 **A widow who had started using:** These accounts come from the buyers' testimony at the trial of USA v. Shropshire.

103 **"The police, man":** Video of controlled buy from Antonio Shropshire.

104 **The undercover cop set up a second buy:** Court records, USA v. Shropshire.

105 **Anderson had been caught:** Pen register application, March 14, 2016.

105 **That struck McDougall as odd:** McDougall, interview, June 25, 2019.

10. VALOR

107   **At midnight, Rayam was sitting in the car:** Jemell Rayam, testimony, USA v. Hersl et al., 2018.

107   **The armed man emerged:** Shores et al. v. Rayam et al. civil lawsuit.

108   **"I called Jemell":** Thomas Finnegan, sentencing hearing, USA v. Finnegan.

108   **"I was law enforcement":** Jemell Rayam, testimony, USA v. Shropshire, October 25, 2017.

109   **"For myself growing up":** Cherelle Rayam, character letter for sentencing.

109   **In June 2007, Rayam shot someone:** Jemell Rayam, statement to investigators, 2007.

109   **Rayam left the Baltimore police force:** Cherelle Rayam's letter. She wrote: "His squad supervisor at the time, Sgt. Kevin Jones, valued Jemell so much that he told him if it doesn't work out up there, he will always have a place on the squad. Jemell trained in New York for only two weeks, then called me to express his strong sentiment on why something in his spirit was urging him to come back to Baltimore. He came back and was welcomed into Sgt. Jones' squad."

110   **The other passenger, Keith Hill:** Transcript of Keith Hill's interview with homicide detectives, 2009. I attempted to follow up with Hill in 2019; through an attorney, he declined to be interviewed.

110   **Rayam received a Citation of Valor:** It should be noted that Rayam was not reported to be involved in another shooting after 2009.

110   **At one point, he teamed up with a woman:** Jemell Rayam, testimony, USA v. Hersl et al., January 30, 2018.

111   **"They was telling me":** Gary Brown, interview, October 19, 2017.

112   **"It was like movie shit":** Ibid.

114   **When Rayam came back:** Sergeant Kevin Jones, who promised a job for Rayam if he returned from the New York State Police, was by this time in charge of the Gun Trace Task Force.

114   **"We pretty much assist patrol units":** Jemell Rayam, 2013 deposition, Estate of Shawn Cannady v. Rayam et al.

115   **His report, released in late 2013:** Anthony Batts, "Public Safety in the City of Baltimore: A Strategic Plan for Improvement," November 21, 2013.

115   **A patrol officer said he thought he recognized:** Court records show that Detective Jay Rose charged the innocent man with seventeen counts on June 30, 2014. The warrant was revoked and charges were dismissed on July 15, 2014. Because the man has not had the charges expunged, they continue to exist in the public record.

II. STRAP IN

116   **"Frankly, if Clewell had called up":** Andrea Smith, interview, September 9, 2019.

117   **Assistant U.S. Attorney Leo Wise:** This assessment of Wise's work ethic is from interviews with colleagues including former Maryland U.S. attorney Rod Rosenstein.

117   **He typically didn't handle drug cases:** Leo Wise interview, August 14, 2019. Some additional background on Wise and Hines: A Harvard Law graduate, Wise joined the Justice Department in 2004 through its honors program and lived out of a suitcase for four years, moving around the country helping on high-profile cases like the racketeering case against the tobacco companies and the Enron case. He left the Justice Department for a newly created position as the first independent ethics watchdog for the House of Representatives. He was just thirty-one years old and asking questions of powerful politicians who were not used to being scrutinized in such a way. He and a small team ruffled feathers in his three years on the job, uncovering abuses while getting screamed at and thrown out of offices. A House committee dismissed most of the cases he brought, and officials were discussing scaling back his office's powers when he joined the U.S. Attorney's Office in Maryland. Wise had attended Johns Hopkins University, where he met his wife, and they wanted to return to Baltimore. He took a $23,000 pay cut and

joined as a fraud and corruption prosecutor. Hines, meanwhile, is nine years younger than Wise. As an undergraduate at Franklin & Marshall College in his hometown of Lancaster, Pennsylvania, he was a double major in government and Spanish and played on the basketball team before attending Villanova for law school. His post–law school jobs included traveling to Louisiana with former FBI director Louis Freeh to investigate fraudulent claims related to the Deepwater Horizon oil spill, then an eleven-month stint in Montana as counsel for the Chippewa Cree Indian tribe, during which he handled the controversial ouster of the tribal chairman.

117   **One day, as Jensen was shuffling:** Erika Jensen, interview, August 16, 2019.

118   **Looking over the new information:** David McDougall, interview, June 25, 2019.

118   **They also found that two years earlier:** This information about Guinn coming forward in 2013 is verified in a search warrant affidavit. Guinn is referred to as Officer-1: "Investigators believe Officer-1's motivation to come forward with the information was based on his employment obligation to report suspicions of inappropriate behavior and further investigators believes [*sic*] Officer-1 to be reliable." Investigators repeatedly referred to Guinn's information in the affidavits to establish their probable cause to believe that Gondo had relationships with drug dealers.

118   **Everything they did:** Ryan Guinn, interview, June 24, 2018.

119   **"A couple guys will pick you up":** Ryan Guinn, interview, March 18, 2019.

119   **a plainclothes officer who reported others:** This refers to the case of Detective Joe Crystal, who said that after he had reported an assault a dead rat had appeared on his windshield. Guinn did not specifically invoke this case, but it occurred in the same time frame.

120   **an analysis of Gondo's phone records:** Search warrants.

121   **"If we get a dirty call, strap in":** Jensen, interview, August 16, 2019.

121   "The best way to keep a secret": Wise, interview, August 14, 2019.

121   **In the midst of the investigation:** Also around this time, in November 2015, Rayam was again flagged for suspected wrongdoing when Circuit Court Judge Barry Williams suppressed all evidence in one of his cases. "There may come a time when I would take [Rayam's] word. But based on the way he presented himself today, this court is unable to take his word for anything," Williams said at the hearing. Rayam, after later pleading guilty and admitting to years of crimes, maintained that he did not lie about the circumstances in the case, however, which underscores the complicated task of sorting through allegations of misconduct.

121   **A decade earlier, a defense attorney:** Julie Bykowicz, "Drug Case Falls Apart," *Baltimore Sun,* March 27, 2006. The defense attorney was Bradley MacFee; the chief legal counsel at the time who replied to MacFee was Karen Stakem Hornig.

122   **By 2014, the city had settled:** Mark Puente, "Some Baltimore Police Officers Face Repeated Misconduct Lawsuits," *Baltimore Sun,* October 4, 2014.

122   **Young Moose:** I covered Young Moose's charges, but the best coverage of his situation came from music writer Lawrence Burney in *Vice,* "How a Dirty Baltimore Cop's Vendetta Derailed a Promising Rapper's Career," which was posted on May 10, 2017.

122   **"Hersl has always been a great detective":** John Burns, email to Captain Kevin Jones, April 6, 2016.

12. MONSTERS

123   **One likened it to baseball's steroid era:** This comment was made by a homicide detective during my reporting from an investigation in which I was embedded in late 2015 for a series in *The Baltimore Sun* called "Chasing a Killer."

123   **Detective Sean Suiter had since risen:** The case referred to here is the killing of Kendal Fenwick, who was gunned down on

November 9, 2015, in Park Heights. Fenwick's case drew considerable media attention, as he was said to have been shot by drug dealers upset that he had built a fence to keep them from cutting through his property. A wide array of community members came together to finish building the fence. By the time the suspect went to trial, prosecutors argued that Fenwick had been killed in mistaken retaliation for another shooting. The prosecutor on the case was Assistant State's Attorney Patrick Seidel, who appears in chapter 22.

124 **Among those killed:** Walter Price was fatally shot on November 22, 2016, in the 500 block of Random Road.

124 **The twenty-year-old was walking home:** Malik McCaffity, interview, November 7, 2018.

124 **McCaffity had lost his father:** Lori Turner, interview, February 22, 2019.

125 **"He was always in the house":** Leedra Turner, interview, February 20, 2019.

125 **Malik was shot for the first time:** Sentencing memorandum, USA v. McCaffity.

126 **McCaffity was booked:** A note on Malik's case. He testified before a federal grand jury, and his case was among those charged in the GTTF indictment. But prosecutors never put him on the stand at the officers' trial; while the case was pending, the twenty-two-year-old held up a Northeast Baltimore liquor store at gunpoint. Body camera footage showed that responding officers found him hiding in a walk-in refrigerator. "If I could find that police officer, I would give him a hug," McCaffity's mother, Lori Turner, said later. "That police officer could've killed him. I feel like he handled it well." The U.S. Attorney's Office took McCaffity's case federal, and he was sentenced to eight years in prison for the robbery: more than some of the corrupt officers received for committing a series of robberies using the power of their badge. McCaffity, whose gun arrest by Jenkins and his squad was dropped, insists as he serves time for the unrelated robbery that the gun Jenkins arrested him for did not belong to him.

127 **"Anytime a grown man":** Maurice Ward, testimony, USA v. Hersl et al., January 23, 2018.

127 **Jenkins pulled his car in front:** Wayne Jenkins, testimony, State v. Stevenson et al., October 31, 2016. Ward, Oreese Stevenson, and Evodio Hendrix also testified at USA v. Hersl et al. that they had pulled in front of the van.

127 **Jenkins asked Stevenson:** The specific language of the conversation comes from the officers' account in the search warrant for Stevenson's home. Hendrix testified at USA v. Hersl et al. that Stevenson had told the officers he had a safe, kilos of cocaine, and guns. Stevenson, however, denied in his testimony at the same trial that he had made such statements to the officers.

128 **Jenkins emerged from the van:** Account of Hendrix's proffer.

128 **A decade earlier:** The indictment referred to here is USA v. Rice et al. While I inspected documents from the case, I also consulted the reporting of City Paper's Van Smith.

128 **"I need you to come to this address":** Donald Stepp, testimony, USA v. Hersl et al., February 1, 2018. Stepp said that Jenkins had said, "I got a monster"; then Stepp corrected himself and said that Jenkins had used the term drug lord on this particular occasion.

128 **Jenkins would occasionally bring Stepp:** Ibid.

129 **Stevenson had purchased:** State property and business records.

129 **The officers could see:** Ward and Hendrix, testimony, USA v. Hersl et al., January 23 and 29, 2018.

130 **Jenkins cradled a kilogram:** Ward, testimony, USA v. Hersl et al., January 23, 2018.

130 **Stepp watched through binoculars:** Stepp, testimony, USA v. Hersl et al., February 1, 2018.

130 **At Central Booking:** Transcript of conversation between Oreese Stevenson and Keona Holloway, application for cellphone records, February 24, 2017.

131 **When they finally got a warrant:** Holloway told investigators that she had returned to the home at around 12:30 A.M. and that that was when Jenkins had arrived and showed her the warrant and asked her to leave. This information is contained

within the federal government's application for cellphone records filed on February 24, 2017.

131 **"Do you know, in this house":** Video of Wayne Jenkins filmed by Marcus Taylor, provided by Taylor.

131 **Inside was more than $200,000:** This amount is disputed. Ward and Hendrix testified that $100,000 was taken and $100,000 was left inside. Stevenson has maintained that he had more; he told the FBI that he had "more than $260,000" in the safe alone, and two bags containing $40,000 total elsewhere in the home. This information is contained within the application for cellphone records filed on February 24, 2017. In his testimony at USA v. Hersl et al., Stevenson testified that he had "$200,000 and some change" in the safe and $40,000 in the bags.

132 **"How much did he [Stevenson] say":** Account of Ward's proffer.

132 **Jenkins put back what he estimated:** Ward and Hendrix, testimony, USA v. Hersl et al., January 23 and 29, 2018.

132 **"Hey Sarge, come downstairs":** Video of safe opening.

132 **The task force officer, Ethan Glover:** Ethan Glover, testimony, USA v. Hersl et al., January 25, 2018.

133 **After wrapping up at Stevenson's home:** Ward and Hendrix, testimony, USA v. Hersl et al., January 23 and 29, 2018.

133 **As Ward drove back:** Ward, testimony, USA v. Hersl et al., January 23, 2018.

133 **Mostly, he told the FBI:** Account of Ward's proffer.

134 **Stevenson was indeed concerned:** Transcript of conversation between Oreese Stevenson and Keona Holloway, application for cellphone records, February 24, 2017.

134 **Jenkins came up with a plan:** Ward, testimony, USA v. Hersl et al., January 23, 2018.

13. THE WIRE

135 **Sergeant John Sieracki:** John Sieracki, interview, September 12, 2019.

135 **Now the previously authorized wiretap:** Indictment, USA v. Shropshire et al., and court testimony of Momodu Gondo, October 25, 2017.

136   "This is it": Erika Jensen, interview, August 16, 2019.

136   It demonstrated a "longtime, personal relationship": Application for pen register, May 16, 2016.

136   On May 4: Ibid.

136   Later, investigators would write: Ibid.

137   "We gonna be able to do that thing": Application to use closed-circuit television, June 8, 2016.

137   Sieracki was out on the streets: Sieracki, interview, September 12, 2019.

138   The gun—a two-shot .22 caliber pistol: Charging documents, State v. Nicholas DeForge.

138   The federal team next decided: Jensen, interview, August 16, 2019.

139   "What happened to your money?": Application to use closed-circuit television, June 8, 2016.

139   DeForge's mother later said: Laura Slater, interview, July 31, 2018.

139   "You're not going to believe": Jensen, interview, August 16, 2019.

139   Jensen, nicknamed "Honey Badger": Ibid.

140   "Even if a confidential informant": Application to use closed-circuit television, June 8, 2016.

140   The FBI rented: Ibid.

140   A supervisor from McDougall's Harford County team: David McDougall, interview.

141   "They, particularly Rayam, were very leery": Erika Jensen, interview, September 19, 2019.

141   A planned attempt: Ibid.

142   They still were confident: Interview with source who spoke on the condition of anonymity.

143   the jury deadlocked—they were one vote away: *Baltimore Sun* reporter Kevin Rector and I wrote a story published January 16, 2016, in which a juror gave this inside account: "Jury in Officer Porter trial was one vote from acquittal on most serious charge."

143   "They are in a high-crime area": This comment was made by Circuit Court Judge Pamela White at a suppression hearing on January 27, 2016.

143   **"Police are allowed"**: This comment was made by attorney Marc Zayon.

14. HORNET'S NEST

145   **"Monday"**: Sean Miller, email to Kevin Jones, June 10, 2016.

146   **"Has Allers been moved?"**: Dean Palmere, email to Sean Miller and Frank Ebberts, also BCC'd to himself, June 6, 2016.

146   **The officers themselves were suspicious**: Wiretapped phone call between Jemell Rayam and Momodu Gondo, June 15, 2016.

147   **"When we first came to GTTF"**: Maurice Ward, interview.

147   **"This is how this boy be"**: Wiretapped phone call between Maurice Ward and Momodu Gondo, June 14, 2016.

148   **Gondo called Rayam with the good news**: Wiretapped phone call between Jemell Rayam and Momodu Gondo, June 14, 2016.

148   **"Wayne's back!!!!!"**: John Burns, email, June 15, 2016.

148   **"As much as I hate doing this"**: Robert Himes, email, July 10, 2016.

148   **In 1998, when he was twenty-seven**: Peter Hermann and Nancy Youssef, "Loot Links Prothero Killing to Drug Ring," *Baltimore Sun*, March 8, 2000.

149   **In May 2009, employees**: Court documents from USA v. Keenan Hughes et al.

149   **Because of Hamilton's prior convictions**: Ibid.

149   **Documents show Hamilton helped**: USA v. Gregory Whyte.

149   **In 2016, two years after his release**: Property records.

149   **An informant—one of Hamilton's own relatives**: Court statements of William Purpura and Jemell Rayam, USA v. Daniel Hersl et al.

150   **But a few days later**: Search warrant application, August 10, 2016.

150   **It would later emerge**: Jemell Rayam, testimony, USA v. Daniel Hersl et al., January 29, 2018.

150   **Gondo arranged for Glen Wells**: Superseding indictment, USA v. Jenkins et al.

150   "Man, I know there was money": Rayam, testimony, USA v. Daniel Hersl et al., January 29, 2018.

150   "We figured Jenkins lied": Maurice Ward, interview.

152   "We have to go back to the drawing board": This quote is from Tessa Hill-Aston, the NAACP president at the time.

152   "I know they had a pattern": Momodu Gondo, testimony, USA v. Shropshire et al., October 25, 2017.

153   Jenkins "was very reckless": Ibid.

153   "I ain't know it's like that": Text messages between Momodu Gondo and Glen Wells, June 28, 2016.

153   He was encouraging the officers: Wayne Jenkins, in wiretapped call with Momodu Gondo, June 29, 2016.

153   By early July, the officers were giddy: Wiretapped call between Jemell Rayam and Momodu Gondo, July 1, 2016.

15. BUILDING GREATNESS

155   "Can we pull them over in the county?": Wiretap transcript, wiretap application, October 21, 2016.

156   "We got you on three controlled buys": Ronald Hamilton, interview, "Charm City," *New York Times* podcast, June 13, 2018.

156   "It was a dud house": Momodu Gondo, testimony, USA v. Daniel Hersl et al., February 5, 2018.

156   "You could basically say he wasn't": Jemell Rayam, testimony, USA v. Jemell Rayam, January 29, 2018.

157   "Just be quiet": Hamilton, "Charm City."

158   "You take care of us": Ronald Hamilton, police interview, search warrant, February 24, 2017.

158   Rayam handed him a business card: Ronald Hamilton, testimony, USA v. Daniel Hersl et al., January 31, 2018.

158   "We can do this three times a year": Jemell Rayam, testimony, USA v. Daniel Hersl et al., February 5, 2018.

158   "I'm counting and counting": FBI recording device, July 8, 2016.

159   Surveillance video showed Rayam: Search warrant application, February 24, 2017.

159 **"I got up [Jenkins's] butt for you"**: Gondo to Wells, wiretapped conversation, July 9, 2016.

159 **After the hearing concluded**: Ronald Hamilton, peace order application, November 21, 2016.

159 **He had earlier texted Rayam**: Hamilton, testimony, USA v. Hersl et al.

160 **"Jesus Christ!"**: Juan Minaya to Wayne Jenkins, email, July 26, 2016.

160 **"Great work, Lt. Wayne!"**: Michael Pool to Wayne Jenkins, email, July 22, 2016.

160 **"If we could get the rest"**: Richard Worley to Wayne Jenkins, email, July 26, 2016.

160 **The next trial**: The state's attorney's office successfully maneuvered to be able to call the charged officers as witnesses against each other. But that required a new team of prosecutors, referred to as a "clean team," to handle the prosecution of Officer Garrett Miller, to ensure that information that Miller testified to did not seep into his own case. As I reported for *The Baltimore Sun*, the "clean team" prosecutors believed the case against Miller should not go forward.

162 **Van driver Caesar Goodson**: Goodson's attorney, Sean Malone, interview, April 24, 2020.

162 **It was almost midnight on August 3, 2016**: Several well-chronicled cases that the officers took part in were left out of this book for narrative reasons. One of those cases happened two days prior to this incident: the August 1, 2016, gun arrest of a man named Albert Brown, who was working for the Safe Streets antiviolence program run by the city health department. The program hires convicts and others with street credibility to mediate disputes outside the purview of police. Brown was another man who had been stopped at a gas station parking lot for not having a seatbelt on. Hersl's body camera was not switched on when Brown allegedly gave the officers permission to search his car and they found a gun and cocaine. The items were said to have been found in the ceiling area—just as in the Walter Price case in 2014. And as in the Price case, they tried to pump him for information on others. "This is like, the third time we got a

guy from Safe Streets with a gun," Jenkins chided him in the gas station parking lot. Then Jenkins's voice dropped: "You wanna go somewhere and talk this out? Do you want to make it look like we're arresting you, and get out of here so people won't see it? I don't care about that gun or the drugs. Want to go somewhere and talk and keep it 100, or not?" From his work mediating conflicts, Brown likely had all sorts of information police would like to know. His job required him to keep it confidential. "You might as well take me to jail," Brown responded. When the officers pulled around the corner six minutes later, Hersl assured Ward that his body camera was off. But Hersl was still getting the hang of the new technology, and the camera was actually still running. They drove to Brown's listed address, directly across the street from the Western District police station, the start of the Freddie Gray uprising eighteen months earlier. "Y'all just gonna go in the house with no warrant?" Brown said from the back seat. "They can secure anything," Hersl responded. "It's called exigent circumstances." He muttered: "Safe Streets, boy I tell you, all them guys are cruddy. That whole program's gotta be shut down." By the time the case went for its first court appearance five months later in January 2017, Brown's attorney Ivan Bates asked the prosecutor in the case if he had any problem with what he had seen. "Do you recognize your officers have some issues; [that] they went into his house without a warrant?" Bates asked. So what, the prosecutor said. "This is a pullover in a gas station. [A warrantless search of the home] has nothing to do with this case." "It does," Bates asserted, "because they lie about everything."

162 **The case had originated with Jenkins:** Baltimore County police records.

163 **Baltimore County police sergeant Bruce Vaughn:** Report of Sergeant Bruce Vaughn, August 9, 2016.

163 **County detective Jason Metz:** Jason Metz, interview, September 9, 2019.

163 **The county officer turned back:** Report of Detective Brian Cowley, August 9, 2016.

164 **"The fugitive task force":** Report of Sergeant Vaughn.

164 **"There's more dope and a gun here"**: Report of Detective Joe Backhaus, August 12, 2016.

164 **A county officer asked him to pipe down**: Report of Detective Cowley.

164 **Two years earlier, Metz**: Baltimore County police records of Donald Stepp investigations.

16. HUNTING

166 **"We'd drive around and kinda go hunting"**: Daniel Hersl, testimony, January 15, 2017.

166 **"The biggest cases you'll ever make"**: footage from Daniel Hersl's body camera, August 10, 2016.

166 **"What we don't see is all those cases"**: David Jaros, interview, spring 2019.

167 **For years, Jenkins and the other officers**: The reference here to officers making their own videos goes beyond the Oreese Stevenson iPhone video; I found numerous instances of the officers, prior to issuance of body cameras, writing in statements of probable cause that they had submitted short iPhone clips in which they recorded themselves speaking to suspects or taking a statement. People arrested by the officers also spoke of being recorded for limited purposes.

167 **One of the men who was stopped**: Hersl's body camera, August 10, 2016.

167 **The security guard**: D'Andre Adams, interview, September 27, 2018.

168 **Immediately after letting Adams go**: Hersl's body camera, August 10, 2016.

169 **At a gas station in Northwest Baltimore**: Ibid.

169 **In the weeks following the Justice Department report**: Indictment, USA v. Kenton Gondo et al.

169 **The officers never activated their body cameras**: I obtained a log of all footage uploaded from the officers' cameras, and no footage matching these incidents was logged. Officers are not able to delete or filter footage from their cameras.

169 **Hersl would later be recorded:** Response in opposition to motion for review of detention order, USA v. Hersl, March 7, 2017.

169 **For almost two months:** Erika Jensen, interview, August 16, 2019.

170 **The device would be rigged:** No video from the device was ever shown; Jensen said that the officers primarily worked at night and that the video quality was poor.

171 **The next night:** Audio from recording device, August 31, 2016.

171 **The fleeing vehicle:** This account comes from video footage I obtained from the University of Maryland, Baltimore Police Department.

172 **she was "really horrified":** Jensen, interview, August 16, 2019.

172 **Federal authorities listened over the wiretap:** Transcription of FBI recording device, September 22, 2016.

172 **the GTTF chased a man:** Body camera footage, September 24, 2016.

173 **Albert Peisinger:** Albert Peisinger, interview, May 25, 2018.

173 **An internal department newsletter went out:** Several well-chronicled cases that the officers took part in were left out for narrative reasons. Another took place around this time, on October 5, 2016: the robbery of Gregory Harding. According to the indictment, the officers embarked on a high-speed chase in which Harding threw more than nine ounces of cocaine out of his window before Jenkins intentionally drove into his vehicle, near Mondawmin Mall. Body camera captured the next moments, with Jenkins saying to Gondo, "Just like last time. There's a half-key [kilo] here; we can get big shit," and later, "This guy's big money. We gotta do the right thing, do all our homework, and get on him." At one point he asked Gondo if his body camera was still running. Rayam would later testify that Jenkins had given him the cocaine and told him to sell it and kick back the proceeds. Two days later, Rayam traveled to Philadelphia to meet with a former BPD officer and, at the time, current Philadelphia police officer Eric Snell, who gave the drugs to a relative to sell. Snell was charged in November 2017 and took his case to trial. Prosecutors presented evidence including text messages

showing Rayam and Snell using coded language to discuss the sale. Jenkins, too, had sent Rayam urgent text messages, which Rayam testified were his sergeant trying to collect the money. A few days prior to Snell's trial, I spoke to Harding, who fretted about being called to testify against officers: "I just want to move on past the situation. It wasn't my first encounter with dirty cops. This has been going on in Baltimore forever." He was not ultimately called. A few months later, on February 26, 2019, Harding, thirty-nine, was gunned down in Northeast Baltimore. Police released no motive and have made no arrests.

174   **Two pages later, the newsletter:** *Your BPD News,* October 2016.

174   **From 2012 to 2016, 40 percent:** Analysis by Christine Zhang for *The Baltimore Sun.* "Cops and Robbers, Part II: Corrupt Squad Scoured Baltimore Streets in Pursuit of Black Men to Search, Arrest—and Steal From," June 12, 2019.

174   **attorney Ivan Bates, who said:** Ivan Bates, interview, October 17, 2018.

174   **He recalled one time:** Ivan Bates, testimony, Commission to Restore Trust in Policing, June 11, 2019.

174   **Now in October:** Video of State v. Oreese Stevenson and Demetrius Brown, October 31, 2016.

175   **Bates followed Jenkins:** Bates, interview, October 17, 2018.

17. READ BETWEEN THE LINES

177   **"I'm sure you remember":** Wayne Jenkins, email, February 2, 2016.

177   **"10-4 Wayne":** Darryl De Sousa, email, February 3, 2016.

178   **"I remember calling my dad":** James Kostoplis, interview, May 8, 2019.

178   **Earlier in the month:** FBI recording, October 5, 2016, described in first indictment on page 26. King, Murray, and Sylvester appear earlier in the book; Kendall Richburg was a detective in the Violent Crimes Impact Section whose phone was wiretapped by the FBI in 2012, revealing that he was conspiring with an informant. He admitted to kicking back seized drugs, discussing the planting of evidence, and telling the informant to rob

someone Richburg had searched. Richburg received eight years in federal prison.

179 **As Gladstone and the officers rolled up:** This arrest took place on October 11, 2016.

179 **"Call Wayne!":** Antonio Shropshire, interview.

180 **McDougall asked Shropshire:** Ibid.

180 **As McDougall and Kilpatrick drove:** Scott Kilpatrick, interview and court testimony.

180 **On the date of his initial court appearance:** Police record of Shropshire proffer session, November 30, 2016.

182 **"They've empowered the criminal element":** Kevin Rector, Justin George, and Luke Broadwater, "Baltimore, Justice Department Reach Consent Decree Agreement on Police Reform," *Baltimore Sun,* January 12, 2017.

182 **Around 2 A.M.:** Baltimore County Police, body camera video, January 29, 2017.

183 **A week later, a man hiking:** Baltimore County Police, body camera and incident report, February 5, 2017.

183 **During his leave:** Internal Affairs report.

183 **"He said, I just want to let you know":** Ivan Bates, interview, October 17, 2018.

184 **One night in February:** James Kostoplis, court testimony and May 8, 2019, interview.

18. COGNITIVE DISSONANCE

189 **The federal investigators continued:** Transcript of recording device.

190 **Most "did not want anything to do with this":** Erika Jensen, interview, August 16, 2019.

190 **Wise recalls sitting down:** Leo Wise, interview, August 14, 2019.

190 **Bates also brought them additional clients:** Ivan Bates, testimony, Commission to Restore Trust in Policing, June 11, 2019.

190 **"The way he put it":** Derek Hines, interview, August 14, 2019.

191 **"No bullshit":** Kevin Davis, interview, May 14, 2019.

191 **Jensen considered a number of options:** Jensen, interview, August 16, 2019.

192   **Commissioner Davis thought it was important:** Davis, interview, May 14, 2019.

192   **As Sieracki drove it:** John Sieracki, interview, September 12, 2019.

192   **"We knew they had this wrecked car":** Jensen, interview, August 16, 2019.

193   **Meanwhile, BPD had cleared off:** Rodney Hill, interview.

193   **At one point, the GPS:** Erika Jensen, interview, September 19, 2019.

194   **"I'm one of you!":** Sieracki, interview, September 12, 2019.

194   **Rayam was arrested eight minutes later:** The times that the officers arrived were provided by FBI Task Force Officer John Sieracki.

194   **"Being arrested was the last thing on my mind":** Maurice Ward, interview.

194   **Davis, the commissioner, moved:** Kevin Davis, interview, August 14, 2018.

195   **Assistant State's Attorney Anna Mantegna:** Anna Mantegna, interview, 2019. Mantegna had more involvement in the case than I was able to portray here: Wise and Hines said that a city prosecutor had tipped Jenkins off to the federal investigation (referred to in chapter 17), and the U.S. Attorney's Office eventually told the state's attorney's office that they believed the prosecutor was Mantegna, on the basis of phone records showing she and Jenkins had had an extended conversation around that time. Though federal prosecutors said they had no basis to charge her, Mantegna was fired by the city prosecutor's office. Mantegna has maintained that she did not know—and would not have known—about the federal investigation. "I had no clue" about a federal investigation, Mantegna told me. "None whatsoever." She said she did speak to Jenkins about concerns that Rayam and Gondo had credibility issues. Mantegna told the FBI that she had told Jenkins, "Those guys are dirty—watch them like a hawk." Mantegna unsuccessfully sued.

195   **Another prosecutor at the time said:** A prosecutor at the time who spoke on the condition of anonymity, 2019.

196   **The department commissioned an internal investigation:** Internal Affairs report.

197   **Another lieutenant:** Ibid.

197   **Jenkins tried to rally the officers:** Maurice Ward, interview, corroborated by accounts of other officers' proffers.

198   **In a separate instance, Jenkins remembered:** Accounts of Momodu Gondo and Evodio Hendrix proffer.

198   **"I've been doin' so much stuff":** Account of Evodio Hendrix proffer.

198   **Wise and Hines, the prosecutors:** Leo Wise and Derek Hines interview, August 14, 2019.

198   **"I didn't do this stuff":** Sieracki, interview, September 12, 2019.

198   **Wise was struck by their lax attitude:** Leo Wise, interview, February 21, 2018.

199   **Jerome Hersl visited:** Archive recording of Harford County Council meeting, June 21, 2017.

200   **One robbery allegedly involved Allers's adult son:** Indictment, USA v. Thomas Allers.

200   **They made eye contact:** Testimony of Lekyle Whitaker, State v. Antwon Frazier. "I'll never forget how he looked at me," Whitaker testified. Frazier, the man charged with killing Robinson, was acquitted by a jury of all charges: a key witness refused to cooperate, and Frazier's defense attorney told jurors there was too much doubt.

200   **He rebuffed requests to cooperate:** Angel Allers, interview, May 10, 2018.

201   **"He said just in case":** Evodio Hendrix, testimony, USA v. Hersl et al., January 29, 2018.

201   **He was in an Oklahoma facility:** Umar Burley, interview, October 7, 2019.

202   **Jenkins, too, had engaged the feds:** Acting U.S. Attorney Stephen Schenning disclosed that Jenkins had entered into a proffer agreement in a February 15, 2018, letter regarding the city prosecutor who they believed had leaked word of the investigation. Additional information about Jenkins's proffers comes from sources.

202   **Among their questions for Guinn:** Ryan Guinn, interview, June 24, 2018.

19. HARLEM PARK

203   **"The writing was on the wall":** Martin Bartness, interview, November 16, 2017.

203   **"He was not only a good cop":** Rick Willard, interview, November 16, 2017.

203   **His partner in the homicide unit:** Jonathan Jones, interview, November 16, 2017.

204   **It was their second visit:** Independent Review Board, "Report to the Commissioner of the Police Department of Baltimore City Concerning an Independent Review of the Nov. 15, 2017 Incident and Its Aftermath," August 27, 2018, 26.

204   **The home was said to be a "hangout":** Justin George, "Police Say Home Where Three Killed Was Gang Hangout," *Baltimore Sun,* December 7, 2016.

207   **"Sean was calling me":** David Bomenka, on body camera of responding officers, as described in Independent Review Board, "Report to the Commissioner," 39.

207   **Others were patted down:** "Baltimore Police Department Monitoring Team: First Semiannual Report," July 18, 2018, 64.

207   **It would be hours:** Nicole Suiter, interview, May 5, 2019.

209   **Ryan Guinn showed up as scheduled:** Ryan Guinn, interview, March 18, 2019.

209   **One person called Metro Crime Stoppers:** From a summary of tips received by police.

210   **The DEA got wiretaps:** Investigative documents from State v. Carey Olivis, 2018.

210   **The BPD had also, without a warrant:** Motions from USA v. Sydney Frazier. Frazier had control over the home next to the vacant lot where Suiter was shot; it was undergoing renovations and appeared vacant. Police entered without a warrant and found a gun box and other contraband inside, then applied for a search warrant claiming that a blood trail led from the lot to the home. No such trail existed.

210 **He said police were searching:** Kevin Davis, press conference, November 16, 2017.

210 **There they located a bullet:** This occurred on Monday, November 20, 2017.

211 **"Just because the guy was scheduled":** Kevin Davis, interview, May 14, 2019.

212 **the department publicly confirmed:** Kevin Davis, press conference, November 17, 2017.

212 **Hundreds of officers:** The funeral took place at the Mount Pleasant Church.

212 **Among the pallbearers:** The sergeant leading the investigation, James Lloyd, would be criminally charged in July 2020 with kidnapping and extortion. He allegedly threatened a contractor who worked on his home with arrest if he did not get a refund, and drove the man to a bank to withdraw money. The department said Lloyd was on the clock when the incident occurred.

213 **Suiter never made it:** The specific language in the indictment said: "After the crash, and after U.B. and B.M. had been arrested, Jenkins told Officer #2 [Guinn] to call a Sergeant who was not at the scene because he had the 'stuff' or 'shit' in his car, or words to that effect. Officer #2 called the Sergeant but the conversation was brief because the Sergeant had arrived at the scene, having heard Officer #2's request for assistance on the police radio. After speaking with the Sergeant, Officer #2 turned his attention to the elderly driver who remained trapped inside his car on the front porch of the row home. After emergency medical personnel arrived on the scene, Officer #2 returned to Jenkins who was standing near U.B. and B.M.'s car. At that time, Jenkins told Officer #2 that the 'stuff' or 'shit' was in the car, referring to U.B. and B.M.'s car, and that Jenkins was going to send Officer #1 [Suiter] to the car to find it because Officer #1 was 'clueless,' or words to that effect. Sometime later, Officer #2 saw Officer #1 searching the car. Officer #1 signaled that he had found something. Officer #1 found approximately 28 grams of heroin that Jenkins had planted in the vehicle."

213 **Guinn would later say:** Ryan Guinn, interview, June 24, 2018.

214 **A few weeks later, Burley:** Court hearing, December 18, 2017.

20. GUILTY

215   **On December 13, 2017:** Baltimore County police reports of Detective Christopher Toland.

216   **A month earlier, Toland:** Baltimore County police records.

216   **"The cooperators all talked about it":** Leo Wise, interview, February 21, 2018.

216   **The county police had previously investigated:** Baltimore County police records.

217   **By 8:31 A.M.:** Derek Hines, email, contained within Baltimore County police investigative files on Stepp.

218   **Jenkins's car that was reported stolen:** Account of Stepp proffer from source. Evodio Hendrix also told authorities that Jenkins had been trying to sell the car and that the story of it being stolen didn't make sense because Hendrix's wife had a similar car and its alarm and special key would make it difficult to steal.

218   **But on January 3:** Information about "considerable negotiations" regarding the statements of facts to the plea agreement comes from a letter from Acting U.S. Attorney Stephen Schenning sent to the city state's attorney's office on February 15, 2018.

21. COPS AND ROBBERS

220   **"This is a dysfunctional police department":** Kevin Davis, interview, January 8, 2018.

221   **"Crime is now spilling out all over":** Catherine Pugh, press briefing, January 19, 2018.

221   **On the first day of trial:** Opening statements took place on January 23, 2018.

221   **theft, not robbery:** In state-level cases of officers who had been accused of stealing, the charges were for theft, not robbery. For example, in 2004, Officer Myron Thornes was charged with taking $500 from an undercover officer and was charged with theft. In 2009, Officer Michael Sylvester, referenced in chapter 10, was charged with theft in another sting involving a cadet; there

are several others. I could not find any examples of officers charged with taking money while on duty who were charged with robbery. Still, Purpura's argument failed.

222 **They talked about overtime fraud:** Ward testified on January 23 and 25, 2018. There were no proceedings on January 24, 2018.

222 **At one point, two duffel bags:** Hendrix testified on January 29, 2018.

222 **When Stepp took the stand:** Stepp testified on February 1, 2018.

223 **Oreese Stevenson, saying candidly:** Stevenson testified on January 31, 2018.

223 **Hines asked a man named Shawn Whiting:** Whiting testified on January 25, 2018.

223 **The defense peppered Hamilton with questions:** Hamilton testified on January 31, 2018.

224 **Rayam also broke down:** Rayam testified on January 29 and 30, 2018.

224 **Gondo was the last:** Gondo testified on February 5, 2018.

224 **Palmere denied the accusation:** Kevin Rector, "Top-Ranking Baltimore Police Official Retires, Denies He Coached Gun Task Force Officer on How to Avoid Punishment," *Baltimore Sun*, February 5, 2018. Palmere told Rector: "It's not true. I would not coach somebody. I've always taken pride in my ethics and integrity."

224 **One of Taylor's defense attorneys:** This question was from defense attorney Christopher Nieto.

225 **Suiter's family pushed back:** The uncle was Kevin Basil.

225 **Prosecutors called Detective James Kostoplis:** Kostoplis took the stand on February 6, 2018.

226 **"Take this all in":** Derek Hines, interview, August 14, 2019.

226 **"The whole thing was such a mess":** Erika Jensen, interview, August 16, 2019.

226 **"Let me make it clear":** Darryl De Sousa, statement to press, February 12, 2018.

22. POSSIBILITIES AND PROBABILITIES

229   The case changed: Frederick H. Bealefeld, interview, 2010.

229   "I was there": Luther Young, "A Partner Remembers," *Baltimore Sun,* December 3, 1985.

229   To this day: Gary Childs, interview, April 19, 2019.

233   They'd exchanged messages: Independent Review Board, "Report to the Commissioner of the Police Department of Baltimore City Concerning an Independent Review of the Nov. 15, 2017 Incident and Its Aftermath," August 27, 2018, made public August 28, 2018.

233   There were other indicators: Ibid.

233   Hersl recounted: Hersl letter, December 10, 2017, via source. Hersl went on to say that Suiter and Gondo had met up with women from the Harlem Park area, and speculated that they could have had something to do with the killing.

233   "The Board concludes": Independent Review Board, "Report."

234   A day after the release: Nicole Suiter, press conference, August 29, 2018.

235   "My husband is a stand-up guy": Nicole Suiter, interview, August 29, 2018.

236   "I was never, ever fucking worried": Jeremy Eldridge, interview, March 21, 2019.

236   As Suiter relayed it: Jeremy Eldridge, interview, March 19, 2020.

236   "It was like kids": Eldridge, interview, March 21, 2019.

236   "I want a clean crack": Ibid.

237   Eldridge sought to pull the documents: Ibid.

237   Suiter seemed to brush off: Eldridge, interview, March 19, 2020.

237   Eldridge tried to think: Ibid.

237   In their conversations: Ibid.

237   After finding out about Suiter's shooting: Eldridge, interview, March 21, 2019.

238   "They were shell-shocked": Ibid.

238   They sparred: Eldridge, interview, March 19, 2020.

238   **Wise and Hines later explained:** Leo Wise and Derek Hines, interview, August 14, 2019.

238   **Eldridge was successful:** Eldridge, interview, March 21, 2019.

238   **The FBI impounded and searched:** Independent Review Board, "Report," 115.

239   **Eldridge lambasted the IRB's claims:** Eldridge, interview, March 21, 2019.

240   **One of the very first things out of Gondo's mouth:** Account obtained via source.

240   **Rayam too, in a proffer session:** Account obtained via source.

240   **Jenkins, meanwhile, insisted:** Account from multiple sources.

240   **"I still don't understand":** Maurice Ward, interview.

241   **Pauling sat down for an interview:** Donte Pauling, interview video.

241   **When footage of Pauling's interview:** The footage first aired on WMAR on November 29, 2018: "Homicide Interview Raises New Questions in Suiter Death Investigation."

241   **The story caught the attention:** Patrick Seidel, email to BPD, November 2019.

242   **"If you wanted to fake a homicide":** David Fowler, interview, March 5, 2020.

242   **Among those who staunchly believe:** Jonathan Jones, interview, July 19, 2020.

243   **Eldridge continues to press investigators:** Eldridge, interview, March 21, 2019.

23. THE ABYSS STARES BACK

247   **Guinn says he himself was the one:** Ryan Guinn, interview, June 24, 2018.

24. THE PLACE TO BE

249   **"You've got to realize":** Richard C. B. Woods, interview, March 11, 2018.

250 **Gladstone had retired:** Gladstone retired on May 1, 2017, according to the police department. It was actually his second retirement: He retired in December 2012 and returned one year later in December 2013.

250 **Around the same time:** Gladstone indictment.

251 **Wise would later remark:** Leo Wise, USA v. Carmine Vignola sentencing hearing, February 6, 2020.

252 **Gladstone and two other officers:** The other two officers were Detectives Ivo Louvado and Victor Rivera; it was Rivera's informant who sold the drugs. This account comes from the criminal information filed against Louvado and Rivera in the spring of 2020.

252 **By comparison, Antonio Shropshire:** I asked Shropshire in the spring of 2020 to reflect on his sentence, compared to those received by the corrupt officers. He acknowledged that he was in line for more time because of his record, but said both he and the officers received sentences that were too long: "It's all too much time," he wrote to me. "Because I been breaking the law since 2005 I should have got more time then [*sic*] them officers and I'm just being honest. [But] any double digit number for a crime other than murder, sex crimes is injustice, no [matter] who you are, Black/white, police or not a police. . . . My sentence was without a doubt unfair. The justice system as a whole is unfair."

253 **Matthew Ryckman, a former officer:** Letter from Assistant U.S. Attorney Timothy Delgado, November 2018.

253 **Marilyn Mosby went into her reelection campaign:** Mosby secured 49.4 percent of the vote in the 2018 Democratic primary, with Bates taking 28.1 percent and Thiru Vignarajah receiving 22.5 percent. In heavily Democratic Baltimore, the election is decided in the primary.

253 **"Some of these individuals":** Marilyn Mosby, Baltimore City Council meeting, June 4, 2018.

254 **Almost all of the direct supervisors:** At the time of this writing, the GTTF commander prior to Allers and Jenkins, Kevin Jones, is a lieutenant colonel in the Patrol Division. Gondo and Rayam were promoted under Jones's command, and he had supervised Jenkins as well. Commissioner Michael Harrison told *Baltimore*

Sun reporter Jessica Anderson only that the FBI had vetted Jones for criminal wrongdoing. Former colonel Sean Miller—who oversaw the Plainclothes Division—was demoted to lieutenant and has been working in the Southern District.

254 **New commissioner Michael Harrison:** Harrison's remarks came at a meeting of the state's Commission to Restore Trust in Policing on September 17, 2019. The city solicitor who expressed concern about liability was Andre Davis, the federal judge who had condemned Keith Gladstone and Thomas Wilson in 2003 for lying in search warrants. It should be noted that Mayor Catherine E. Pugh, who appointed Harrison and Davis, herself resigned over a children's book scandal and was indicted on federal fraud and tax evasion charges that would result in a guilty plea and three years in prison. Federal prosecutor Leo Wise had helped build the case when he wasn't investigating corrupt police.

254 **The city sought to be excused:** Solicitor Davis put the question to the state's highest court, seeking to release the city from liability in lawsuits over the GTTF officers' conduct. He argued that their behavior was so far "outside the scope of their employment" that the city should not have to cover their legal bills. The court of appeals rejected the argument in an April 24, 2020, ruling.

254 **Early in the summer of 2019:** Ryan Guinn, interview, March 18, 2019.

258 **"I'm a sitting duck":** Umar Burley, interview, October 7, 2019.

258 **"I'm hoping once we hit that":** James Kostoplis, interview, October 22, 2019.

259 **"Sometimes I look back":** Erika Jensen, interview, August 16, 2019.

259 **Though he did have work done:** Records for work done to the property from Baltimore County Department of Permits, Approvals and Inspections; other property records show Jenkins had acquired at least two other homes in the Middle River area.

260 **One officer told the FBI:** Account of Gondo's proffer, obtained via source.

260 **The plaintiff, Andre Crowder:** Crowder took part in a February 2, 2018, news conference in which he said the officers

searched his car on September 28, 2016, and had found a gun. He said $10,000 was taken later during a search of his home. During the three days he was jailed, his three-year-old son passed away. "It's bigger than the charge they put on me," Crowder said. "The mark they put on my record, the cash that was took, all of that, it doesn't matter, because I wasn't there to spend the last moments of my son's life with him because of this situation." His lawsuit was dismissed by his attorneys after the body camera video surfaced.

261   **Hersl, Taylor, and Allers have also continued:** Hersl has written a series of letters to the state legislature's Commission to Restore Trust in Policing; Taylor and I corresponded for months following his conviction; in 2018, I interviewed Allers's family and friends who spoke to his good character and said he was innocent and would have never taken money. In a postconviction motion that Allers himself filed on June 10, 2019, Allers wrote that he "did not believe he was guilty of a serious crime that to the extent of his conduct was wrong, and that his conduct was miniscule compared to others." Rather than protest his complete innocence, Allers wrote that he had "received approximately $5,000, not more than $100,000."

INDEX

Names with (LEO) indicate law enforcement officers.

ABOUT THE AUTHOR

A crime reporter for the *Baltimore Sun*, Justin Fenton was part of the Pulitzer Prize finalist staff recognized for their coverage of the events surrounding the death of Freddie Gray. This is his first book.

ABOUT THE TYPE

This book was set in Caslon, a typeface first designed in 1722 by William Caslon (1692–1766). Its widespread use by most English printers in the early eighteenth century soon supplanted the Dutch typefaces that had formerly prevailed. The roman is considered a "workhorse" typeface due to its pleasant, open appearance, while the italic is exceedingly decorative.